"Those who think that there is nothing new to learn about the Holy Spirit should read *An Unconventional Go'* 'r from merely rehashing well-worn themes, Levison freshly 'he Spirit's role and work in the Gospels. Marked by i' 'etical insight, a studied familiarity with the Scrir 'ortant reflections, lively prose, and an o' ,pic, this book will make you think aga' perplexing, often challenging, and alw? , the Spirit in the life of Jesus—and in th(

—Marian. ,i, Fuller Theological Seminary

"Jack Levison has establish. .self as the keenest of eyes when it comes to anything about Spirit—spirit, breath, wind, Spirit—in the Old Testament and Judaism, but in *An Unconventional God* Levison explores a section of Scripture rarely given the attention it deserves for pneumatology: the four Gospels. Levison's nuanced attentiveness to the Old Testament and Judaism is brought into play to see the Gospels' understanding of the Spirit in a way that is both comprehensive and unconventional. This book will replace the standard studies of Spirit in the Gospels."

—**Scot McKnight**, Northern Seminary

"Are you looking for a Holy Spirit who lifts you up when you are down? Inspires a felicitous reply when you are arguing? Guides you to the lone empty parking spot? Then Jack Levison's *An Unconventional God* may not be the book you want—although perhaps it is exactly the book you need. In this elegant and convicting exposition of the Spirit's role in the canonical Gospels, Levison shows us that the Holy Spirit portrayed in them is one who drives Jesus into the wilderness and who may drive *us* there also. The good news, in Levison's telling, is a promise not of easy deliverance from our trials but of divine presence to accompany us through the hard places."

—**Susan R. Garrett**, Louisville Seminary

"This book offers an unconventional biography, a beautifully written history of the Holy Spirit in the life of Jesus. Treating one anecdote at a time, Levison carves out the facets of each report, painting a colorful picture of the Holy Spirit with the ink of the Scriptures, a portrait never to be captured in a single line or thought. His interpretations show the precision of an exegete and yet the openness of an ancient biographer to different reports or versions of the same incident. This fascinating book offers something for everyone."

—**Rainer Hirsch-Luipold**, University of Bern

An
Unconventional
GOD

An Unconventional GOD

THE SPIRIT
according to
JESUS

JACK LEVISON

Ⅱ𝔅

Baker Academic
a division of Baker Publishing Group
Grand Rapids, Michigan

Published by Baker Academic
a division of Baker Publishing Group
PO Box 6287, Grand Rapids, MI 49516-6287
www.bakeracademic.com

Printed in the United States of America

Library of Congress Cataloging-in-Publication Data
Names: Levison, John R., author.
Title: An unconventional God : the Spirit according to Jesus / Jack Levison.
Description: Grand Rapids, Michigan : Baker Academic, a division of Baker Publishing Group, 2020. | Includes index.
Identifiers: LCCN 2020007053 | ISBN 9781540961198 (paperback) | ISBN 9781540963437 (casebound)
Subjects: LCSH: Holy Spirit—Biblical teaching. | Bible. Gospels—Criticism, interpretation, etc.
Classification: LCC BT121.3 .L49 2020 | DDC 231/.3—dc23
LC record available at https://lccn.loc.gov/2020007053

20 21 22 23 24 25 26   7 6 5 4 3 2 1

To Priscilla

Contents

Acknowledgments

The book is done, the corrections and additions entered—except for this part. I left this single, satisfying assignment to the end. It is a cold, gray, and uncharacteristically frigid winter day in Dallas; I am in my Southern Methodist University office with the room heater blazing and a cup of tea at my elbow. It is time now to indulge in reminiscence.

I owe the origin of this book, as I did *A Boundless God*, to Bob Hosack of Baker Academic. Bob took both ideas to his team and came away with a green light. That team, it turns out, has been adept, efficient, and amenable—every one of them: Jeremy Wells, Mason Slater, Jennifer Hale, Shelly MacNaughton, Sarah Gombis, Kara Day, Amy Donaldson, Kristie Berglund, Robert Maccini, and Paula Gibson, who produced a cover twice over and captured the spirit of this book.

I am grateful, too, to Perkins School of Theology, Southern Methodist University, on several counts: a yearlong sabbatical, which Dean Craig Hill granted; a Scholarly Outreach Award, which left summers free of teaching; the research support of the W. J. A. Power Chair of Old Testament Interpretation and Biblical Hebrew, of which I am, for these fortunate years, the occupant. Thanks to these resources, I was able to revise *A Boundless God*, complete a nearly final draft of *An Unconventional God*, and accomplish the late-stage work on *The Holy Spirit before Christianity*.

While most of my writing took place in the ordinary and comfortable confines of my SMU office and our townhome in Dallas,

Priscilla and I were able to write and revise our books in two more enviable locales. We spent two stunning weeks at the Mount Tabor Ecumenical Centre for Art and Spirituality—a Tuscan villa owned by the Community of Jesus, which ably operates Paraclete Press. The fresh cappuccinos Brother Benedict brought to Priscilla and me on the veranda, followed by lavish lunches, turned the otherwise onerous task of revision into an indulgence. Priscilla and I also spent five months in a small apartment under the eaves in Munich, thanks to a resumption of my Alexander von Humboldt Fellowship and the hospitality of Loren Stuckenbruck, professor of New Testament at Ludwig-Maximilians-Universität in Munich. Priscilla and I tackled more work than we could have imagined, though I did come home five pounds heavier, thanks to the irresistible density of *Bauernbrot* from the Kistenpfennig bakery and *Käse* from the nearby *Ökomarkt*.

Thanks, too, to my children, Chloe and Jeremy, whose care rims my writing and keeps it squarely in perspective. The unlikely presence of our adult children in Dallas over the past few years is a gift I had not foreseen.

There is a line in William Butler Yeats's poem *Adam's Curse* that reads, "A line will take us hours maybe." I have staggered and lurched for hours, days really, in search of words while writing this book, but no more so than now, when it comes time to acknowledge my wife, Priscilla, whom I have known and loved—it *was* love at first sight, I think—for nearly four decades. These are the hardest words by far to find. How to capture the memories of life alongside her—writing, yes, but playing too? Outdoor dinners in Barga, snowshoeing in Bad Kohlgrub, walks along the Ammersee, *Kaffee mit Milch* at the Munich Hauptbahnhof on chilly Saturday mornings, strolls in the English Garden. How to express, as well, the elation I feel still at the sound of her footsteps outside my office door? I have acquired no language to thank Priscilla for a marriage that is at once eternal and diurnal, as elusive and visceral as love itself. A dedication is not enough, but it is what I have to give. And Priscilla, with characteristic grace, will accept it, meager though it be. I know this because I know this woman well, and well she loves me.

Abbreviations

General

//	parallel(s)
alt.	altered
LXX	Septuagint (Greek Old Testament)
MT	Masoretic Text (Hebrew Old Testament)

Bible Versions

CEB	Common English Bible
KJV	King James Version
MSG	*The Message*
NETS	New English Translation of the Septuagint
NIV	New International Version
NRSV	New Revised Standard Version

Old Testament

Gen.	Genesis	2 Kings	2 Kings
Exod.	Exodus	1 Chron.	1 Chronicles
Lev.	Leviticus	2 Chron.	2 Chronicles
Num.	Numbers	Ezra	Ezra
Deut.	Deuteronomy	Neh.	Nehemiah
Josh.	Joshua	Esther	Esther
Judg.	Judges	Job	Job
Ruth	Ruth	Ps(s).	Psalm(s)
1 Sam.	1 Samuel	Prov.	Proverbs
2 Sam.	2 Samuel	Eccles.	Ecclesiastes
1 Kings	1 Kings	Song	Song of Songs

Isa.	Isaiah	Jon.	Jonah
Jer.	Jeremiah	Mic.	Micah
Lam.	Lamentations	Nah.	Nahum
Ezek.	Ezekiel	Hab.	Habakkuk
Dan.	Daniel	Zeph.	Zephaniah
Hosea	Hosea	Hag.	Haggai
Joel	Joel	Zech.	Zechariah
Amos	Amos	Mal.	Malachi
Obad.	Obadiah		

New Testament

Matt.	Matthew	1 Tim.	1 Timothy
Mark	Mark	2 Tim.	2 Timothy
Luke	Luke	Titus	Titus
John	John	Philem.	Philemon
Acts	Acts	Heb.	Hebrews
Rom.	Romans	James	James
1 Cor.	1 Corinthians	1 Pet.	1 Peter
2 Cor.	2 Corinthians	2 Pet.	2 Peter
Gal.	Galatians	1 John	1 John
Eph.	Ephesians	2 John	2 John
Phil.	Philippians	3 John	3 John
Col.	Colossians	Jude	Jude
1 Thess.	1 Thessalonians	Rev.	Revelation
2 Thess.	2 Thessalonians		

Old Testament Apocrypha

Sir.   Sirach (Ecclesiasticus)

Dead Sea Scrolls

1QM	*War Scroll*	4Q521	*Messianic Apocalypse*
1QS	*Community Rule*	11Q5	*Psalms Scroll*

Josephus

Ant.   *Antiquities of the Jews*

Gnostic Texts

Gos. Thom.   Gospel of Thomas

Introduction

Glance at the number of times the word *spirit* occurs in the New Testament, and you will understand why Christians tend to look to the letters of Paul for their understanding of the Holy Spirit. References to *pneuma* (the Greek word usually translated as "spirit") in his letters are, by the numbers, more conspicuous than in the Gospels. For every thousand words he writes, Paul refers to *pneuma* 4.78 times in his letter to the Romans, 5.85 times in 1 Corinthians, and a whopping 8.05 times in Galatians—nearly 1 percent of the words in this letter, counting even conjunctions such as *kai* and *de*.[1]

With these numbers from Paul's Letters in mind, turn now to the Gospels. In the Gospel of Matthew, *pneuma* makes up just over one (1.03) in a thousand words—one-tenth of a percent. In the Fourth Gospel, the word *pneuma* occurs just 1.53 times out of every thousand words. Luke's Gospel contains 1.85 occurrences out of a thousand—surprisingly low, given that it is often identified as the Gospel of the Spirit. In the Gospel of Mark, *pneuma* occurs 2.03 times out of a thousand.[2]

---

1. At times, I will refer to *pneuma*, but since this is a Greek word, it is subject to case declensions (nominative, genitive, dative, accusative), which result in a change of form. Occasionally I will refer to *pneuma* in the singular genitive case as *pneumatos* and in the singular dative case as *pneumati*.

2. These numbers are based on the analysis of Accordance software, using Barbara Aland, Kurt Aland, Johannes Karavidopoulos, Carlo M. Martini, and Bruce M. Metzger, eds., *Novum Testamentum Graece*, 28th rev. ed. (Stuttgart: Deutsche Bibelgesellschaft: 2012).

The disparity between Paul's Letters and the Gospels becomes particularly conspicuous when we consider that most of the references to *pneuma* in the Gospels are not to the Holy Spirit. Of the nearly two dozen references to *pneuma* in Mark's Gospel, for instance, only six refer to the Holy Spirit,[3] while thirteen—more than twice as many—refer to *unclean* spirits.[4] Paul's Letters, then, are far denser when it comes to the Holy Spirit.

Numbers are hardly inspiring, but they are indicative. A batting average of .350 is far more impressive than a batting average of .225. A shooting percentage in basketball of 50 percent, rather than 30 percent, can be the difference between advancing to the championship game and taking a long ride home. And most readers of this book know the difference between a 95 percent and a 65 percent on an exam. By the numbers, *pneuma* features much more prominently in the letters of Paul than the Gospels.

Yet numbers do not tell the whole story. The Holy Spirit, grasped from the vantage point of the Gospels, is uncommon, astonishing, *unconventional* even, because the Spirit becomes enmeshed in the tortured—literally, *tortured*—life of Jesus of Nazareth. The Spirit is part of a lifelong drama, consisting of conflicts whose flames Jesus fans.

As they remember his story, the authors of the four Gospels recollect that the uncommon presence of the Holy Spirit spanned Jesus's life. The Spirit is, in a real sense, the tensive presence that holds together their narratives. Before Jesus even takes a step, some recall that the Holy Spirit inspired Elizabeth, Mary, Zechariah, and John the Baptist (still in Elizabeth's belly) to pray or praise or find themselves—Mary, at least—pregnant. They remember the descent of the Holy Spirit at Jesus's baptism, the force of the Holy Spirit in the wilderness, Jesus's dire warning about blasphemy against the Holy Spirit, his assurance of the Holy Spirit for martyrs, and even the promise of the Holy Spirit after his death.

---

3. Mark 1:8, 10, 12; 3:29; 12:36; 13:11.
4. Mark 1:23, 26, 27; 3:11, 30; 5:2, 8, 13; 6:7; 7:25; 9:17, 20, 25. Two references are to Jesus's spirit (2:8; 8:12), and one is to Jesus saying that the spirit is willing, though the flesh is weak (14:38).

The four Gospels, of course, are not homogeneous.[5] No one ironed out the creases in the story so that all four Gospels speak with one voice, but the presence of the Spirit with Jesus is decisive in all four Gospels. It is almost inconceivable, for example, to imagine Jesus's life without the descent of the Holy Spirit at his baptism. So crucial, so critical was that moment for what was about to unfold that the descent of the dove is one of those rare scenes that appear in all four Gospels.

The impact of the Holy Spirit on Jesus is pivotal to all four Gospels, and recognizing that the life of Jesus gives the Holy Spirit a unique tenor that occurs nowhere else in the annals of early Christian literature is just as essential. The impact of Jesus's story on the portrayal of the Holy Spirit in the Gospels is dramatic: there is just one moment in the whole of Jesus's life when he rejoices in the Holy Spirit, and this in only one of the Gospels (Luke 10:21). One moment of joy. One glimpse of gladness. When the Holy Spirit is taken up in the currents that would lead to Jesus's death, a certain grimness, a foreboding emerges. Jesus never engenders a naive hope of tranquility. Determined rather to ensure the fidelity of his followers after his death, Jesus understands the Holy Spirit in terms other than joy and gladness. Faithfulness to the point of death, yes. Reliability, to be sure. An exacting imitation of Jesus, absolutely. These are a few of the unmistakable marks of the Holy Spirit in the Gospels.[6]

The Gospels offer what is not presented elsewhere in the New Testament, where the fruits of the Holy Spirit are love, joy, peace, patience, kindness, generosity, faithfulness, gentleness, and self-control (Gal. 5:22–23) and where the gifts of the Spirit are an utterance of wisdom, an utterance of knowledge, faith, healing, miracles, prophecy, the discernment of spirits, various kinds of tongues, and

5. My assumption is that the Gospel of Mark is the earliest Gospel and that the authors of the Gospels of Matthew and Luke had access to Mark's Gospel as they wrote their own. The Gospel of John—the Fourth Gospel—may be related to the Synoptic Gospels (Matthew, Mark, and Luke), though what I have written in this book is not dependent on a decision about whether the author of the Fourth Gospel knew any or all of the others.

6. The birth stories of Luke 1–2 present the Holy Spirit as the source of blessing and praise, but these are about the impact of the Spirit before Jesus is an adult. You will find an analysis of these birth stories in chap. 1.

the interpretation of tongues (1 Cor. 12:8–10). There is, of course, some overlap between the letters of Paul and the stories of Jesus. For instance, there is the inspiration of a message focused on the cross (1 Cor. 2:1–5).[7] There is the association of joy with the Holy Spirit in the Pauline Letters (Rom. 14:17; 15:13; Gal. 5:22; 1 Thess. 1:6) and words that express joy early in Luke's Gospel (Luke 1:41, 67), as well as Jesus's single instance of rejoicing in the Spirit (Luke 10:21). There is also a connection between the Holy Spirit and healing (1 Cor. 12:9), as in the Gospels and Acts (e.g., Matt. 12:9–21; Acts 10:37–38).

Yet those who remembered the impact of the Holy Spirit on Jesus did not transform the Spirit wholesale into a source of abiding joy and peace and patience and kindness or anything that resembles speaking in tongues. Nor could they, bound as they were by the memory of Jesus—a memory that gave the Holy Spirit a dimmer tenor, a darker hue, overshadowed as it was by the long obedience of Jesus.

Refracted through the prism of Jesus's life and death, therefore, the Holy Spirit shows up in the oddest situations and the most baffling teachings of Jesus—in desert sojourns, in a strange saying about scorpions and snakes, in puzzling adages about birth from above and springs from below. The Gospels disclose an alien world of the Spirit, a world that mystifies, challenges, and invigorates. This is the unconventional yet ultimately inspiring world of the Holy Spirit—the Spirit of the Gospels—that fills the pages of this book.[8]

---

7. In 1 Cor. 2:1–5, Paul writes, "When I came to you, brothers and sisters, I did not come proclaiming the mystery of God to you in lofty words or wisdom. For I decided to know nothing among you except Jesus Christ, and him crucified. And I came to you in weakness and in fear and in much trembling. My speech and my proclamation were not with plausible words of wisdom, but with a demonstration of the Spirit and of power, so that your faith might rest not on human wisdom but on the power of God."

8. Some books on the Holy Spirit in the Gospels proceed Gospel by Gospel. For example, George Montague, *Growth of a Biblical Tradition* (New York: Paulist Press, 1976); Craig Keener, *The Spirit in the Gospels and Acts: Divine Purity and Power* (Grand Rapids: Baker Academic, 2010); and John Carroll, *The Holy Spirit in the New Testament* (Nashville: Abingdon, 2018). I proceed for the most part episode by episode. For instance, rather than treating the baptism of Jesus in four different places, each under a separate Gospel, I treat all four interpretations of Jesus's baptism in the same chapter.

1

Spirit and the Swell
of Expectation

This is how the birth of Jesus Christ took place. When Mary his mother was engaged to Joseph, before they were married, she became pregnant by the Holy Spirit. Joseph her husband was a righteous man. Because he didn't want to humiliate her, he decided to call off their engagement quietly. As he was thinking about this, an angel from the Lord appeared to him in a dream and said, "Joseph son of David, don't be afraid to take Mary as your wife, because the child she carries was conceived by the Holy Spirit."

Matthew 1:18–20 CEB

The angel said, "Don't be afraid, Zechariah. Your prayers have been heard. Your wife Elizabeth will give birth to your son and you must name him John. He will be a joy and delight to you, and many people will rejoice at his birth, for he will be great in the Lord's eyes. He must not drink wine and liquor. He will be filled with the Holy Spirit even before his birth. He will bring many Israelites back to the Lord their God. He will go forth before the Lord, equipped with the spirit and power of Elijah. He will turn the hearts of fathers back to their children, and he will turn the disobedient to righteous patterns of thinking. He will make ready a people prepared for the Lord."

Luke 1:13–17 CEB

When Elizabeth was six months pregnant, God sent the angel Gabriel to Nazareth, a city in Galilee, to a virgin who was engaged to a man named Joseph, a descendant of David's house. The virgin's name was Mary. When the angel came to her, he said, "Rejoice, favored one! The Lord is with you!" She was confused by these words and wondered what kind of greeting this might be. The angel said, "Don't be afraid, Mary. God is honoring you. Look! You will conceive and give birth to a son, and you will name him Jesus. He will be great and he will be called the Son of the Most High. The Lord God will give him the throne of David his father. He will rule over Jacob's house forever, and there will be no end to his kingdom."

Then Mary said to the angel, "How will this happen since I haven't had sexual relations with a man?"

The angel replied, "The Holy Spirit will come over you and the power of the Most High will overshadow you. Therefore, the one who is to be born will be holy. He will be called God's Son. Look, even in her old age, your relative Elizabeth has conceived a son. This woman who was labeled 'unable to conceive' is now six months pregnant. Nothing is impossible for God."

Then Mary said, "I am the Lord's servant. Let it be with me just as you have said." Then the angel left her.

Luke 1:26–38 CEB

When Elizabeth heard Mary's greeting, the child leaped in her womb, and Elizabeth was filled with the Holy Spirit. With a loud voice she blurted out, "God has blessed you above all women, and he has blessed the child you carry. Why do I have this honor, that the mother of my Lord should come to me? As soon as I heard your greeting, the baby in my womb jumped for joy. Happy is she who believed that the Lord would fulfill the promises he made to her."

Luke 1:41–45 CEB

John's father Zechariah was filled with the Holy Spirit and prophesied,

> "Bless the Lord God of Israel
> because he has come to help and has delivered his people."

Luke 1:67–68 CEB

A man named Simeon was in Jerusalem. He was righteous and devout. He eagerly anticipated the restoration of Israel, and the Holy Spirit rested on him. The Holy Spirit revealed to him that he wouldn't die before he had seen the Lord's Christ. Led by the Spirit, he went into the temple area. Meanwhile, Jesus' parents brought the child to the temple so that they could do what was customary under the Law. Simeon took Jesus in his arms and praised God. He said,

> "Now, master, let your servant go in peace according to your
>   word,
>   because my eyes have seen your salvation.
> You prepared this salvation in the presence of all peoples.
> It's a light for revelation to the Gentiles
>   and a glory for your people Israel."

His father and mother were amazed by what was said about him. Simeon blessed them and said to Mary his mother, "This boy is assigned to be the cause of the falling and rising of many in Israel and to be a sign that generates opposition so that the inner thoughts of many will be revealed. And a sword will pierce your innermost being too."

Luke 2:25–35 CEB

Two Stories, One Source

The story of Jesus's birth is really *two* stories. The first two chapters of Matthew's Gospel could hardly be more different from the first two of Luke's Gospel.

Matthew's birth stories are taut with mathematical precision, like the work of the ancient astrologers who navigated deserts and seas, oceans and mountains, by calculating the stars and their movements. One miscalculated degree could bring devastation and disaster. Matthew writes of magi and a brilliant star settling over a nondescript house; he writes, too, as if he were one of the magi, with astronomical fastidiousness, with immense control, as if life depended on it, which it did for ancient sailors and nomads. Even Matthew's genealogies occur in three precise sets of fourteen generations each, as if to say, "You should have known this would happen! You could have *counted* on it." The stories he tells are crisp and methodical. He tells five of them—this number evoking the five books of Torah, the Pentateuch—each one bristling with accuracy. These are not random stories collected ad hoc but stories collated, specially selected, gauged to drive home one point: the events surrounding Jesus's birth, five in all, happened to fulfill what had been spoken earlier by Israel's prophets. When we read Matthew's genealogies and birth stories, which open the curtain to the drama ahead, we are audience to an algorithm, captives to theological calculation. Numbers don't lie—at least not these numbers. Matthew points this out with forty-two generations, five stories, two parents, and one child.

Compare this with Luke's take on the action surrounding Jesus's birth, which, so unlike Matthew's Gospel, bursts with the unfathomable. The birth of a baby to an old couple is so shocking that the old man is struck dumb until his son's birth; he simply cannot fathom what has happened through his own rumpled frame or what is happening to his wife's geriatric body, in which the Holy Spirit has concocted a strange alchemy of life. Then there is the young unmarried woman, who is just as shockingly pregnant. "How can this be?" she asks. It's a wonder that leaves one wondering. All of these people, old Zechariah and Elizabeth, along with young Mary—Joseph is nowhere to be seen (not yet, anyway)—are shocked and elated at this pair of births. Each of them also has something to say—something full of praise and blessing and joy and glee. So does Simeon, another old man who has waited and waited for this day—Simeon, who meets the poor young parents in the temple and thanks God that his eyes have finally seen God's salvation. This is a time of yearning and surprise, expectation and bewilderment. It is a time of birth and babies, of pregnancies and praise. Angels sing above; shepherds scuttle below. The joy is immeasurable.

Luke's Gospel begins with an infinity of grace, Matthew's with the calculus of hope. At the center of both sets of stories—Matthew's measured five and Luke's rush of canticles—lies an uncannily similar perspective. Not just the baby Jesus, whose birth is the glue. There is also a hue, an atmosphere, an ambience. For both Matthew and Luke, the Jewish Scriptures are essential, indispensable for grasping what went on in those early, heady days. They are the leaven, the bread that is baking in the oven. They are a background scent, yes, rich and undeniable and welcoming. Yet there is something more to these stories. The Holy Spirit is also essential, indispensable for grasping what went on with the first glimmer of inspiration. And here is the rub: the Spirit is essential not because something altogether *new* was happening—the birth of Christianity, let's say—but because something *old*, ancient, yet timeless was coming to fruition. The Holy Spirit is central to the birth of Jesus not so much to spawn something new as to spark something old, not so much to invent as to ignite.

Born of Holy Spirit

In Matthew's Gospel, there is no gush of the Spirit, no filling, no songs of celebration. There is, however, political intrigue: a paranoid king destined to destroy his family and anyone else who gets in his way—the Jewish historian Josephus tells us as much. There is propriety too: the impulse to divorce a woman like Mary, who seems patently promiscuous to her betrothed. There is urgency as well: the struggle to survive as refugees in Egypt. Whereas angelic canticles in heaven, the poetry of wonder on earth, and an uncommon concatenation of praise and prayer belong in the Gospel of Luke, Matthew's Gospel features unforgiving lines of political and personal scandals.

It is here, at risk of personal scandal, that a staid Matthew introduces the Holy Spirit. Matthew's Jesus dots his i's and crosses his t's: he claims that not a jot or tittle will pass away from Torah.

So does Joseph before him. Joseph, too, wants to get it right in the face of potentially ruinous scandal. He will dismiss Mary properly, inconspicuously—but Joseph's plans are shattered. Enter the Holy Spirit, who changes everything by transforming a disgraceful pregnancy into a virtuous birth. The Holy Spirit does not just *avert* scandal; the Holy Spirit *converts* scandal into virtue. When Joseph resolves to dismiss Mary quietly—itself an exercise in constraint— "an angel of the Lord appeared to him in a dream and said, 'Joseph, son of David, do not be afraid to take Mary as your wife, for the child conceived in her is from (the) Holy Spirit'" (Matt. 1:20 alt.).

There is something surprisingly eerie and inexact about Matthew's language here. He does not say that what is conceived is from *the* Holy Spirit but "from holy spirit" (Greek, *ek pneumatos estin hagiou*). At no time in this short scene does he deploy the definite article so that we can say, "Oh, *that* Holy Spirit." Matthew could just as well be saying, "The child conceived in her is from *a* holy spirit." It may be that mystery has eclipsed accuracy, and we should leave it at that. Probably not—because lying in the background of this story wafts the inevitable scent of the Old Testament.

Two passages in the Old Testament—and only two—refer to "holy spirit." They are so different from each other that they call for entirely different interpretations of Jesus's birth, depending on which one you think lies behind Matthew's Gospel. Both Old Testament passages endow this story with richness and resonance—without them our understanding of Jesus's birth sounds tinny by comparison.

The first passage occurs in a lament in Isaiah 63, where the prophet pleads, "Where is the one who put within them his holy spirit?" (Isa. 63:11). The prophet is perplexed by the absence of the Spirit in his day, especially when he looks back to the exodus, the story of Israel's liberation, when God put God's Holy Spirit within Israel. At that distant time, he believes, God led the people from Egypt into the promised land by means of God's Holy Spirit. The Holy Spirit took on the role of the pillars of cloud and fire and of the angel God authorized to lead the people to safety.[1]

---

1. You will find an interpretation of this poem in the eighth chapter of my *A Boundless God: The Spirit according to the Old Testament* (Grand Rapids: Baker Academic, 2020). Key biblical texts include Exod. 13:21–22; 14:19; 23:20–24. For a

Is it any surprise that the Holy Spirit, who inspired the exodus, should now show up to inspire the birth of the Messiah? After all, Matthew himself sees the parallel between Israel's secure ascent from Egypt over a thousand years earlier and the ascent of Jesus's family from Egypt in safety (Matt. 2:13–23). Imagine this: Mary's pregnancy is not due to happenstance or infidelity—not at all! The Holy Spirit in her is the same Holy Spirit that liberated Israel from an irascible tyrant; Herod the Great stands no chance against the sway of this Holy Spirit. From the vantage point of Isaiah 63, the birth of Jesus, occasioned by the Holy Spirit within Mary, is the culmination of a long story of leading, designing, and delivering. Is it too much to say, in light of Isaiah 63, that the water of Mary's womb, awake now with the Holy Spirit, is like a latter-day Red Sea, through which Israel, alert to the Holy Spirit within them, can be liberated? This is a great deal to invest in a single birth, but this is the birth of the Messiah (as Matthew puts it), after all.

The lament in Isaiah 63, then, is a perfect backdrop to Jesus's birth—or is it? Psalm 51 also refers to holy spirit, but this poem from the Old Testament understands this spirit in a dramatically different way from Isaiah 63. The psalmist begs God,

> Create in me a clean heart, O God,
> and put a new and right spirit within me.
> Do not cast me away from your presence,
> and do not take your holy spirit from me.
> Restore to me the joy of your salvation,
> and sustain in me a willing spirit. (Ps. 51:10–12)[2]

The sacrifice acceptable to God is "a broken spirit; a broken and contrite heart" (Ps. 51:17).

In this Old Testament poem, the spirit is something within a human being—a new spirit, a right spirit, a willing spirit, a *holy* spirit. From this perspective, the holy spirit in Mary may be *her own*

---

detailed analysis of the fusion of the agents of the exodus with the Holy Spirit, see my *The Holy Spirit before Christianity* (Waco: Baylor University Press, 2019).

2. You will find a more thorough analysis of this psalm in my *Filled with the Spirit* (Grand Rapids: Eerdmans, 2009), 28–33.

holy spirit; Mary could be pregnant because of the sanctity of *her* spirit. This reading is possible because the original Greek twice lacks the definite article, *the*; Mary is pregnant because of *a* holy spirit— *her* holy spirit. Had Matthew intended to refer to *the* Holy Spirit, he might easily have said so with the definite article, but he does not. His grammar, which is usually cautious and careful, leaves open the possibility that Mary's sanctity makes her the right woman to bear the Messiah, Jesus. She was pregnant due to a holy spirit, or as the angel puts it, the child conceived in her is the product of a holy spirit. Joseph need not worry; Mary's spirit remains holy, appearances to the contrary.

There is irony here. According to tradition, David wrote Psalm 51 after his ill-conceived affair with Bathsheba. (Bathsheba, remember, is one of the sexually suspect women—along with Tamar, Ruth, Rahab, and Mary—who populate the genealogy that opens Matthew's Gospel.) Guilty, the adulterous king begs for a willing, upright, and holy spirit. Where is the irony? Mary, whose pregnancy looks like the product of an illicit tryst, has the willing, upright, and holy spirit for which a chastened David pleaded.

With this particular Old Testament foreground, we are a long way from the traditional Christian belief that Jesus was "conceived by the Holy Ghost." That interpretation fits the birth stories if Isaiah 63 lies in the background—if the Holy Spirit who led Israel from within now works within Mary to bring about a new exodus through the leadership of the Messiah. That interpretation does *not* fit the birth stories if Psalm 51 lies in the background—if Mary has the sanctity of spirit that makes her the perfect mother of the Messiah. The angel assures Joseph, therefore, that this pregnancy arises not from Mary's infidelity or a lapse in discipline but from her peculiar holiness.

This discussion is not an effort to undermine a cherished Christian belief. It is an attempt to give grammar its due. The brevity of Matthew's prose permits a variety of interpretations but also prevents us from holding any one too tightly. This story may set Mary's pregnancy into Israel's narrative of exodus (Isa. 63), or it may recall Psalm 51, in which a fallen king begs for a willing, upright, and holy spirit. Whatever we make of Matthew's telling of the story, the scent of the Jewish Scriptures is there, taking us back to a distant past.

The birth of the Messiah "from holy spirit" evokes the thrill of the exodus and the chill of a contrite king.

But it is not a *birth* at all—not exactly. Matthew begins the story in this way: "Now the *genesis* of Jesus the Messiah took place in this way" (Matt. 1:18, my translation). His selection of a single Greek word, *genesis*, translated too often and too blandly as "birth," takes us back over the entire span of the Spirit in Scripture to the poetry of creation. The majestic poem of creation concludes, "This is the book of the origin [*genesis*] of heaven and earth" (Gen. 2:4 NETS). The cadence of creation rises with this solitary word. By writing so economically, so efficiently, Matthew opens the curtain to the entire scope, the breathtaking compass, of Israel's Scriptures.

The birth of Jesus, therefore, is less an impregnation than a cosmic creation—a *genesis*—that evokes the Spirit's hovering over the water: "Yet the earth was invisible and unformed, and darkness was over the abyss, and a [spirit of God swept] over the water" (Gen. 1:2 NETS).[3] Already in some of Scripture's first words,[4] the Spirit is active, even before a word is spoken. Now, that Spirit swirls in Mary's womb.

The Birth of the Baptist

An economy of words opens to the divine economy in Matthew's Gospel. The Spirit may not rush or clothe or pour or rest, as the Spirit does throughout the Jewish Scriptures. The Spirit may not fill the faithful, as in the book of Acts. Yet in a measured and meaningful way, the Spirit evokes the entire sweep of Israel's history—creation, exodus, kingship—in spare but significant words: *genesis* and *from holy spirit*.

Luke's Gospel is less tidy when it comes to the Spirit—less spare, certainly less measured, more unkempt, and altogether imbalanced. Praise gushes untrammeled in the wake of both Zechariah's and Mary's bewilderment. Whereas the Holy Spirit appears in only one scene, though a notable and puzzling one, in the Gospel of Matthew,

---

3. I have modified the NETS translation because I think the Greek words *pneuma theou* demand a stronger translation than "a divine wind."

4. This number applies to the Greek translation, which Matthew probably used. In the Hebrew, *rûaḥ* appears as the seventeenth word.

that Spirit—not *a* spirit—dominates the drama in the Gospel of Luke, from gestation to Jesus's guest appearance as a young man in his hometown synagogue. This is no pedestrian drama. In this Gospel, the Holy Spirit is hard at work before Jesus's birth, inspiring pregnancy, praise, and promise.

John the Baptist is the first to fall prey to the Spirit's power, not in the guise of something new but in the garb of something old. The angel's predictions are bathed in the Jewish Scriptures: "For he [John] will be great in the sight of the Lord. He must never drink wine or strong drink; even from the womb of his mother he will be filled with holy spirit. He will turn many of the people of Israel to the Lord their God. With the spirit and power of Elijah he will go before him, to turn the hearts of parents to their children, and the disobedient to the wisdom of the righteous, to make ready a people prepared for the Lord" (Luke 1:15–17 alt.). Virtually every ingredient of this prediction enhances the prophetic character of John's vocation. Like both the Israelite judge Samson (Judg. 13:4–5) and the seer Samuel, who anointed David (1 Sam. 1:9–15), the Baptist will abstain from wine. Like the famed prophet Jeremiah (Jer. 1:5), the Baptist will be set apart before birth (Luke 1:15). Living in "the spirit and power of Elijah" (Luke 1:17), the Baptist will follow in the steps of Elisha, who received a double portion of Elijah's spirit when his mentor ascended in a chariot of fire (2 Kings 2:9–15). And his ability to "turn the hearts of parents to their children" (Luke 1:17) will identify him as Elijah returned; this is what the prophet Malachi predicted in what are the last words of the last prophet in the Old Testament:[5] "Lo, I will send you the prophet Elijah before the great and terrible day of the LORD comes. He will turn the hearts of parents to their children and the hearts of children to their parents, so that I will not come and strike the land with a curse" (Mal. 4:5–6).[6] Finally, the angel's last words to Zechariah, "to make ready a people prepared for the Lord" (Luke 1:17), are the ones that stick. They appear in one form or another in each of the four Gospels. Like so much in the angelic announcement, they too erupt from the Old Testament—from Isaiah 40 to be exact:

5. This order represents the Christian Old Testament. The order in the Jewish Scriptures ends with 2 Chronicles.

6. See Sir. 48:10.

> A voice of one crying out in the wilderness:
>> "Prepare the way of the Lord;
>> make straight the paths of our God." (Isa. 40:3 NETS)

Extract the Old Testament phrases from the angel's announcement, and you have virtually nothing left. No threads. No fabric. Nothing. And at the heart of this announcement is the Spirit. Before birth the Baptist will be filled with the Spirit. He will live in the spirit and power of Elijah—the grand stream of the prophetic Spirit.

The Gospel of Luke dispels the myth that the Holy Spirit was not at work until Pentecost, until the birth of Christianity. These were not Christians who received the Spirit; these were Jews. They were the first to play a role in the story of Jesus, who was yet another in a line of Jews filled with the Spirit.

We should hardly be surprised that the Spirit erupts months before Jesus's birth or years before Pentecost. These are faithful people, good people. Zechariah and Elizabeth, long in the tooth but childless, were not willing to shirk the disciplines of faith for that reason; they were both "righteous before God, living blamelessly according to all the commandments and regulations of the Lord" (Luke 1:6). Even after the angel spoke and chastised Zechariah with speechlessness for not believing on the spot—in a moment of ill-founded unfaith, Zechariah happened to raise the problem of their age to the angel Gabriel—Zechariah continued to serve in the temple. Only "when his time of service was ended," that day, and not a moment before, did he go "to his home" (1:23). No excuses for the old man, no eluding the necessary work of the righteous, no shirking or skulking away from daily trudges to the temple.

And the old couple might have found a reason to give up on God. Their barrenness had cost them dearly in a culture that prized the production of heirs. After hearing about the angelic promise, Elizabeth would say only this (that we know of) in five months of seclusion: "This is what the Lord has done for me when he looked favorably on me and took away the disgrace I have endured among my people" (Luke 1:25). God did not just look favorably; God also took away disgrace. Disgrace may not yet be forgotten, but it lingers in the shadow of grace.

A Burst of Inspired Blessing

It is difficult to imagine what Elizabeth felt as she cradled a baby. Luke does not describe her experience in terms of a swollen belly, an aching back, seasons of gestation, the glow of pregnancy, or the precarious straits of birth. Luke describes her experience in terms of the Holy Spirit. Then, six months after Zechariah was told Elizabeth would bear a prophet, Mary visits with the news of her own pregnancy: "When Elizabeth heard Mary's greeting, the child leaped in her womb. And Elizabeth was filled with the Holy Spirit and exclaimed with a loud cry, 'Blessed are you among women, and blessed is the fruit of your womb. And why has this happened to me, that the mother of my Lord comes to me? For as soon as I heard the sound of your greeting, the child in my womb leaped for joy. And blessed is she who believed that there would be a fulfillment of what was spoken to her by the Lord'" (Luke 1:41–45). Praise and blessing gush, inspired, from Elizabeth. Twice she calls her younger cousin "blessed" (*eulogēmenē*) and once more, "blessed" (*makaria*). Elizabeth, filled with the Holy Spirit, blesses, blesses, and blesses again.

This is not a tame telling, a whispered word of encouragement or murmured sisterly advice. Elizabeth "was filled with the Holy Spirit and exclaimed with a loud voice" (Luke 1:41 alt.). For a sense of the intensity of that experience, we need to pause over these words.

Elizabeth was *filled* with the Holy Spirit. Throughout the Hebrew Bible, the word translated "fill" (*mālē'*) means absolute fullness. A pregnancy that comes to term is filled (Gen. 25:24). A period of purification that is completed is filled (Lev. 12:4, 6).[7] Spaces, too, are filled. When Egyptian houses are filled with swarms of flies, more than a few flies can be expected (Exod. 8:21; 8:17 MT).[8] When the

---

7. Jacob's wait for Rachel was filled when it was over (Gen. 29:21). A vow is fulfilled (Num. 6:5). Banquets that end are filled (Esther 1:5). When the Babylonian exile ended, it was filled (Jer. 25:12).

8. Frequently the verse numbers in the Hebrew are different than in English because they were added long after the original writings were penned and at a time when many versions existed. The process, in other words, was not seamless or controlled. My friend Ben Wright, editor of an English translation of the Septuagint (an early Greek translation of the Hebrew Old Testament that contains many other books besides), wrote that verses differ for different reasons in different books: "With books like Joshua and Judges different translations were preserved. In

hem of God's robe fills the temple, more than a tip of the garment occupies the inner sanctum (Isa. 6:1). When Jeremiah protests that the land is filled with idols, he means to say the land is polluted to the full (Jer. 16:18). When the Jordan fills its banks, the river floods those banks (Josh. 3:15).[9] Birthing, swarming, polluting, flooding, *filling*. Elizabeth was filled to the brim with the Holy Spirit.

Filled with the Spirit, Elizabeth *exclaims (anaphōnein)*. This Greek word occurs only five times in the Greek translation of the Old Testament, all in the books of Chronicles, where worship is raucous, riotous, and rambunctious. In the very last use of this word, the Israelites gathered in unison with trumpets and harps and singing and acclamation, and "raised a sound with trumpets and cymbals and instruments of songs. . . . And the house was filled with a cloud of the Lord's glory" (2 Chron. 5:13 NETS). Just as the house was filled with a cloud of God's glory in a moment of unbridled praise, so now Elizabeth is filled with the Holy Spirit in a moment of unbridled—perhaps even raucous, riotous, and rambunctious—praise.

Finally, Elizabeth exclaims with a *loud voice (kraugē megalē)*. If this seems at odds with her persona as the righteous, blameless, elderly, dutiful wife of Zechariah, it is. Luke adopts this phrase in just one other instance, toward the close of the book of Acts, where he describes a violent confrontation between Pharisees and Sadducees prompted by none other than the apostle Paul. The skirmish grows so violent that the Romans send in soldiers to squelch it (Acts 23:9–10). Perhaps Elizabeth, after five months of seclusion with a baby in her

---

Daniel and its additions, there is an Old Greek and a Theodotion translation fully preserved. In fact Theodotion was the common translation [of Daniel] in antiquity. These [translations] will often have a different relationship to the Hebrew, where the translation has additional or fewer verses. In Jeremiah Gk [Greek] is shorter than the MT [Hebrew] . . . and chapters are in a different arrangement. The translation of Exodus is a different case, where Gk omits material found in the MT and it occasionally has a longer, shorter, or rearranged text" (email message to author, March 26, 2020). The difference in the numbering of psalms occurs because Greek translators divided Pss. 116 and 147 into two each (making four out of two) and joined Pss. 9 and 10, as well as Pss. 114 and 115, into a single psalm each (making two out of four).

9. Similar understandings of filling occur in 1 Kings 8:10, 15; 2 Chron. 6:4; Jer. 23:24; 44:25; Ezek. 43:5; 44:4; Hab. 2:14. You will find a more thorough analysis in my *Filled with the Spirit*, 55–58.

belly, can't help but shout blessings at the top of her lungs, filled as she is with the Holy Spirit.

The Birth of a Savior

Surprises mount in Luke's story of wondrous births, and so does bewilderment. This time it is not an old married man but a young single woman who is baffled by an angel's words. The angel Gabriel visits Mary, announces her pregnancy, and then responds to her question, "How can this be, since I am a virgin?," with still another pronouncement: "The Holy Spirit will come upon you, and the power of the Most High will overshadow you; therefore the child to be born will be holy; he will be called Son of God" (Luke 1:34–35). Mary is doubly bewildered, both by being told she is favored (1:28, 30) and by being told she will conceive a son.

It is difficult to know what a Galilean peasant girl would have understood about sex and conception, but we do know that, in the annals of ancient Greek physiology, the man was thought to have the power of conception, since *pneuma*—spirit-breath—vitalized his sperm. The woman's uterus, in essence, was thought to function as a vessel for his vitality. The angel might have said, along the lines of ancient biology, "A *pneuma* will enter you and create a son inside you." Now *that* a Galilean girl might have understood.

However, Mary understands enough to know that the angel is not saying that Joseph's *pneuma*/sperm will become vital in her. That is why she asks, "How can this happen, since I don't know a man?" (Luke 1:34, my translation). Something else is being promised—or threatened—here. Mary, young and unsophisticated, knows this full well.

This explosive conversation between angel and virgin has cast a spell over centuries of Christian thought. But is it a conversation about the virgin birth? Not necessarily. Gabriel does not say, "The Holy Spirit will come upon you, and you will be pregnant." Gabriel does say, "The Holy Spirit will come upon you, and the power of the Most High will overshadow you; therefore the child to be born will be holy; he will be called Son of God" (Luke 1:35). Understood in this way, the pronouncement is less about the mechanics of Mary's pregnancy than about the character of her son. The "therefore" that links the first and second halves of the promise connects the Holy Spirit with the holiness of the child and the power of the Most High with the Son of God. When the Greek is read in this way, the Holy Spirit will not *cause* Mary to become pregnant; the Spirit will ensure that her child will be *holy*. Holy Spirit, holy son.[10]

We have seen this move before. When the angel talked to Zechariah about his soon-to-be son, nearly everything in the promise, a kaleidoscope of Old Testament phrases, was about that son. The focus was not on conception; the accent did not fall on a miraculous birth. That is why when Zechariah, filled with the Holy Spirit, prophesies later, he waxes eloquent not about the conception or birth of John the Baptist, as marvelous and miraculous as they may be, but about God's decisive action in the world, about raising up a savior, about remembering promises and covenants and oaths, about making space for a people who will worship in holiness and justice all their days. Zechariah knows that his son will be pivotal to this grand plan, so he concludes his prophecy with a word to his son that is, as we have come to expect, full of Old Testament hopes and dreams:

> And you, child, will be called the prophet of the Most High;
>> for you will go before the Lord to prepare his ways,
> to give knowledge of salvation to his people
>> by the forgiveness of their sins.
> By the tender mercy of our God,
>> the dawn from on high will break upon us,
> to give light to those who sit in darkness and in the shadow
>> of death,
>> to guide our feet into the way of peace. (Luke 1:76–79)

Luke does not paint a picture of Zechariah adoringly rubbing Elizabeth's distended belly. It is not the conception that matters so much as the impact this child will have as a prophet preparing the way

---

10. This discussion does not dispense with belief in the virgin birth; it does suggest that the Greek syntax can be read in different ways, at least one of which may not have a virgin birth in view at all.

of the Lord (Isa. 40:3), breaking the dawn (Isa. 58:8), bringing light to those who sit in darkness (Isa. 42:7), doing the hard labor of God's work. There is not an ounce of soppiness or a whiff of sentimentality in Zechariah's prophecy—as if Luke is daring us to romanticize this pregnancy, which is itself pregnant with *political* impact.

The angel's announcement to Mary follows the same pattern: "And now, you will conceive in your womb and bear a son, and you will name him Jesus. He will be great, and will be called the Son of the Most High, and the Lord God will give to him the throne of his ancestor David. He will reign over the house of Jacob forever, and of his kingdom there will be no end" (Luke 1:31–33). There is no promise here of the glow of a second trimester or the cooing of a baby in the soft light of dawn. Mary's son will be Joshua by name, a military leader and Moses's successor; her son will occupy the throne of David and rule over the house of Jacob with an eternal kingdom. Small wonder that Mary is bewildered by what she hears. So Gabriel explains, "The Holy Spirit will come upon you, and the power of the Most High will overshadow you; therefore the child to be born will be holy; he will be called Son of God" (Luke 1:35). Again, he responds to her question not with the mechanics of birth but with a description of her son. In both Gabriel's initial promise (1:31–33) and his response to her question (1:35), the weight of angelic words rests heavily on the upcoming rule of Mary's unborn child.

It is not the biology of conception, even inspired conception, that grabs the spotlight in Luke's Gospel—or Matthew's, for that matter. It is not the physiology of birth, even a miraculous one, nor anatomy, even inexplicable anatomy, that lies at the center of this story. It is the scope of God's story—a story about a remembering, rescuing, redeeming God who catalyzes these births to reshape history.

In Matthew's Gospel, the *genesis* of Jesus *from holy spirit* recalls a story that spans the magnificence of creation, the miracle of exodus, and the misery of an errant king. In Luke's Gospel, the Holy Spirit is joined at the hip to the power that will overshadow Mary. This verb "overshadow" (*episkiazein*) is an evocative one because it, like so many of the nouns and verbs that cluster around the Holy Spirit in Matthew and Luke, is embedded in Israel's history. Israel's poets, the psalmists, lay claim to this power. They know that God's pinions can *overshadow* those who live in the shelter of the Most High (Ps. 91:4; 90:4 LXX). The psalmist claims that God is a strong deliverer who "*overshadowed* my head in the day of battle" (Ps. 140:7 alt.; 139:8 LXX). And most poignant of all, when Israel, fresh from the exodus, builds a tabernacle—a sacred tent in which Moses meets God—they recognize the cloud of God's glory, which *overshadows* the tabernacle in the wilderness so forcefully that "Moses was not able to enter the tent of meeting because the cloud settled upon it, and the glory of the LORD filled the tabernacle" (Exod. 40:35).

Divine rescue. Divine guidance. Divine glory. All of this was palpable in those earliest days of liberation from Egypt, long before the advent of Rome, which overshadowed Zechariah, Elizabeth, Mary, and Joseph. Later in Luke's Gospel, the verb *overshadow* reinforces another renewal of God's glory. At the transfiguration of Jesus, "a cloud came and overshadowed them; and they were terrified as they entered the cloud. Then from the cloud came a voice that said, 'This is my Son, my Chosen; listen to him!'" (Luke 9:34–35). This is tabernacle language. The overshadowing cloud, coupled with the divine voice that reiterates what Jesus heard at his baptism, communicates that God is present with Jesus, Elijah, and Moses on the Mount of Transfiguration, just as God safeguarded Israel in the mountain at Sinai.

For now, the power of God, the Holy Spirit, will overshadow a girl from Galilee who receives a straightforward if unsettling promise. The Holy Spirit again descends on a sacred space—not a tent in an unforgiving wilderness but the belly of a suddenly pregnant woman.

The Spirit and Simeon

The Holy Spirit appears next at the fringes of the temple, in the world of widows and old men and peasants from Galilee. Luke describes an old man with unusually lavish language, including three rapid-fire references to the Spirit: "Now there was a man in Jerusalem whose name was Simeon; this man was righteous and devout, looking forward to the consolation of Israel, and the Holy Spirit rested on him. It had been revealed to him by the Holy Spirit that he would not see death before he had seen the Lord's Messiah. Guided by the Spirit, Simeon came into the temple" (Luke 2:25–27). Though it is invisible to the powers that be, Simeon is inspired—three times inspired. The Spirit rests on him. The Spirit reveals to him. The Spirit guides him.

What he says as the result of the inspiration is surprising only to those who have failed to read what precedes Simeon's story in the Gospel of Luke. When Simeon sees the child, he lifts the baby in his arms and praises God in words known to the church as the Nunc Dimittis:

> Lord, now lettest thou thy servant depart in peace, according
>   to thy word.
> For mine eyes have seen thy salvation,
> Which thou hast prepared before the face of all people;
> A light to lighten the Gentiles, and the glory of thy people
>   Israel. (Luke 2:29–32 KJV)

Like every canticle, every promise, and every prediction about John the Baptist and Jesus, this prayer, too, drips with the Old Testament. Simeon's song, though it seems extemporaneous and unplanned, is in fact deliberately suffused with the dream of the Old Testament—Isaiah 40–55 to be exact. If his song were a jigsaw puzzle and every phrase of it a separate piece, we would likely discover that each piece of the puzzle is a snippet of Isaiah 40–55. Take those phrases away and, like Gabriel's promise to Zechariah, nothing would be left on which to hold.

This is not surprising; Simeon has waited for the consolation of Israel. This is a shorthand reminder of Isaiah 40:1–2, which begins, "Comfort, O comfort my people, says your God." Simeon, like Zechariah and the angel before him, understands that the advent of the baby is the inauguration of the liberation that this ancient prophet anticipated. Simeon's belief that Jesus will be "a light to lighten the Gentiles" stems from Isaiah 42:6, "I have given you as . . . a light to the nations." Even Simeon's belief that Jesus comes "for glory to your people Israel" echoes Isaiah 46:13: "I will put salvation in Zion, for Israel my glory."

Simeon's private words to Mary, "This child is destined for the falling and the rising of many in Israel, and to be a sign that will be opposed" (Luke 2:34), also grow from the soil of Isaiah 40–55.

Opposition will be the hallmark of the child's destiny. He will become, in short, the suffering servant, whose uncompromising expansion of God's reign to all nations—not just Israel—leads him to personal anguish (Isa. 42:2–3), to the torment of having his beard torn out and his back beaten (50:4–7), and to an early, ignominious death (53:7–12). With the inspiration of the Holy Spirit, Simeon captures the majesty of Jesus's ministry—he will be a light to the nations—and the misery of his death, like the servant long before him. This is a remarkable perception, a truly astute—Luke would say *inspired*—observation about Jesus's destiny, a destiny that would thrust a sword through Mary's soul.

When we realize that Simeon's song is a collage of words and ideas originally lodged in Isaiah 40–55, we learn something important about the Holy Spirit. Simeon, who receives guidance and revelation because the Spirit rests on him, is a figure of epic inspiration. We know nothing else about him—except that he was a student of the book of Isaiah. Simeon is ripe to lift this peasant son in his arms because the whole of his being is saturated by the prophetic vision of Isaiah 40–55. Simeon is inspired, in other words, because he is vigilant, because he is regular in devotion, and because he has studied the poignant prophecies of Isaiah 40–55, which he now sees taking shape in a small Galilean boy who will be a light to the nations and offer salvation to all the world's peoples.

Though set against the backdrop of Jewish kings (Luke 1:5) and Roman emperors (2:1), the characters occupying the stage of John the Baptist's and Jesus's birth are negligible. No lucre need be pried from their clenched fists; they are not the stuff of Plutarch's *Lives*. They are inconspicuous—but faithful, too—disciplined in prayer and study, and committed to a regimen of Jewish fidelity. If these first stories in Luke's Gospel teach nothing else, it is that an experience of the Holy Spirit rises from regular devotion. Prophecy and blessing arise from singular dedication. Such discipline, such devotion, such dedication—the crucible of inspiration—angle toward that single significant moment, when all that has been learned will come together in a dazzling, long-awaited, yet still unexpected salvation of God, as surprising as a Nazarene baby carried to the temple by his peasant parents with two turtledoves in tow.

2

Spirit, Fire, and a
Vital Message

Matthew 3:11–12	Mark 1:7–8
I baptize with water those of you who have changed your hearts and lives. The one who is coming after me is stronger than I am. I'm not worthy to carry his sandals. He will baptize you with the Holy Spirit and with fire. The shovel he uses to sift the wheat from the husks is in his hands. He will clean out his threshing area and bring the wheat into his barn. But he will burn the husks with a fire that can't be put out. (CEB)	He announced, "One stronger than I am is coming after me. I'm not even worthy to bend over and loosen the strap of his sandals. I baptize you with water, but he will baptize you with the Holy Spirit." (CEB)

The Spirit and Prophetic Power

The heavenly angel may have promised that the prophet would "turn the hearts of parents to their children" (Luke 1:17), but an earthly ruler would have none of it. A father may have thought that his son's job was "to guide our feet into the way of peace" (Luke 1:79), but a king saw in that son the threat of war. It would be utterly wrong to consign John the Baptist to the realm of religion, the sphere of spirituality, or the purely personal. He was to prepare a *people*—not a person. He was to guide *our* feet into the way of peace.

The political ripples of John's vocation and the spacious sweep of his appeal are present in the Gospels: "Though Herod wanted to put him to death," they tell us, "he feared the crowd, because they regarded him as a prophet" (Matt. 14:5). The politician, in other words,

Luke 3:15–17	John 1:19–28
The people were filled with expectation, and everyone wondered whether John might be the Christ. John replied to them all, "I baptize you with water, but the one who is more powerful than me is coming. I'm not worthy to loosen the strap of his sandals. He will baptize you with the Holy Spirit and fire. The shovel he uses to sift the wheat from the husks is in his hands. He will clean out his threshing area and bring the wheat into his barn. But he will burn the husks with a fire that can't be put out." (CEB)	This is John's testimony when the Jewish leaders in Jerusalem sent priests and Levites to ask him, "Who are you?" John confessed (he didn't deny but confessed), "I'm not the Christ." They asked him, "Then who are you? Are you Elijah?" John said, "I'm not." "Are you the prophet?" John answered, "No." They asked, "Who are you? We need to give an answer to those who sent us. What do you say about yourself?" John replied, *"I am a voice crying out in the wilderness, Make the Lord's path straight, just as the prophet Isaiah said."* Those sent by the Pharisees asked, "Why do you baptize if you aren't the Christ, nor Elijah, nor the prophet?" John answered, "I baptize with water. Someone greater stands among you, whom you don't recognize. He comes after me, but I'm not worthy to untie his sandal straps." This encounter took place across the Jordan in Bethany where John was baptizing. (CEB)

was cowed by the prophet's popularity. It would have cost Herod too much to put John to death, even though John had upended Herod for taking Herodias, the wife of his brother Philip, as his mistress. Herod never did have the courage to murder John; he crumpled in the face of pressure. Only when his back was to the wall (after he promised Herodias's daughter whatever she wished for dancing at his birthday party) did his will deflate. What Herodias's daughter demanded, of course, was the head of John the Baptist on a platter (Matt. 14:6–11).

While the force of John's latent political power is present in the Gospels, they are not our only source of information. Before the end of the first century, the Jewish historian Josephus, writing under the largesse of the Flavians, an exceptionally wealthy Roman family, includes a snippet about John the Baptist in his prodigious retelling of history titled the *Antiquities of the Jews*.[1] Josephus tells his wealthy readers that some Jews believed God destroyed Herod's army in revenge for what Herod did to John the Baptist. Herod killed John, Josephus goes on to say, although John was a good man. Politics—ever and always, politics.

Ever the storyteller, Josephus allows the plot to thicken. Herod was convinced, Josephus tells us, that John might spark a revolt—though Josephus does not say why Herod believed this. But the Gospels do—at least they supply the missing link. According to Luke's Gospel, "Tax collectors came to be baptized, and they asked him, 'Teacher, what should we do?' . . . Soldiers also asked him, 'And we, what should we do?'" (3:12, 14). Herod might have tolerated politically innocuous religious teachers, like the Pharisees, listening to John. He might even have tolerated the effete upper class, the Sadducees, listening to John. But tax collectors? They were his source of disposable income. And soldiers? They could threaten a coup d'état should John say the word. These Herod could not tolerate.

And so, writes Josephus, Herod launched a preemptive strike against John and sent him in chains to Machaerus, a mountain fortress, where he was murdered. This is why (Josephus repeats this) Herod's army was destroyed—to avenge John the Baptist. God, in essence, wanted to inflict harm on Herod.

We have come a long way from angelic promises and a father's prophecy to his long-awaited son. Or have we? There was no sentimentality in that promise, no treacle tones in that prophecy before John was born. John was always to be a prophet to the people. He was always to wrest peace from Realpolitik. Filled with the Holy Spirit from before his birth, he was destined to "turn back [*epistrepsei*] many of the people of Israel to the Lord their God" (Luke 1:16 alt.)—not "turn," as in the gradual nudging of a wheel, but "turn back," as in the returning, restoring, and wrenching of a whole people. He was destined to do this "with the spirit and power of Elijah," who had antagonized King Ahab and Queen Jezebel and was known to kings as the "troubler of Israel" (1 Kings 18:17–18) for having brought

---

1. Josephus, *Ant.* 18.116–19.

Israel—and Israel's royal house—to its knees with a hideous drought. Finally, John would turn back the "disobedient to the wisdom of the righteous" (Luke 1:17). Again, not "turn" but "turn back"—and not the pliant but the disobedient, the resistant, and the recalcitrant.

This is what it would mean for John to be filled with the Holy Spirit from before his birth. This is what it would mean, too, for John to be filled with the Holy Spirit at the moment of his death at Herod Antipas's hand. He would hold sway but never power. He would grasp truth but never control. Herod had every reason to fear John the Baptist, not because he was a political usurper but because he was a prophet, not because he was filled with ambition but because he was filled with the Holy Spirit. This is the sort of inspiration that makes the powerful appear pathetic, that renders the formidable foolish—which is precisely what Herod became in the face of John's frankness and fullness with the Holy Spirit.

And this is why when John the Baptist finally speaks for himself his speech lacks flamboyance; it is void of polished rhetoric. The power of John's speech—the fullness of the Holy Spirit—lies not in delicate turns of phrase or in a knack for perfect timing or even in his mastery of Israel's Scriptures; the power of John's speech lies exclusively in its straightforwardness, its ability to strip bare, to clarify the essentials of life in the crucible of another's coming.

The Spirit and Humility

In the earliest Gospel, John the Baptist announces (repeatedly—insistently—if the imperfect tense of the Greek verb *ekēryssen* ["proclaimed"] is any indication): "The one who is more powerful than I is coming after me; I am not worthy to stoop down and untie the thong of his sandals. I have baptized you with water; but he will baptize you with the Holy Spirit" (Mark 1:7–8). Short and to the point—but not insignificant.

John's words are full of *humility*. Though he is the voice preparing the way in the wilderness, though he leads Israel in the spirit and power of Elijah, though he will "turn the hearts of parents to their children, and the disobedient to the wisdom of the righteous, to make ready a people prepared for the Lord" (Luke 1:15–17 alt.), John knows full well that his work is only preparatory.

Jesus knows this too. Long after the baptism, John, while languishing in prison, sends messengers to see if Jesus is the one coming after him. Jesus turns to the crowd and says,

> What did you go out into the wilderness to look at? A reed shaken by the wind? What then did you go out to see? Someone dressed in soft robes? Look, those who put on fine clothing and live in luxury are in royal palaces. What then did you go out to see? A prophet? Yes, I tell you, and more than a prophet. This is the one about whom it is written,
>
> > "See, I am sending my messenger ahead of you,
> > who will prepare your way before you."
>
> I tell you, among those born of women no one is greater than John; yet the least in the kingdom of God is greater than he. (Luke 7:24–28)

More than a prophet but still *preparing* the way—he is not the way itself. And so John, the focus of great expectations, describes himself as less than Jesus's slave, less laudable than someone authorized to strap on Jesus's sandal. There is remarkable restraint in what John says, an utter abandonment of self-promotion and an absolute awareness of his vocation. This is a clear sign of the Holy Spirit in John: he relentlessly resists the temptation to overstep his bounds, to point to himself rather than the way ahead. He refuses to occupy a space that is not his.

The tinge of humility is especially conspicuous in the Fourth Gospel, where John the Baptist says, "I baptize with water. Among you stands one whom you do not know, the one who is coming after me; I am not worthy to untie the thong of his sandal" (John 1:26–27). Notice that the contrast of water and Spirit, though familiar in the Synoptic Gospels, is missing here. The Baptist does not dare to draw a connection between his baptism with water and Jesus's baptism with Spirit. There is a connection between water and Spirit a day later, when John the Baptist mysteriously says, "I myself did not know him, but the one who sent me to baptize with water said to me, 'He on whom you see the Spirit descend and remain is the one who baptizes with the Holy Spirit'" (John 1:33). But this is not a matter of John's baptism with water and Jesus's baptism with Spirit. The association of John with Jesus is more oblique in the Fourth Gospel, where the emphasis lies more on the identity of Jesus than on the relationship—or contrast—between John's and Jesus's baptisms. Jesus will baptize in the Spirit because he himself received the Spirit. So John does not say something like, "I baptize with water, but he will baptize with Spirit." He says something more like, "I baptize with water, but I am unworthy to untie his shoelaces."

The Spirit and Hope

There is something else compelling in these simple words of Mark's Gospel: "The one who is more powerful than I is coming after me; I am not worthy to stoop down and untie the thong of his sandals. I have baptized you with water; but he will baptize you with the Holy Spirit" (Mark 1:7–8). As succinct as it is, what John the Baptist says is full of hope and oriented to a fertile future. This promise of the Spirit is not in dribbles or drips but in a full dunk, in a baptism like the baptisms in the Jordan River that people came from all over Judea to experience. With a promise such as this, John recalls the great prophetic promises of the Spirit outpoured, of transformation, of deserts turned into forests and servants made into prophets.

> For the palace will be forsaken,
>   the populous city deserted;
> the hill and the watchtower
>   will become dens forever,
> the joy of wild asses,
>   a pasture for flocks;
> until a spirit from on high is poured out on us,
>   and the wilderness becomes a fruitful field,
>   and the fruitful field is deemed a forest. (Isa. 32:14–15)

> Thus says the LORD who made you,
>   who formed you in the womb and will help you:
> Do not fear, O Jacob my servant,
>   Jeshurun whom I have chosen.

> For I will pour water on the thirsty land,
>   and streams on the dry ground;
> I will pour my spirit upon your descendants,
>   and my blessing on your offspring. (Isa. 44:2–3)

> Then afterward
>   I will pour out my spirit on all flesh;
> your sons and your daughters shall prophesy,
>   your old men shall dream dreams,
>   and your young men shall see visions.
> Even on the male and female slaves,
>   in those days, I will pour out my spirit. (Joel 2:28–29)[2]

John's is such a simple saying, such a modest promise, yet it is buoyed by promises given long before of outpourings, of rain showers, of deluges.

The power of this promise escalates when we realize that John was a voice in the *desert*, a real wilderness with limestone canyons and unforgiving cliffs so porous that they could not hold water. Parched, the prophet promises refreshment. "I am not worthy to strap his sandals," he knows, "but the one to come will immerse you in the Holy Spirit."

The Spirit and Repentance

It looks as if John the Baptist, drenched in humility but driven by hope, draws a sharp contrast between his baptism in water and Jesus's baptism in the Holy Spirit. The two seem to be entirely different—not water *but* Spirit. Most English Bible translations (e.g., KJV, NRSV, NIV, CEB) make it seem this way. In Greek this is not necessarily the case. The word *de* (but) is like clearing your throat. It can mean "but," "and," or even "ahem." So John's words could just as well mean, "I have baptized you with water, *and* he will baptize you with Holy Spirit."

If John intends a contrast, then the repentance he demands applies only to his water baptism and not to Jesus's Spirit baptism. He

---

2. You will find an analysis of these passages in my *A Boundless God: The Spirit according to the Old Testament* (Grand Rapids: Baker Academic, 2020), 89–103.

demands repentance when he baptizes in water, but Jesus, by way of contrast, will bring the Holy Spirit. Yet if John projects continuity rather than contrast—if the Greek particle *de* suggests "and" rather than "but"—then repentance is requisite to both baptisms. People must repent because John will baptize in water and Jesus in Holy Spirit. Repentance is essential to both baptisms. In short, baptism in the Holy Spirit will *complete* the process of purification that John's water baptism—a baptism of repentance for the forgiveness of sins—begins.

A baptism of repentance, in other words, is not the antithesis of baptism with the Holy Spirit. It is not an act of the will as opposed to an act of grace; repentance is the *precursor* to a baptism with the Holy Spirit. If there is evidence of baptism in the Holy Spirit in a person's life, it is not so much spiritual gifts, not even speaking in tongues, but a life of repentance, of lifelong penitence. It is the discipline of constantly turning back, which is precisely what the angel said John the Baptist would do: "He will turn *back* many of the people of Israel to the Lord their God. With the spirit and power of Elijah he will go before him, to turn *back* the hearts of parents to their children, and the disobedient to the wisdom of the righteous, to make ready a people prepared for the Lord" (Luke 1:16–17 alt.).

John the Baptist was hardly novel in making this connection between repentance, water, and the Spirit. More than five centuries earlier, Ezekiel's promise, given to the people of Judah after they were plunged into exile, had connected turning back—or moving forward afresh—with water: "I will sprinkle clean water upon you, and you shall be clean from all your uncleannesses, and from all your idols I will cleanse you. A new heart I will give you, and a new spirit I will put within you; and I will remove from your body the heart of stone and give you a heart of flesh. I will put my spirit within you, and make you follow my statutes and be careful to observe my ordinances" (Ezek. 36:25–27).[3] Closer to John's time, the Qumran community (it is possible that John had at some point associated with them) took up Ezekiel's promise. During their initiation ceremony, which took

---

3. For an analysis of this text, see my *A Boundless God*, 131–37.

place annually around the Jewish feast of Pentecost, they probably recited something like this:

> For it is by the spirit of the true counsel of God that are atoned the paths of man, all his iniquities, so that he can look at the light of life. And it is by the holy spirit of the community, in its truth, that he is cleansed of all his iniquities. And by the spirit of uprightness and of humility his sin is atoned. And by the compliance of his soul with all the laws of God his flesh is cleansed by being sprinkled with cleansing waters and being made holy with the waters of repentance.[4]

When the dust settles, we can see similarities between initiation into the community at Qumran and John's baptism. Cleansing by water, cleansing by Spirit, and the necessity of repentance—these offer a stunning counterpart to John's declaration and promise, "I have baptized you with water [Matthew's Gospel even adds "for repentance"], and he will baptize you with the Holy Spirit."

The people at Qumran were drawn by the alchemy of the Spirit, repentance, and water baptism into an established community with buildings, a hierarchy of priests, pooled economic resources, and a daily routine of study and prayer. The sort of community into which John called his followers became clear slowly, as Jesus gathered a ragtag but devoted group around him—a group with no buildings, no hierarchy, no clear financial plan, no routine, and certainly no initiation ceremony. Most important of all, John's community was itinerant, focused on turning Israel back to lost ways, while the community at Qumran was sequestered from Israel, which it tended to regard as irredeemably lost.

John, in his inauspicious way and far from the trappings of power in Jerusalem, opened the door to those who gathered around him when he announced "a baptism of repentance for the forgiveness of sins" (Mark 1:4). And the people of Israel, by all counts, responded with alacrity. People from all over the Judean countryside came to be baptized in the Jordan River, "confessing their sins" (1:5). Small wonder that Herod felt threatened. A man of the masses, a man aware of the limits of his vocation, a man of few words and fewer

4. 1QS column 3, lines 6–9.

possessions, John held an almost mystical spell over those who came to hear him. We do not need the Gospels, with their clear bias toward John and Jesus, to tell us this. Josephus, who had nothing to gain from praising John the Baptist (and Josephus was an expert at calculating gain), says that John's preaching struck such a chord that Herod fretted over John's potential power. Herod needn't have been vexed, of course. John, filled with the Holy Spirit, eschewed political power because he knew precisely the limits and promise of his vocation, which pointed his hearers to someone who would baptize them in the Holy Spirit.

The Spirit and Judgment

Humility, hope, penitence, and purification are effects of the Holy Spirit that conjure images of virtue and portraits of faith. Think of the fidelity of John the Baptist's father as he heard the angel's promise after decades of disappointment. Consider the face of John's mother as she, filled with the Spirit, blessed and blessed again. Ruminate upon the open visage of Jesus's mother, puzzling over the angel's greeting. Think of the eyes of the man who lifted the baby Jesus in his arms and told God it was time now for him to die in peace. These are paragons of virtue, people of humility, models of hope. These are, simply put, people of the Spirit.

The Spirit and humility. The Spirit and hope. The Spirit and a life of penitence. These are vital, even vibrant, associations, but these are not the only dimensions of the Spirit in the stories of John the Baptist and Jesus. Matthew and Luke apparently had at hand another version of John's baptism—a trickier one than Mark's or the Fourth Gospel's—a version that associated the Spirit with *fire*. In the Gospels of Matthew and Luke, the association "Holy Spirit and fire" tells us that judgment is afoot.

Together, fire and *rûaḥ* (Hebrew, "spirit") symbolize in the Jewish Scriptures a single act of judgment, as in the words of Isaiah: "Once the Lord has washed away the filth of the daughters of Zion and cleansed the bloodstains of Jerusalem from its midst by a *rûaḥ* of judgment and by a *rûaḥ* of burning . . ." (Isa. 4:4 alt.). In this saying, *rûaḥ* is the midpoint that connects judgment and fire. Isaiah also imagines judgment for the whole world when he predicts,

> See, the name of the LORD comes from far away,
>   burning with God's anger, and in thick rising smoke;
> God's lips are full of indignation,
>   and God's tongue is like a devouring fire;
> God's *rûaḥ* is like an overflowing stream
>   that reaches up to the neck—
> to sift the nations with the sieve of destruction,
>   and to place on the jaws of the peoples a bridle that leads
>   them astray. (Isa. 30:27–28 alt.)

Rûaḥ is an overflowing stream—baptism by fire.

It would soothe to expunge this association of the Holy Spirit with fiery judgment; it would be ill-advised too. Fire is a ready symbol of judgment in the Gospels. Throughout the Gospel of Matthew, fire accompanies final judgment (Matt. 3:10, 12; 5:22; 7:19; 13:40, 42, 50; 18:8–9; 25:41). Even in what precedes and follows the message of baptism, Spirit and fire are closely related. John the Baptist, as a lead-up to his word on baptism, imagines a fiery judgment: "Even now the ax is lying at the root of the trees; every tree therefore that does not bear good fruit is cut down and thrown into the fire. I baptize you with water for repentance, but one who is more powerful than I is coming after me; I am not worthy to carry his sandals. He will baptize you with the Holy Spirit and fire" (3:10–11). What follows his word of baptism is equally spattered with judgment: "His winnowing fork is in his hand, and he will clear his threshing floor and will gather his wheat into the granary; but the chaff he will burn with unquenchable fire" (3:12). It is not difficult to imagine the distinct association of the spirit with the wind—*pneuma* as spirit-wind—that is necessary to winnow grain (when grain is tossed into the air so that the chaff may be whisked away and the grain fall straight to the threshing floor). Then follows the gathering of chaff and fire, the chaff alight and smoky, the billowing gray of finality, of judgment. Spirit-wind and fire—both images reinforce what John has just said, that Jesus will baptize with Holy Spirit and fire.

No, we cannot be rid of this fiery spirit of judgment that characterizes Jesus's ministry, brings a change in epoch, and catalyzes an unparalleled division between believers and unbelievers, between followers and opponents of Jesus, and even between family members, though it will not always be easy to discern the insiders from the outsiders. Even presumed insiders like prophets and miracle workers will not escape judgment if their works do not match their words:

> Every tree that does not bear good fruit is cut down and thrown into the fire. Thus you will know them by their fruits. Not everyone who says to me, "Lord, Lord," will enter the kingdom of heaven, but only the one who does the will of my Father in heaven. On that day many will say to me, "Lord, Lord, did we not prophesy in your name, and cast out demons in your name, and do many deeds of power in your name?" Then I will declare to them, "I never knew you; go away from me, you evildoers." (Matt. 7:19–23)

This is an unsettling word for insiders to the Christian faith who think the Holy Spirit inspires prophecies or healing or brilliant teaching. If their deeds do not match their words, these insiders will be judged with Holy Spirit and with fire—with fiery, not friendly, spirit.

In Luke's Gospel, John's prediction of Spirit and fire is the culmination of practical teaching about how to live. John teaches in three clusters. The first is replete with judgment, from the words "you pit of snakes" to the prediction that every tree with bad fruit will be "cut down and thrown into the fire" (Luke 3:7–9, my translation). There is no escaping judgment here.

The second cluster of teaching is straightforward and also inescapable. John delivers practical advice on what exactly bearing good fruit means (Luke 3:10–14). This is simple advice. Those in the crowd with two coats or with food must give to those who have none. The tax collectors should collect the prescribed amount and no more. The soldiers should not harass or extort money and should be happy with their provisions and pay. In sum, John's hearers should be satisfied with little and contented with slim pickings. They should be grateful, generous, and good. Those who do this are trees that bear good fruit. Goodness is a matter of money, virtue a simple economic equation.

There is no escaping this. For John the Baptist, the quintessence of goodness is straightforward.

The directness of John's teaching evidently left the people spellbound, wondering if John himself was the Messiah. This growth of anticipation provides the backdrop for John's third cluster of teaching, in which he predicts that another "will baptize you with the Holy Spirit and fire. His winnowing fork is in his hand, to clear his threshing floor and to gather the wheat into his granary; but the chaff he will burn with unquenchable fire" (Luke 3:16–17). With these nature images, John turns the crowd's attention from practical advice about simple living back to the judgment of trees that fail to bear good fruit. In such a context, *pneuma* appears to be the wind that blows away the chaff that will be burned. There is, however, much more in this brief rebuttal, for it is not wind but holy *pneuma* that, with fire, is the material of a baptism that not only extends but also far exceeds John's water baptism.

John the Baptist's teaching is not a how-to primer on the good life. John's advice to soldiers, for example, is hardly about how to discover personal fulfillment in their vocations; it is an appeal for daily justice. His language is feisty, even quarrelsome; his images consist of axes, eternally burning trees, and the spirit-wind and fire that would purify Jerusalem. If this is good news—as Luke says, "So, with many other exhortations, he proclaimed the good news to the people" (3:18)— it is good news only to the practical penitents who give away coats and food. To others who consider themselves insiders in the divine economy, it comes as judgment. These people are of less use to God than stones, which God can raise to become Abraham's children.

The association of the Holy Spirit with fire suggests finality. Annihilation would be easy and final—like a firestorm of death in one fell swoop, like the apocalyptic figure in 4 Ezra 13:10–11, who scorches his enemies with the spirit-breath of his mouth. In the Gospels, judgment is more protracted, more complex. Think of Jesus's statement about avoiding the fire of hell: "If your hand or your foot causes you to stumble, cut it off and throw it away; it is better for you to enter life maimed or lame than to have two hands or two feet and to be thrown into the eternal fire. And if your eye causes you to stumble, tear it out and throw it away; it is better for you to enter life with one eye than to have two eyes and to be thrown into the hell of fire" (Matt. 18:8–9). Here, avoiding final judgment demands judging one's actions *in the meantime*.

In the end, an encounter with Jesus is not just an encounter with love; his demands are so rigorous, his standards so severe, that only the Holy Spirit, with its fiery presence, can burn away, bit by bit, what otherwise destines even his followers to an eternal fire.[5] Purification by the Spirit in the presence of Jesus (preserved for us in the Gospels) keeps the fire of judgment away in the end, even though it burns, scalds, and scars.

There is, therefore, a genuine harshness in the introduction of the Holy Spirit at the start of Jesus's public life in the Gospels of Matthew and Luke. The gentle dove has not yet descended. Demons have not yet been driven out by the Spirit of God. Healing miracles have not yet come about through the presence of the Holy Spirit. The commission to baptize in the name of Father, Son, and Holy Spirit has not yet been extended by a resurrected Lord. For now, nearly at the start of the Gospels of Matthew and Luke, the Holy Spirit is experienced harshly, with fire as a means of judgment, but this is judgment that cleanses now, Spirit that purifies now, fire that refines now—not in mystical journeys or quests for personal fulfillment, not even in the exercise of astonishing spiritual gifts, but in simple gratitude, sustained generosity, prolonged contentment. *Give your second coat away. Give extra food away. Be satisfied with your wages.* There is no straight path from time to eternity, from sin to justice, except through a penitence-rich, sustained and simple daily experience— *practice* might be a better word—of the Holy Spirit and fire.

The Spirit and Praise

The Gospels offer no clear moment at which a reader can say, "Finally! John's promise is fulfilled! The Holy Spirit and fire are ours!" This

---

5. Naturally, in association with fire, I opt to use the pronoun *it* to refer to the Holy Spirit here. Yet I tend also to prefer the neuter pronoun in general to avoid assigning gender to the Spirit. No pronoun is adequate, of course. On this issue, see my *A Boundless God*, 160–62.

is especially true of Mark's Gospel. Jesus selects disciples, teaches them, and is exasperated by their failure to grasp the meaning of his teaching. He never baptizes his followers with the Holy Spirit, as John the Baptist promised. Instead, they finish out the Gospel of Mark flawed, failing even to show up early at the tomb with the women who brought spices. The disciples end up quite as obdurate as when they began, quite as uncomprehending in Jerusalem as they had proven to be in Galilee.

Though a good bit longer on the whole, Matthew's Gospel offers little more than Mark's to suggest that Jesus baptized those around him with Holy Spirit and fire. The trial his followers endure is his trial and death, but they give no evidence of having come through it any more pure or penitent—certainly no more humble and hopeful—than when they began.

Luke does offer fulfillment, though not in the Gospel itself. Only in his second volume, the book of Acts, do Jesus's followers receive Spirit and fire. After his resurrection, Jesus orders them "not to leave Jerusalem, but to wait there for the promise of the Father. 'This,' [Jesus] said, 'is what you have heard from me; for John baptized with water, but you will be baptized with the Holy Spirit not many days from now'" (Acts 1:4–5). Luke alters John's promise in revealing ways. He adds, first of all, "not many days from now," a chronological detail that paves the way for Pentecost, the point at which a reader can say, "Finally! John's promise is fulfilled!" He also omits the element of fire, though it is there in the Gospel version of John the Baptist's word of baptism. Consequently, Luke rather tidily eviscerates judgment and accentuates the Holy Spirit, the driving force of the early church in the book of Acts.

When Spirit and fire do finally come, on the Jewish harvest feast of Pentecost, they do not bring judgment, at least not overtly so. The experience of Jesus's followers aligns with those of Zechariah, Elizabeth, and Simeon. Like them, the followers wait (Acts 1:7–8). They pray together in the upper room (1:14). And clearly they study the Scriptures as Simeon did, for when tongues as of fire settle on them and each is filled with Holy Spirit, they recite God's praiseworthy acts and mighty deeds in languages they do not know (2:1–13). "God's praiseworthy acts" is shorthand for a recitation of Israel's history. In the Torah, Moses encourages the Israelites to "acknowledge God's praiseworthy acts [*megaleia*], God's mighty hand and God's outstretched arm" (Deut. 11:2, my translation).[6]

Luke resurrects John's saying again when, later on, gentiles receive the Holy Spirit in the city of Caesarea (Acts 10:34–48). Summoned by Cornelius, Peter treks to Caesarea to meet gentiles, who were not compelled to adhere to Jewish customs. While Peter is preaching, the Holy Spirit pours over the gentiles, who speak in tongues and praise (*megalynontōn*) God (10:46).

In his report to church leaders in Jerusalem afterward, Peter reflects again on this outpouring of the Spirit upon gentiles—this time in light of John the Baptist's promise (not as it appears in the Gospel but as it appears in Acts 1): "And as I began to speak," Peter recollects, "the Holy Spirit fell upon them just as it had upon us at the beginning. And I remembered the word of the Lord, how he had said, 'John baptized with water, but you will be baptized with the Holy Spirit.' If then God gave them the same gift that God gave us when we believed in the Lord Jesus Christ, who was I that I could hinder God?" Those in the Jerusalem church are silenced by this, so they praise God, saying, "Then God has given even to the Gentiles the repentance that leads to life" (Acts 11:15–18 alt.).

The Jewish followers of Jesus praise God when they hear that the gentiles, too, have praised God. This note of praise takes us back to Pentecost, when the Holy Spirit first filled Jesus's followers and they proclaimed the praiseworthy acts of God in a swath of languages (Acts 2:1–13). The same Jewish followers who proclaimed God's praiseworthy acts at Pentecost now praise God when they hear that the Holy Spirit has led the gentiles to praise God.

The common denominator of the Holy Spirit's presence is praise: praise in Jerusalem when the Holy Spirit first fills them (Acts 2:11), praise among gentiles in Caesarea when the Holy Spirit falls upon them (10:46), and praise again in Jerusalem when Jesus's followers hear that the Holy Spirit has fallen on the gentiles (11:18). Finally, John the Baptist's prediction has become reality in mouths full of

6. The Greek translation of the Hebrew represented by the English "praiseworthy acts" in Deut. 11:2 is *ta megaleia autou*.

praise, Jewish and gentile mouths, from Jerusalem to Caesarea and back again.

But of course, John the Baptist's promise had long been fulfilled, in a way, before the marvel of Pentecost and the days of wonder that followed. Zechariah had been refined by the fire of waiting, Elizabeth by the flare of shame. Mary had been singed by the surprise of illicit birth and again by the whispered words of Simeon that she carried with her until her heart was pierced along with her son. Simeon himself—Anna the prophet, too—had been refined by years of waiting and studying and praying.[7] Even John the Baptist, who had endured the self-imposed penitence of life in the desert, would die at the hands of a jealous king. In a real sense, we have come full circle back to the joy of Zechariah, to the praise of Elizabeth as the baby bounced in her belly, to the acclaim of Simeon as he lifted the baby into the air, and even to the fur-clad, locust-fed prophet who spent his days guiding Israel into the path of peace. All of them were full of the Holy Spirit. Each of them was full of praise, of Israel's story experienced afresh.

If *a life of repentance* is evidence of baptism with both water and the Holy Spirit, and if *refinement* is evidence of baptism with the Holy Spirit and fire, then *praise* is also evidence of baptism with the Holy Spirit.

Penitence. Purging. Praise. These are the fruits of John the Baptist's reckoning that someone whose sandal he was not worthy to untie would baptize with the Holy Spirit—and fire.

---

7. Anna appears as a prophet in Luke 2:36–38.

3

Spirit and the Sway
of Baptism

Matthew 3:13–17	Mark 1:9–11
At that time Jesus came from Galilee to the Jordan River so that John would baptize him. John tried to stop him and said, "I need to be baptized by you, yet you come to me?" Jesus answered, "Allow me to be baptized now. This is necessary to fulfill all righteousness." So John agreed to baptize Jesus. When Jesus was baptized, he immediately came up out of the water. Heaven was opened to him, and he saw the Spirit of God coming down like a dove and resting on him. A voice from heaven said, "This is my Son whom I dearly love; I find happiness in him." (CEB)	About that time, Jesus came from Nazareth of Galilee, and John baptized him in the Jordan River. While he was coming up out of the water, Jesus saw heaven splitting open and the Spirit, like a dove, coming down on him. And there was a voice from heaven: "You are my Son, whom I dearly love; in you I find happiness." (CEB)

Just an Ordinary Day

It is all so ordinary: "In those days Jesus came from Nazareth of Galilee and was baptized by John in the Jordan" (Mark 1:9). Like the crowds from Judea, Jesus is drawn to the Baptist, and with the crowds he is baptized along the muddy banks of the Jordan River. Luke puts it this way: "Now when all the people were baptized, and when Jesus also had been baptized" (Luke 3:21). Jesus is one of—not even the first of—many. The Fourth Gospel says that "the next day [John] saw Jesus coming toward him" (John 1:29). Just a day, the next day, an ordinary day.

It is not even a public spectacle. In the earliest Gospel, Mark stresses that Jesus, rising from the water, sees the heavens opened and the Spirit's descent as a dove. The crowds are apparently oblivious—only Jesus sees. For them, at least, it is an ordinary day.

Matthew's Gospel is ambiguous as well: "the heavens were opened," presumably for everyone to see (Matt. 3:16). Some important ancient manuscripts even add the words "to him"—the heavens were opened *to him*, as if only Jesus and no one else saw the clouds torn apart. The story goes on to say that *Jesus* saw the dove's descent. This, too, may imply that the experience of the Spirit was Jesus's alone rather than the public's. On balance, then, Matthew's story of

Luke 3:21–22	John 1:29–34
When everyone was being baptized, Jesus also was baptized. While he was praying, heaven was opened and the Holy Spirit came down on him in bodily form like a dove. And there was a voice from heaven: "You are my Son, whom I dearly love; in you I find happiness." (CEB)	The next day John saw Jesus coming toward him and said, "Look! The Lamb of God who takes away the sin of the world! This is the one about whom I said, 'He who comes after me is really greater than me because he existed before me.' Even I didn't recognize him, but I came baptizing with water so that he might be made known to Israel." John testified, "I saw the Spirit coming down from heaven like a dove, and it rested on him. Even I didn't recognize him, but the one who sent me to baptize with water said to me, 'The one on whom you see the Spirit coming down and resting is the one who baptizes with the Holy Spirit.' I have seen and testified that this one is God's Son." (CEB)

Jesus's baptism suggests that the opening of the heavens was not a public event, and the descent of the dove was a private affair. Add to this another clue: Matthew's disinterest in the reaction of the crowds to the breach in heaven.

Luke, for his part, writes that "the heaven was opened" after "all the people were baptized" (Luke 3:21); he removes the verb *he saw*, which in Mark's Gospel gives the experience a private tenor (Mark 1:10). Presumably all of them basked in the light of heaven, yet Luke makes nothing of it. Luke is perfectly capable of describing a group experience—like Pentecost, when he emphasizes that tongues as of fire rested on each one of them (Acts 2:1–4). But in the baptismal scene, Luke does not say who saw the heavens opened one way or the other. He certainly does not record a reaction from the crowds—no one was blinded by a heavenly light like Saul on the road to Damascus (Acts 9:3).

In the Fourth Gospel, the story is narrated differently—through John the Baptist's eyes: "I saw the Spirit descending from heaven like a dove, and it remained on him" (John 1:32). Did the crowds see the Spirit too? Or just John? The Fourth Gospel reveals no interest in this question.

Whether the crowds saw the heavens torn open and the dove fluttering downward cannot be said for sure. All three accounts in the

Synoptic Gospels are ambiguous, even discreet. It is just a day—probably just an ordinary day—for the crowds of people on the banks of the Jordan. They listen to John the Baptist teach about contentment, justice, and generosity, and they repent. They confess their sins. They are baptized by the prophet. They go home.

It is puzzling that not one of the Gospel writers makes this a public spectacle. The prophet in the spirit and power of Elijah is there. The crowds, who even Josephus tells us were spellbound by John the Baptist, are there. The Son of God is there. Even the occasion is there: an entrée to ministry, an inauguration.

All of this privacy is puzzling—or is it? Vocation and commitment that lasts—God knows Jesus will need this kind of commitment—are personal to the core. What the crowds see as they look skyward is immaterial. What John feels in their baptismal embrace is irrelevant. This experience has to be Jesus's own.

And Jesus's own it is.

People Being Faithful

One of Mark's favorite words is *immediately*. Immediately Jesus goes here and does that, and just as immediately he leaves. Mark's story of Jesus takes off with the same breakneck pace. When it comes to the start of it all, Mark's Gospel gets right to the point: Jesus arrives, Jesus is baptized, the dove descends, the voice speaks, and he is thrown *immediately* into the desert. Hardly a glimpse of what brings Jesus to this poignant moment, apart from John's preaching in the wilderness, is available in Mark's story.

This precipitous start raises all sorts of questions. The purpose of this baptism, for instance, is repentance, the forgiveness of sins (Mark 1:4), which suggests, of course, that Jesus is baptized for the sake of repentance, the forgiveness of sins; it suggests that Jesus is a sinner. Matthew resolves this dilemma by introducing a conversation between Jesus and John in which John initially refuses to baptize Jesus. Jesus responds by telling John that he must do this to "fulfill all righteousness" (Matt. 3:15). This is a classic expression of Matthew's commitment to demonstrate that Jesus obeys Torah. He is baptized not because he needs to repent but in order to fulfill every jot and tittle of Torah (Matt. 5:17–20).

It would be shortsighted to interpret this conversation exclusively on theological grounds: as an effort to exonerate Jesus, to extract him from sin, or to present him as someone who, in the words of the Letter to the Hebrews, was tested in all respects but was without sin (Heb. 4:15). This may well be true, but this conversation expresses something more basic: Jesus's faithfulness.

The conversation in this regard is almost cinematic. The scene begins with a throng gathered along the shores of the Jordan River: "Then the people of Jerusalem and all Judea were going out to him, and all the region along the Jordan, and they were baptized by him in the river Jordan, confessing their sins" (Matt. 3:5–6). Enter the Pharisees and Sadducees, whose presence seems to unnerve John the Baptist. He labels them a pit of snakes and lambastes them for trying to escape God's anger. He launches into a tirade about burning trees and winnowing forks and threshing floors and smoldering chaff. Into this raw scene, populated by peasant and priest and Pharisee and prophet alike, enters Jesus, straight from Galilee, with one purpose and one purpose alone: to be baptized by John.

All of a sudden the crowds fall away. The Pharisees lose their foothold in the scene. The Sadducees fade into the background. Only what John and Jesus have to say to each other matters. And what Jesus has to say is simple. He tells John to leave it alone, to let it go for now because it is fitting, suitable, and appropriate to fulfill all that is righteous. So John lets it go; it is that simple.

But Jesus's response is not. It is enigmatic, though a glimmer of its meaning can be captured by a conversation Jesus would have later. Challenged in the temple by a defiant group of chief priests and elders who question his authority, Jesus asks a question about the authority of John the Baptist: "I will also ask you one question," he begins. "If you tell me the answer, then I will also tell you by what authority I do these things. Did the baptism of John come from heaven, or was it of human origin?" Trapped, they argue with each other and then respond: "We do not know," they concede. So Jesus retorts, "Neither will I tell you by what authority I am doing these things" (Matt. 21:24–27).

Jesus then puts his opponents on notice with a deceptively simple story: "What do you think?" he asks. "A man had two sons; he went to the first and said, 'Son, go and work in the vineyard today.' He answered, 'I will not'; but later he changed his mind and went. The father went to the second and said the same; and he answered, 'I go, sir'; but he did not go. Which of the two did the will of his father?" The chief priests and scribes respond, "The first." This story of simple obedience leads Jesus back to the Baptist: "Truly I tell you, the tax collectors and the prostitutes are going into the kingdom of God ahead of you. For John came to you in the way of righteousness [*en hodo dikaiosynēs*] and you did not believe him, but the tax collectors and the prostitutes believed him; and even after you saw it, you did not change your minds and believe him" (Matt. 21:28–32). John came in the path of justice, of *dikaiosynē*, of simple obedience.

John had traveled the way of righteousness (*dikaiosynē*); Jesus would now be baptized to fulfill all righteousness (*dikaiosynē*). John had walked along the fringes of society; Jesus, too, would stay the course of justice in the company of tax collectors and prostitutes by demanding allegiance to a kingdom that requires discipline and simplicity—the very contentment and gratitude the Baptist had urged for the soldiers, the tax collectors, and the crowds. This is the very contentment and gratitude that Jesus would also demand of his own disciples when he urged them to live by an exceptional righteousness (*dikaiosynē*), understood in the simplest of terms: giving one's cheek to an attacker, one's cloak to a beggar, and one's livelihood to anyone who asks (Matt. 5:38–42).

The way of righteousness evinces an unavoidable simplicity that permeates not just the exceptional flashes of intense piety or unbridled enthusiasm but those quotidian moments that call for contentment, gratitude, and generosity. So Jesus comes from Galilee, walking not so much the trade routes and byways as the way of righteousness, paving the way for the descent of the dove.

The Descent of the Spirit

Though emblematized in icon and painting, sculpture and stained glass, the descent of the dove was understood from the start in different ways.

Mark, as we would expect, gets right to the point: Jesus arrives, Jesus is baptized, the dove descends, and the voice speaks. The scene lacks personality except for a small Greek preposition, *eis*: the Spirit descends *into* Jesus after his baptism (Mark 1:10). Although the Greek preposition *eis* (into) may at times be synonymous with the preposition *epi* (upon)—as in Mark 13:3—it usually means "into." The Spirit descends *into* Jesus. Clearly the Spirit is not an actual dove that somehow disappears into Jesus's body; the Spirit descends *like* a dove and enters him.

For Mark, and Matthew after him, the words "like a dove" are adverbial, describing the way in which the Spirit descends: in a dove-like manner. It flutters through the violent rupture of the clouds, not like the thunder at Sinai or the rushing wind of Pentecost and unlike the Spirit that clobbered the soon-to-be-king Saul and the tragic hero Samson. The Spirit descends lightly, like a dove.

▬ ▬ ▬

Luke fashions his own aura of the dove's descent. He adds conspicuously that Jesus was praying while the dove descended on him. Prayer, of course, plays a key role in Luke's Gospel, so it is only natural that Luke should portray Jesus as a person of prayer at this focal point in his life. As after healing a leper, Jesus "would withdraw to deserted places and pray" (Luke 5:16). Before selecting twelve apostles, "he went out to the mountain to pray; and he spent the night in prayer to God" (6:12). Unlike in Matthew's Gospel, Jesus gives his disciples a model prayer—the Lord's Prayer, or the Our Father—only after "praying in a certain place" (11:1). He even sums up this session on prayer: "If you then, who are evil, know how to give good gifts to your children, how much more will the heavenly Father give the Holy Spirit to those who ask him!" (11:13). It is only natural, then, that the Spirit should enter Jesus's life while he is praying.

Yet the act of prayer preceding reception of the Spirit is not just a literary motif in the Gospel of Luke. It drives home Jesus's receptivity and openness and sets him in an ordinary but auspicious line of faithful people who experience the Spirit in profound ways: (1) John the Baptist's aged parents, both of whom "were righteous [*dikaioi*] before God, living blamelessly according to all the commandments and regulations of the Lord" (Luke 1:6); (2) Elizabeth, who, filled with the Holy Spirit, gushed with a threefold blessing; (3) Zechariah, who had anticipated the birth of a son in angel-enforced silence, was filled with the Holy Spirit and prophesied; (4) old man Simeon, who was righteous (*dikaios*) and devout, looking forward to the consolation of Israel, and who, with the Holy Spirit resting on him, had received a revelation "by the Holy Spirit that he would not see death before he had seen the Lord's Messiah" (2:26). Simeon came to the temple, to the peasant parents with small son in tow, "guided by the Spirit." Each of these who experienced the Spirit was forward looking, faithful, dogged, and determined. Their demeanor and their discipline determined their experience of the Spirit.

Jesus now prays and in the posture of prayer receives the Spirit. Perhaps he has learned from the learned, the venerable, the likes of Elizabeth, Zechariah, Simeon, and Anna. Perhaps he knows already what he will later tell his disciples, that "if you then, who are evil, know how to give good gifts to your children, how much more will the heavenly Father give the Holy Spirit to those who ask him!" (Luke 11:13).

What Jesus experiences in the Gospel of Luke he experiences dramatically. Luke writes not that the Holy Spirit descended *like* a dove but that the Spirit descended *in bodily form* as a dove (Luke 3:22). The dove is as real as the bread Jesus breaks on the road to Emmaus (Luke 24:30–32) and the tongues as of fire at Pentecost (Acts 2:1–4). For Luke, the Spirit is not present silently, softly, inconspicuously, or unobtrusively—Elizabeth, at least, exclaimed with a loud voice. Experience of the Spirit at this early point in the Gospel is *visceral*. Small wonder, therefore, that the Holy Spirit descended, according to the Gospel of Luke, *in bodily form* as a dove.

▬▬   ▬▬   ▬▬

In the Fourth Gospel, John the Baptist delivers the theological thrust of the entire Gospel. You will find no obliqueness here, no theological timidity, not an ounce of reticence. In this Gospel, whereas he does not actually *do* the baptizing, John the Baptist testifies to both what happened and what it means. John the Baptist recognizes that Jesus ranks higher than he does because he was before John as the Word of God who became flesh (John 1:14–15). Then, the day after Jesus's baptism, the Baptist recognizes that Jesus is the Lamb of God, who takes away the sin of the world (1:29). John recognizes as well that Jesus is "the Son of God" (1:34). The whole of the theology of the Fourth Gospel is here in a nutshell a day after Jesus's baptism.

Through John the Baptist's eyes, we as readers gain a bird's-eye view of the descent of the dove. Not once but twice the Baptist makes a momentous claim: "I saw the Spirit descending from heaven like a dove, and it remained [*emeinen*] on him" (John 1:32). Then, as if to underscore its importance, he essentially repeats himself, though this time with reference not to the event but to a revelation that would point him to that event: "I myself did not know him, but the one who sent me to baptize with water said to me, 'He on whom you see the Spirit descend and remain is the one who baptizes with the Holy Spirit'" (1:33). Revelation and repetition combine to create the stunning impression of a plan hatched long ago.

Still, in a Gospel that is ripe with theological nuance, a noble simplicity permeates the story of Jesus's baptism. In both the revelation John the Baptist received and the event itself, John knows that the Spirit will not come and go, thrash and leave. In both iterations of the descent of the dove, the Spirit *remains*. This idea of remaining—in more colloquial terms, *abiding*—is indispensable to the Fourth Gospel.[1]

Those who eat my flesh and drink my blood remain in me, and I in them. (6:56 alt.)

If you remain in my word, you are truly my disciples. (8:31 alt.)

I have come as light into the world, so that everyone who believes in me should not remain in the darkness. (12:46)

---

1. Those who do not believe are also characterized by the verb "remain" (*menein*): the wrath of God remains on the unbeliever (John 3:36). Jesus also says to unbelievers, "You do not have [the Father's] word remaining in you, because you do not believe him whom he has sent" (5:38 alt.).

The Father who remains in me does his works. (14:10 alt.)

Remain in me as I remain in you. . . . I am the vine, you are the branches. Those who remain in me and I in them bear much fruit, because apart from me you can do nothing. Whoever does not remain in me is thrown away like a branch and withers; such branches are gathered, thrown into the fire, and burned. If you remain in me, and my words remain in you, ask for whatever you wish, and it will be done for you. . . . As the Father has loved me, so I have loved you; remain in my love. If you keep my commandments, you will remain in my love, just as I have kept my Father's commandments and remain in his love. (15:4–10 alt.)

Remaining means more than accompaniment, though even accompaniment would be welcome. But accompaniment is not a concept that is strong enough to express the force of *remain* in the Fourth Gospel. There is *intimacy* here—picture a parent and a child in a single pool of light, stooped over a shared school project. There is *synergy* here—imagine the thrall of loyal students engrossed in a passionate lecture by their beloved teacher. There is *continuity* here—try to find that single point in a vine where its roots and stock and branches and grapes begin and end. God is not an auxiliary presence in Jesus's life, just as Jesus cannot be an auxiliary presence in his disciples' lives. They have to eat his flesh and drink his blood; they must *absorb* him (John 6:53–56). When the Spirit remains on Jesus, it does not rest like a bluebird on his shoulder. It fuses heaven and earth, merges a father's vision with his son's, creates a seamless synthesis of vocation, of shared lives, of love.

We can see now how the author of the Gospel of Mark expresses the relationship between Jesus and the Spirit—though less elegantly, less gracefully—when he says that the Spirit, descending like a dove, entered *into* Jesus. The scene is awkward—even more awkward than Luke's Spirit in bodily form resting *upon* Jesus. Still, in light of the Fourth Gospel, we are able to catch a glimpse of the shared life of parent and child even in the Gospel of Mark, in which Jesus dashes here and there immediately, rather than settling into slow-cooked theological reflection, as in the Fourth Gospel.

The Significance of a Dove

The Gospel authors, with a detail here, a verb there, express the significance of the dove's descent: *into*, *bodily*, *remain*. These words do not exhaust the significance of the dove. We can discover even more insight, as we have been led to expect from our expedition so far, in the traditions of Israel and early Judaism, which Jesus inhabited.

The image of a dove takes us back to the first lines of the Bible, when God's *rûaḥ* hovered, when "God's Spirit brooded like a bird above the watery abyss" (Gen. 1:2 MSG). The same verb, *hover*, evokes the hovering of a bird of prey over her nestlings in Deuteronomy 32:11. The Spirit that once soared over an unformed creation now descends like a dove toward Jesus.[2] In the Babylonian Talmud, *Hagigah* 15a, the hovering of the *rûaḥ* in Genesis 1:2 is even seen as the fluttering of a dove over her young without actually touching them. *Rûaḥ*, water, and the hovering of a bird, perhaps even a dove, usher in the first creation; now, again, the hovering of a dove, the presence of Spirit, and the murky waters of the Jordan River usher in a new creation.

The dove may signal creation, but the newly formed heaven and earth did not endure for long before a flood turned order to chaos, grandeur to wreckage, symmetry to bedlam. In the wake of destruction, Noah launched a dove

> to see if the waters had subsided from the face of the ground; but the dove found no place to set its foot, and it returned to him to the ark, for the waters were still on the face of the whole earth. So he put out his hand and took it and brought it into the ark with him. He waited another seven days, and again he sent out the dove from the ark; and the dove came back to him in the evening, and there in its beak was a freshly plucked olive leaf; so Noah knew that the waters had subsided from the earth. Then he waited another seven days, and sent out the dove; and it did not return to him any more. (Gen. 8:8–12)

We could pinpoint a great deal in this story as a backdrop to the baptism of Jesus: the tenderness in Noah's outstretched hand; the

2. You will find a discussion of Gen. 1:2 in my *A Boundless God: The Spirit according to the Old Testament* (Grand Rapids: Baker Academic, 2020), 20–21, 160–62.

olive branch as a symbol of fertility (Ps. 128:3), beauty (Jer. 11:16), perpetual benefit (Ps. 52:8; 52:10 MT), and dignity (Judg. 9:9); and the dove as a sign of promise—of those seven days that stretched from a freshly plucked olive leaf in a dove's beak to the final journey marking the end of chaos.[3]

The dove may also symbolize the divine voice, an extremely important means by which God communicates, according to rabbinic literature. In the Babylonian Talmud, *Berakhot* 3a, God's voice is described as the cooing of a dove.

In an Aramaic targum that is a paraphrase of Song of Songs 2:12, the voice of the dove is the voice of the spirit of salvation from Egypt at the exodus. The Hebrew poem reads simply,

> The flowers appear on the earth;
>   the time of singing has come,
> and the voice of the turtledove
>   is heard in our land. (Song 2:12)

The Aramaic paraphrase, which may represent the interpretation of this passage in the synagogue, reads, "And Moses and Aaron, who were like date-palm branches, appeared in order to do miracles in the land of Egypt. And the time of the cutting off of the firstborn has arrived, and as for the voice of the spirit of holiness, concerning the deliverance of which I spoke to your father, you have already heard what I said to him, 'But even the people that they will serve will I judge, and afterwards they will go out with many possessions.' And now, to fulfill what I promised to him through My Memra."[4] The voice of the dove, in this targum, has become the voice of the spirit of holiness—or Holy Spirit.

The dove at the baptism may also indicate precisely what we might expect: Jesus is the Messiah. In the *Messianic Apocalypse* from the Dead Sea Scrolls, the Spirit and an eternal throne are promised to the righteous poor. In this important text, the verb *hover*—the same

---

3. 1 Pet. 3:20–21 states that salvation through water in the story of Noah's ark prefigures salvation through water baptism.

4. This translation is by Christopher Dost for Accordance, Oak Tree Software, 2015.

Hebrew word as in Genesis 1:1–2—portrays the Spirit in imagery like that of a bird:

> For the Lord will consider the pious, and call the righteous by name, and his spirit will hover upon the poor, and he will renew the faithful with his strength. For he will honor the pious upon the throne of an eternal kingdom, freeing prisoners, giving sight to the blind, straightening out the twisted. . . . And the Lord will perform marvelous acts such as have not existed, just as he sa[id,] [for] he will heal the badly wounded and will make the dead live, he will proclaim good news to the poor . . . and enrich the hungry.[5]

This description of the Messiah looks almost exactly like Jesus's response to John the Baptist in the Gospel of Luke. From prison, with time at a standstill, John sends his disciples to ask Jesus if they should look for someone else or remain loyal to Jesus. Jesus's response mirrors the *Messianic Apocalypse*: "Go and tell John what you hear and see: the blind receive their sight, the lame walk, the lepers are cleansed, the deaf hear, the dead are raised, and the poor have good news brought to them. And blessed is anyone who takes no offense at me" (Matt. 11:4–6; see also Luke 7:18–23). The signs of Jesus's messianic status are the characteristics of the Messiah in the *Messianic Apocalypse* with remarkable precision. Remarkable especially is the raising of the dead in both the *Messianic Apocalypse* and Jesus's response. What members of the Qumran community expected, including the Messiah's capacity to raise the dead, Jesus claims to fulfill. And he does fulfill these expectations, because he has received the Spirit that descended on him like a dove or, in the words of the *Messianic Apocalypse*, because the Spirit "hovers upon" the poor, of whom the Messiah—Jesus in the Gospels—is the premier representative.

It would be futile and shortsighted to pick just one of these foregrounds. They resonate in the Gospels, even reverberate, especially since the scene is told in such spare terms with so little commentary. Creation, restoration, the divine voice, the advent of a Messiah for the poor—these do not compete with one another. The Jewish world

5. 4Q521, fragment 2, column 2, lines 5–8, 11–13.

John and Jesus inhabit is rich with texts, rampant with traditions, and rife with expectations. Baptism by a man who will come to be identified as the voice of Isaiah 40 and as the prophet Elijah in Malachi 3 is enough to rouse expectations and to awaken hope. When the Spirit descends *as a dove*, hope for a new creation, rescue from ruin, the inbreaking of a divine word, and liberation for the poor naturally stir—if only the crowd has eyes to see.

A Voice from Heaven

The crowd may have anticipated a divine word or a heavenly voice, but it is Jesus who hears the words. Not in the Fourth Gospel, of course, in which no divine voice accompanies the descent of the dove. The vocation of Jesus is evident only in what John the Baptist has to say about Jesus: that he is the "Lamb of God who takes away the sin of the world" and the "Son of God" (John 1:29, 34). Jesus will sacrifice his life for the world and rule as the Son of God, the royal descendant of King David (2 Sam. 7:13–14). This is a paradox, of course—royal rule and self-sacrifice. It is a paradox expressed succinctly in the Synoptic Gospels through the divine voice at Jesus's baptism: "You are my Son, the Beloved; with you I am well pleased" (Mark 1:11; see Matt. 3:17; Luke 3:22).[6] These are rich words, spoken briefly but rich with meaning—because they are rooted in Israel's Scriptures. The opening words, *You are my Son*, pick up a line from Psalm 2:7, where God addresses the king of Israel at his enthronement. The king testifies to God's promise to him:

> I will tell of the decree of the LORD:
> He said to me, "You are my son;
>   today I have begotten you.
> Ask of me, and I will make the nations your heritage,
>   and the ends of the earth your possession.

6. In the Gospels of Mark and Luke, God addresses Jesus directly; in the Gospel of Matthew, God employs the demonstrative pronoun *this*. Whether *this* points to a public statement is difficult to say, though it does so more than the other Synoptic Gospels' accounts.

> You shall break them with a rod of iron,
> and dash them in pieces like a potter's vessel." (Ps. 2:7–9)

With the evocative words *You are my Son* the baptism of Jesus in the Jordan River becomes a peculiar enthronement of Jesus as David's rightful heir.

The closing words, "with you I am well pleased," recall God's opening words to the inspired servant in Isaiah 42:1:

> Here is my servant, whom I uphold,
> my chosen, in whom my soul delights;
> I have put my spirit upon him;
> he will bring forth justice to the nations.

That inspired servant, a light to the nations and glory to Israel, would die a silent, ignominious death, though not before his opponents would ridicule him, spit on him, pull out his beard, and put him on trial.[7] That servant, full of vision and light, would die at the hands of those who could not embrace his brilliant vision of a world living in the light. This vision was too much for his fellow exiles, who had seen Babylon destroy and desecrate their nation, its temple, and its king. They could not embrace a vision that included other nations, especially oppressor nations, so they destroyed the visionary.

This identification of Jesus as a king destined to suffer should come as no surprise to a student of Israel's Scriptures. Once God had given up on Israel's first king, Samuel anointed David, "and the spirit of the LORD came mightily upon David from that day forward" (1 Sam. 16:13). The servant of Isaiah, too, was chosen, delightful, and anointed with the Spirit to bring justice to the nations (Isa. 42:1).

The strange portrait of Jesus as an inspired king destined to suffer comes as no surprise, especially to a student of Luke's Gospel. Right at the start, the angel Gabriel connects the dots of the Holy Spirit to Jesus as the Son of God and the king of Israel when he says to Mary, "The Holy Spirit will come upon you, and the power of the Most High will overshadow you; therefore the child to be born will be holy;

---

7. These are descriptions of the servant figure, who features in Isa. 42:1–9; 49:1–6; 50:4–9; and 52:13–53:12.

he will be called Son of God" (Luke 1:35). Then, within a year, an aged Simeon understands that Jesus will be the suffering servant of Isaiah, and he takes a baby in his arms and drills deep into Isaiah 42, calling the child "a light for revelation to the Gentiles" (Luke 2:32).

"You are my Son . . . ; with you I am well pleased." These are tender but ominous words. This brief combination of biblical snippets—as fleeting as the dove's descent and the rupture in the clouds—is carefully chosen to communicate Jesus's dual vocation as king and servant, which will transport him over the months ahead from where he is now (the Jordan Valley) to the hill of Golgotha.

But this is not just a job description. There is something tender in these words, despite the inevitability of suffering they portend. Jesus is also beloved. Tying together the sonship and the servanthood of Jesus is the most intimate word of all: *beloved*. There is shared love here, not just vocational clarity. There is affection here, not just a job description.

The scene is a relatively simple one. A crowd that fades into the background. A prophet and his friend deep in conversation. A muddy river. A baptism. A prayer. A cloudy day. It seems like an ordinary day.

Yet it is full of meaning. The dove, in the light of Israel's Scriptures, may be the harbinger of a new creation, of restoration, of a just nation. The divine words, too, are drawn from the well of Israel's Scriptures—Psalm 2:7 and Isaiah 42:1 to be exact. There is meaning in the mundane that can be wrested from Jesus's past, from his traditions, from the texts that fed Zechariah, Elizabeth, Mary, Simeon, and John the Baptist. Jesus, like those who raised him, was poised to hear these words and to understand them, to recognize in them the immeasurable privilege of rule and the menacing prospect of service.

But it all happened so quickly—the heavens, the dove, and the divine words. But as fleeting as the experience was, it defined the entire life and death of Jesus in the months to come, and it transformed an ordinary day—an ordinary *life*—into an extraordinary one.

4

Spirit and the Torment of Temptation

Matthew 4:1–11	Mark 1:12–13
Then Jesus was led up into the wilderness by the Spirit* so that the devil might tempt him. After Jesus had fasted for forty days and forty nights, he was starving. The tempter came to him and said, "Since you are God's Son, command these stones to become bread."	At once the Spirit forced Jesus out into the wilderness.
Jesus replied, "It's written, *People won't live only by bread, but by every word spoken by God.*"	He was in the wilderness
After that the devil brought him into the holy city and stood him at the highest point of the temple. He said to him, "Since you are God's Son, throw yourself down; for it is written, *I will command my angels concerning you, and they will take you up in their hands so that you won't hit your foot on a stone.*"	for forty days, tempted by Satan. He was among the wild
Jesus replied, "Again it's written, *Don't test the Lord your God.*"	animals, and
Then the devil brought him to a very high mountain and showed him all the kingdoms of the world and their glory. He said, "I'll give you all these if you bow down and worship me."	the angels took care of him. (CEB)
Jesus responded, "Go away, Satan, because it's written, *You will worship the Lord your God and serve only him.*" The devil left him, and angels came and took care of him. (CEB alt.)	

Driven Out

Lifted by John the Baptist from the muddy waters of the Jordan River, "just as he [Jesus] was coming up out of the water, he saw the heavens torn apart and the Spirit descending like a dove into him. And a voice came from heaven, 'You are my Son, the Beloved; with you I am well pleased'" (Mark 1:10–11 alt.). The flurry of activity in this scene triggers Jesus's senses—sight and hearing and touch. Wet to the touch with baptismal waters, he looks up to a schism in the clouds and watches the dove's descent while he stands in earshot of divine words spoken to him and him only. This is Jesus's secluded moment before the incessant ambush of crowds, from which he will need to withdraw regularly, and the unremitting opposition of the leaders of the people, who will see themselves steadily losing ground to Jesus. Here, on the ordinary banks of the Jordan, which are nonetheless

Luke 4:1–13

Jesus returned from the Jordan River full of the Holy Spirit, and was led by the Spirit *in*† the wilderness. There he was tempted for forty days by the devil. He ate nothing during those days and afterward Jesus was starving. The devil said to him, "Since you are God's Son, command this stone to become a loaf of bread."

Jesus replied, "It's written, *People won't live only by bread.*"

Next the devil led him to a high place and showed him in a single instant all the kingdoms of the world. The devil said, "I will give you this whole domain and the glory of all these kingdoms. It's been entrusted to me and I can give it to anyone I want. Therefore, if you will worship me, it will all be yours."

Jesus answered, "It's written, *You will worship the Lord your God and serve only him.*"

The devil brought him into Jerusalem and stood him at the highest point of the temple. He said to him, "Since you are God's Son, throw yourself down from here; for it's written: *He will command his angels concerning you, to protect you* and *they will take you up in their hands so that you won't hit your foot on a stone.*"

Jesus answered, "It's been said, *Don't test the Lord your God.*" After finishing every temptation, the devil departed from him until the next opportunity. (CEB alt.)

* This is my translation of the first clause, which reflects the passive voice in the original Greek.
† I have altered the CEB translation at this point to reflect the original Greek, which has the preposition "in" (*en*) rather than "into" (*eis*).

reminiscent of Joshua's ancient and auspicious crossing into the promised land,[1] Jesus has his own moment, his own vision, his own crossing from anonymity to renown.

This is an enviable vision—with an air of certainty, of clarity, anchored by the words of poet and prophet, Psalm 2:7 and Isaiah 42:1. This is one of those moments of absolute lucidity that come about rarely in life. Such lucidity proved elusive even for Jesus. Perhaps he experienced this sort of clarity once more on the Mount of Transfiguration, when he heard the words "This is my Son, my Chosen; listen to him!" (Luke 9:35), which in Matthew's Gospel are even more reminiscent of his baptism: "This is my Son, *the Beloved*; with him I am well pleased; listen to him!" (Matt. 17:5, italics added). Closer to his death, as the menace of a Roman trial unfolded, he

1. The story of the crossing of the Jordan is told principally in Josh. 3–4.

lacked this certainty in the hollows of divine silence, into which he uttered the fateful words, "Father, if you are willing, remove this cup from me; yet, not my will but yours be done" (Luke 22:42 // Matt. 26:39). Centuries later, scribes would resolve the dilemma of an unresponsive God by introducing an angel who strengthens Jesus (Luke 22:43), but this angel is a figment of later hopes for a responsive God rather than a realistic appraisal of the raw scene of Jesus alone in the garden, having to make up his own mind about the way ahead. This is not the baptism, when God identifies the Messiah-servant. Nor is this the transfiguration, when God allies with Jesus. In the garden, Jesus faces death—the rigor of a Roman criminal's death—on his own.

But today, in the Baptist's embrace, Jesus sees the Spirit through the cloven cloud and hears the tender voice quoting familiar words of Scripture applied exclusively to him. There is even heavenly affection here—Jesus is God's beloved—binding together two statements about missional purpose.

No sooner does he have this moment of clarity than it is torn from him, because the truest measure of clarity emerges for Jesus not in the singular confines of a moment's revelation—however idyllic it may be—but in the dogged days of testing in the desert. Jesus is not entitled to a lifetime supply of perfect springtimes; he is destined to endure late summer as well. Those are the dog days, the desert days, that test his mettle.

The gentle descent of the Holy Spirit, therefore, belies its true purpose, which is to drive Jesus violently away from his private respite into a world of rampant hostility: "And the Spirit immediately drove him out into the wilderness. He was in the wilderness forty days, tempted by Satan; and he was with the wild beasts; and the angels waited on him" (Mark 1:12–13). What is certain is this: in Mark's Gospel, the activity of the Spirit borders on violence—on violation. The animals provide companionship, and the angels serve him. But the Spirit's task is singular: to drive Jesus into the wilderness.

The irenic experience following Jesus's baptism, then, is ruptured *immediately*—this is Mark's characteristic word—when the Spirit *drives out* Jesus into the wilderness. This is an explosive verb— *ekballein*—related to the English word *ballistic*. The Holy Spirit drives Jesus out in the same way that Jesus *drives out* demons (Mark 1:34, 39), *drives out* mourners from the room of a dead child (5:40), and *drives out* the money changers from the temple precincts (11:15). With this powerful verb, Jesus even communicates how high the stakes are as he commands his disciples, "If your eye causes you to stumble, *drive it out*; it is better for you to enter the kingdom of God with one eye than to have two eyes and to be thrown into hell" (9:47 alt.). The word also surfaces in Jesus's story about the owner of a vineyard who sent a series of slaves to receive payment from recalcitrant tenants, who just as repeatedly rejected them. The tenants beat the slaves and eventually killed one, so the owner sent his son, thinking that the tenants would respect him at least. They did not. The mutinous vineyard workers recognized the owner's son and "seized him, killed him, and *drove him out* of the vineyard" (12:8 alt.). The verb *ekballein* could not be more violent than in this story. The gentleness of a dove following Jesus's baptism has been left behind by the violent force of the Spirit, driving Jesus out into the battlefield of Satan.

This first action of the Spirit is jarring, grating against the gentle descent of the Spirit. Jesus is not permitted for a split second to remain in the pleasant confines of his vision, with heaven opened, a divine voice directed at him, and a Spirit-dove's docile descent into him. He is not allowed for a moment to remain on the shores of the Jordan River, basking in the words *beloved* and *my Son*. He cannot do so because the Spirit, which arrived as gently as a dove, now drives him into the wilderness *immediately*. There is no hiatus to breathe in the majesty and mystery of his visionary experience.

There may be something even more disturbing in this verb: Jesus drives out demons (Mark 1:34, 39; 3:15, 22; 7:26; 9:18, 38), visitors from the private room of a dead child (5:40), and money changers from the temple (11:15) *against their will*. The Spirit, which now thrusts Jesus out with the fierceness of an exorcist, forces him to exit an experience of divine revelation. The significance of this verb, *drive out*, may be terribly—terrifyingly—clear: *the Spirit drives Jesus into the wilderness against his will*. The Spirit does not comfort Jesus; the Spirit contravenes his comfort. The Spirit does not soothe Jesus; the Spirit banishes him to a godforsaken wilderness.

Though it descends with the grace and promise of a dove, the Spirit now drives Jesus into an antagonistic arena. There, in desolation, Jesus puts to the test his vocation as a Spirit-endowed ruler. Only there, in misery and deprivation, can Jesus begin his work in earnest. The Spirit, therefore, drives him away from the blessed assurance that he is God's anointed, God's beloved, and God's servant, to a world in which all of these assurances are tested and tried in the crucible of hostility.

A Peculiar Inversion

This is not as it should be. The Spirit is a good spirit, a *holy* spirit, a spirit of *truth*. The "fruit of the Spirit," the apostle Paul writes to the Galatians, "is love, joy, peace, patience, kindness, generosity, faithfulness, gentleness, and self-control" (Gal. 5:22–23). But this Spirit, so early in the story of Jesus—right at the start in Mark's Gospel— shows little love, sparse joy, and no peace. The Spirit expels Jesus into the desert rather than nurturing his experience at the Jordan River.

No, this is not as it should be. The world Jesus inhabits is rather neatly suspended between demons and angels, heaven and hell, God and Satan. It is not dualistic in the strict sense, with equal and opposite powers warring against each other. Neither Jews nor Christians ever accepted that Satan could rival God, that demons could challenge angels, or that the gates of hell could prevail against the onslaught of heaven. But there is, nonetheless, a delicate balance between good and evil—what we might call an apocalyptic tension—between above and below, this world and the next.

In this world, the spirits of truth and falsehood can be pitted against each other. Jesus himself, when accused of deriving power from Satan, replies that a house divided against itself cannot stand (Matt. 12:22–28). The author of the letter known as 1 John does precisely this as well when he writes, "By this you know the Spirit of God: every spirit that confesses that Jesus Christ has come in the flesh is from God, and every spirit that does not confess Jesus is not from God" (1 John 4:2–3). In an agonizing effort to come to grips with people who have left the church, who precipitated a schism, he concludes matter-of-factly, "We are from God. Whoever knows God listens to us, and whoever is not from God does not listen to us. From this we know the spirit of truth and the spirit of error" (4:6).

This is a chilling assessment of the situation, which sheds light on the grisly inversion that takes place in the moments following Jesus's baptism. The Spirit descends like a dove through broken clouds. Jesus hears words of assurance, even love. Then the Spirit throws him away into the desert. This is not as it should be. The good spirit acts like the evil spirit; the breath of heaven smells more like belching smoke from the pits of hell.

This good spirit should not drive Jesus out; it should instead ally with him, advocate for him, ensure his well-being. Even the small Jewish community at Qumran, probably within walking distance of where John baptized Jesus, knew this. In their charter document, the *Community Rule*, they discuss how God created "humankind to rule over the world, appointing for them two spirits in which to walk until the time ordained for His visitation. These are the spirits of truth and falsehood. Upright character and fate originate with the Habitation of Light; perverse, with the Fountain of Darkness."[2]

Within this framework, which may have permeated the Jewish world Jesus occupied, "God's love for one spirit lasts forever."[3] "All who walk in this spirit will know healing, bountiful peace, long life, and multiple progeny, followed by eternal blessings and perpetual joy through life everlasting. They will receive a crown of glory with a robe of honor, resplendent forever and ever."[4] But there is a flip side to this coin. The "spirit of falsehood" is known by its ability to inspire "greed, neglect of righteous deeds, wickedness, lying, pride and haughtiness," and a slew of other depravities.[5] "The judgment of all who walk in such ways will be multiple afflictions at the hand of all the angels of perdition, everlasting damnation in the wrath of God's furious vengeance, never-ending terror and reproach for all eternity, with a shameful extinction in the fire of Hell's outer darkness."[6]

2. 1QS column 3, lines 17–19.
3. 1QS column 4, lines 11–12.
4. 1QS column 4, lines 6–8.
5. 1QS column 4, lines 9–11.
6. 1QS column 4, lines 11–12.

Set the Spirit's action just moments after the baptism of Jesus in this context, and an inversion becomes *perversion*. In a world of two spirits, a good and an evil spirit, a false and a true spirit, only one protects those in its care, inspiring them to unalloyed virtue. Jesus experiences—or seems to experience—just the opposite, raising the question of which spirit, in fact, has taken him by the nape of the neck and thrown him into the heap of desolation west of the Jordan River. The spirit of light or the spirit of darkness?

The Spirit turns on a dime, from inspiration to eviction, as if the dove were only a guise, a ruse, a mask for the evil spirit. We know, of course, the end of the story, so we know the spirit that banished Jesus was not an unholy spirit of falsehood. Still, at this early moment in the story of Jesus, the Spirit did the unexpected by driving Jesus out, by doing precisely what we might have expected of the spirit of *falsehood*, if we were first-century Palestinian Jews like the people of the Dead Sea Scrolls or John the Baptist—or Jesus himself.

The shock of this realization makes of Jesus's temptation something more than an arcane or isolated tale told of Jesus and Jesus only. It becomes rather a cautionary tale about taming the Spirit, which, at the start of Jesus's public life, was anything but benign. A conversation about Aslan (who represents Jesus) between Susan and Lucy and the Beaver family in C. S. Lewis's *The Lion, the Witch and the Wardrobe* communicates precisely the gist of the chink between baptism and temptation. Although they are talking about Aslan, what they say applies no less to the Holy Spirit of the Gospels.

> "Why, Daughter of Eve, that's what I brought you here for. I'm to lead you where you shall meet him," said Mr. Beaver.
>
> "Is—is he a man?" asked Lucy.
>
> "Aslan a man!" said Mr. Beaver sternly. "Certainly not. I tell you he is the King of the wood and the son of the great Emperor-Beyond-the-Sea. Don't you know who is the King of Beasts? Aslan is a lion—*the* Lion, the great Lion."
>
> "Ooh!" said Susan, "I'd thought he was a man. Is he—quite safe? I shall feel rather nervous about meeting a lion."
>
> "That you will, dearie, and no mistake," said Mrs. Beaver; "if there's anyone who can appear before Aslan without their knees knocking, they're either braver than most or else just silly."

"Then he isn't safe?" said Lucy.

"Safe?" said Mr. Beaver; "don't you hear what Mrs. Beaver tells you? Who said anything about safe? 'Course he isn't safe. But he's good. He's the King, I tell you."[7]

Those who care to find safety in the Spirit—solace, succor, support—will have to run with their eyes closed, their gaze averted, past the story of the expulsion of Jesus. Jesus, of course, did not run past the experience; he ran instead with the Spirit at his back—or within—straight *into* the belly of the beast, into Satan's snare, the devil's lair.

East of Eden

The Spirit thrusts Jesus into the unforgiving limestone wilderness to the west of the Jordan River, craggy with rocks, perilous with drought, festering with snakes and scorpions. While he is banished to the west geographically, in another sense he is banished to a different region altogether, to the east—east of Eden. One story of temptation takes place in the wilderness west of the Jordan River; the other story takes place in the wilderness east of Eden. On the bleak surface of the temptation, this is Jesus's story; underneath that bleak surface, this is Adam and Eve's story.

Why see the testing of Jesus as a struggle for paradise? For starters, because the verb *drive out*, in addition to occurring in the Gospel of Mark, occurs in the Greek translation of Genesis 3:24 to depict the expulsion of Adam from paradise: God drives out Adam and causes him to dwell opposite the forbidden garden. The occurrence of the same verb in Mark 1:12 is telling. Adam and Eve were driven out of Eden, and now Jesus is driven into the wilderness like they were.

Jesus's role as a new Adam surfaces as well in the phrase "with the wild beasts" (Mark 1:13). The simple phrase "he was with" elsewhere in Mark's Gospel usually indicates peaceful coexistence. Jesus names apostles to be *with* him (3:14). A man released from demons asks to

7. C. S. Lewis, *The Lion, the Witch and the Wardrobe* (New York: Macmillan Collier, 1970), 75–76.

be *with* Jesus (5:18). During Jesus's trial, Peter is pressed and accused of being *with* Jesus (14:67). The phrase "to be with" suggests companionship. In the wilderness, then, Jesus has companionship with the animals; there is none of the typical hostility between human and beast here. Like the first couple, who ruled paradise (Gen. 1:26–28), and like Adam, who named the animals one by one (Gen. 2:19–20), Jesus is now in the amiable presence of the animals.

The simple detail that Jesus coexisted with the animals fulfills all sorts of Israelite hopes for a restoration of Eden, for return to a peaceful coexistence with wild beasts. According to the Israelite prophet Ezekiel, God promises, "I will make with them a covenant of peace and banish wild animals from the land, so that they may live in the wild and sleep in the woods securely" (Ezek. 34:25). Equally close at hand lies the vision of the prophet Isaiah, which contains the memorable description of an anointed leader—a messianic ruler—on whom the Spirit rests, a ruler who will exercise utter equity and usher in universal peace.

> The wolf shall live with the lamb,
> the leopard shall lie down with the kid,
> the calf and the lion and the fatling together,
> and a little child shall lead them.
> The cow and the bear shall graze,
> their young shall lie down together;
> and the lion shall eat straw like the ox.
> The nursing child shall play over the hole of the asp,
> and the weaned child shall put its hand on the adder's den.
> (Isa. 11:6–8)[8]

In a later vision, the curse of the serpent in Genesis 3:14 surfaces more directly:

> The wolf and the lamb shall feed together,
> the lion shall eat straw like the ox;
> but the serpent—its food shall be dust! (Isa. 65:25)

8. You will find a thorough analysis of this text, and others related to it, in chap. 3 of my *A Boundless God: The Spirit according to the Old Testament* (Grand Rapids: Baker Academic, 2020), 53–60.

This apparently negligible phrase in Mark's brief story of Jesus's testing—that he was with the animals—suggests that Jesus will be the one to restore Eden to its rightful state of peace. He will be the anointed ruler, the king of Isaiah 11, who receives the Spirit, establishes justice, brings the world of wild animals serenely to its knees, and conquers finally the serpent, through whom the first couple was brought to its knees.

But it is not a serpent that tests Jesus; it is Satan. In the Bible, of course, the serpent—not Satan—ensnares the first man and woman. Still, in a fascinating and fanciful ancient retelling of Genesis, the Greek *Life of Adam and Eve* (which may have been popular in Jesus's day, perhaps in oral form), Satan is the primary tempter, who uses the serpent to ensnare Eve.[9] In this version of the story of Adam and Eve, Satan approaches the serpent first so that he can approach Eve through the serpent.

> And the devil spoke to the serpent, saying, "Get up. Come to me." And, having gotten up, he went to him. And the devil says to him, "I hear that you are shrewder than all the wild animals. Listen to me, and I will become friends with you. Why are you eating from the weeds of Adam and not from paradise? Get up and come, and let us make him to be thrown out of paradise, as also we were thrown out through him." The serpent says to him, "I am frightened that perhaps the Lord will be angry with me." The devil says to him, "Stop being frightened. Become a tool for me, and I myself will speak through your mouth one word aimed at deceiving them." And immediately he became suspended next to the walls of paradise. And when the angels of God ascended to worship, then Satan was transformed into the appearance of an angel and praised God with hymns—just like the angels. And peeping out of the wall, I saw him—similar to an angel. And he says to me, "Are you Eve?" And I said to him, "I am." And he says to me, "What are you doing in paradise?"[10]

9. In the Greek *Life of Adam and Eve*, the first couple are not together—they occupy separate portions of paradise—so Satan ensnares Eve rather than both of them; cf. Gen. 3:8.

10. Greek *Life of Adam and Eve* 16:1–17:2. The translation is mine (alt.), from the Greek in "Life of Adam and Eve," in *Early Jewish Literature: An Anthology*, ed. B. Embry, R. Herms, and A. Wright (Grand Rapids: Eerdmans, 2018), 454.

In this version of the Genesis story, Satan is the prime mover in the testing of Eve. Now, not on the edge of paradise but in the desiccation of the desert, Jesus reverses Satan's first move.

There may even be an inkling of the story of Adam and Eve in the way in which the Spirit descends *into* Jesus. Unlike the Gospels of Matthew and Luke, we saw already, in which the dove rests *on* Jesus, Mark writes that the Spirit descended *into* Jesus after his baptism (Mark 9:10).[11] It is a difficult image to grasp, of course—the dove's entering *into* Jesus—though less so in light of the creation of the first man, which reads, in the Greek translation, "And God formed man, dust from the earth, and breathed into his face a breath of life, and the man became a living being" (Gen. 2:7 NETS). The breath went *into* his face, just as the Spirit went *into* Jesus. Like Adam, who received God's breath, Jesus now receives God's Spirit.[12]

We have noted time and again how the New Testament story corresponds to Old Testament stories. Whether through the simple word *genesis* in Matthew's Gospel to depict the birth of Jesus or a kaleidoscope of Old Testament images and phrases, as in Simeon's song, the Old Testament is woven into the New. The story of Jesus's testing, even in Mark's succinct version, is yet another of those occasions when the new story is part and parcel of the old story. Like Adam, Jesus receives the life-giving breath of God. Like Adam, Jesus lives companionably with wild animals. Like Adam and Eve, Jesus is driven out into the hostile wilderness. *Unlike* Adam and Eve, Jesus does not succumb to Satan's trickery. Instead, he succeeds where Adam and Eve failed and returns from the desert empowered—Luke would say "full of the Holy Spirit"—to teach and heal, "proclaiming the good news of God, and saying, 'The time is fulfilled, and the kingdom of God has come near; repent, and believe in the good news'" (Mark 1:14–15). Jesus is not beleaguered and defeated like the first couple but poised to do God's bidding. He knows that the time has arrived. The kingdom is at hand. He has learned this right at the heart of Satan's domain—in hunger, isolation, and vulnerability. If Jesus is

11. Although the Greek preposition *eis* (into) may at times be synonymous with the preposition *epi* (upon), as in Mark 13:3, it more typically means "into."

12. *Spirit* and *breath* are different words, but they occur together in the Old Testament (e.g., Gen. 6:17; 7:22; Job 27:3; 33:4; 34:14–15).

the anointed ruler of Isaiah 11, the king of Psalm 2:7, and the servant of Isaiah 42, then he must confront the horrid face of evil and bring a broken world, even vicious animals, into a peaceable kingdom.

He can do this only in the face of hazard, east of Eden—or in his case, just west of the Jordan River.

A New Exodus

In Mark's Gospel, the Spirit drives Jesus into the wilderness, just as God drove Adam and Eve from Eden. In Matthew's Gospel, the words "was led up into the wilderness" evoke something else: vivid memories of Israel's exodus from Egypt through the Red Sea. For example, not long after their liberation, the Israelites complain to Moses, "Why have you *brought us up* out of Egypt, to bring us to this wretched place?" (Num. 20:5, italics added). The wretched place, of course, is a wilderness. On a more felicitous note, one of Israel's poets recalls (on God's behalf),

> I am the LORD your God,
>> who *brought you up* out of the land of Egypt.
>> Open your mouth wide and I will fill it. (Ps. 81:10, italics
>>> added; 80:11 LXX)

The Spirit's ability to lead Jesus *up* into the wilderness smacks of the exodus, when God led Israel *up* from Egypt.

Luke also sets the testing of Jesus against the background of the exodus from Egypt. After ascending from the river full of the Holy Spirit, Jesus "was led by the Spirit in the wilderness, where for forty days he was tempted by the devil" (Luke 4:1–2). The Spirit leads Jesus *in* the wilderness, to be tested for forty days and nights, just as God guided Israel in the wilderness for forty years.

This image of a new exodus sets the story of Jesus within the story of Israel: the Spirit descends on Jesus and leads him *up* to (in Matthew's Gospel) or *in* (in Luke's Gospel) the wilderness for forty days, just as Israel had been led *up* to the wilderness from Egypt and then *in* the wilderness for forty years. Jesus will succeed where Israel failed. Jesus will emerge from the wilderness not just intact but, as Luke would have it, filled with the Holy Spirit.

This setting for the testing of Jesus—coming up out of the water, the leading of the Spirit, a forty-day sojourn in the wilderness— seems a picture-perfect way to underscore Jesus's larger-than-life role in relationship to his Israelite heritage. Perfect in all but one way.

In the story of the exodus, the Spirit did not lead Israel up to or in a wilderness; other agents did. The tradition begins simply enough, with two pillars—one of cloud by day, the other of fire by night— which lead the people: "The LORD went in front of them in a pillar of cloud by day, to lead them along the way, and in a pillar of fire by night, to give them light, so that they might travel by day and by night" (Exod. 13:21). Alongside these pillars traveled a formidable angel. Introduced first to protect Israel from Egypt (14:19–20), the angel became Israel's long-standing guard, an imposing figure not to be trifled with: "I am going to send an angel in front of you, to guard you on the way and to bring you to the place that I have prepared. Be attentive to him and listen to his voice; do not rebel against him, for he will not pardon your transgression; for my name is in him. But if you listen attentively to his voice and do all that I say, then I will be an enemy to your enemies and a foe to your foes" (23:20–22).

Newly liberated from Egypt, Israel was well protected—but not by the Spirit.[13]

By 586 BCE, Babylon had brought many Israelites to their knees in exile. About fifty years later (539 BCE), after the fall of Babylon to Persia, the Persian ruler Cyrus authorized some of Israel's exiles to return to Jerusalem from Babylon. Mired by drought and distress, they were slow to rebuild the temple, so the prophet Haggai cajoled them into action with a remarkable promise that had never before been made: "Yet now take courage, O Zerubbabel, says the LORD; take courage, O Joshua, son of Jehozadak, the high priest; take courage, all you people of the land, says the LORD; work, for I am with you, says the LORD of hosts, according to the promise that I made

---

13. Except in two brief passages from Israel's prophets. You can find a more detailed analysis of Hag. 2:5 and Isa. 63:7–14 in chap. 8 of my *A Boundless God*, 139–55. For a thoroughgoing scholarly study of these texts, you may consult my *The Holy Spirit before Christianity* (Waco: Baylor University Press, 2019).

you when you came out of Egypt. My spirit stands among you; do not fear" (Hag. 2:4–5 alt.).

What promise did God make? According to Haggai, "My spirit stands among you."[14] This is a bizarre promise. God had made many promises to Israel—but not this one. God had said many things on Mount Sinai—just not this. Haggai refers to a promise that does not exist, at least not verbatim, anywhere else in the Hebrew Bible.

Still, it is not hard to determine why Haggai adopts the word *stand* to describe the Spirit's presence among the beleaguered band that had returned from Babylonian exile. The verb *stand* evokes the pillar's presence at a particularly threatening moment in Israel's distant past when they came out of Egypt. Pinned between the Egyptian army and the Sea, on the night before the exodus, with the Egyptian army in hot pursuit, Israel faced annihilation. Yet all of a sudden, as evening set and peril reared its head, "the angel of God who was going before the Israelite army moved and went behind them; and the pillar of cloud moved from in front of them and *stood* behind them. It came between the army of Egypt and the army of Israel. And so the cloud was there with the darkness, and it lit up the night; one did not come near the other all night" (Exod. 14:19–20 alt.).

The pillar of cloud—and the angel by association—*stood* between Israel and the Egyptian army and protected Israel on the cusp of escape. Without this movement from fore to aft, without the pillar's shift from guide to rear guard, Israel would never have crossed the sea, traversed the wilderness, and settled in the land of promise. Without the shift of the angel and pillar, there would be no comparable history of Israel, no Judaism, no Christianity. This was a singular moment of salvation.

Now, centuries later, shortly after return from exile, the Spirit takes on the role of the pillar in Haggai's promise. What the pillar did during the exodus from Egypt—standing in Israel's midst—the

14. The NRSV tends not to capitalize Old Testament references to the spirit or Spirit but capitalizes New Testament references. I follow the NRSV here but think "spirit" should be capitalized to indicate that this is the Spirit of God—what in Isa. 63:10–11 is called the "Holy Spirit" and in Isa. 63:14 is called the "Spirit of the LORD" (though the NRSV does not capitalize even these obvious references to God's Holy Spirit in the Old Testament).

Spirit will now do during a new exodus from Babylon. The Spirit will stand where the pillar once stood. Haggai could not promise his people a visible pillar of cloud or fire, but he could promise that the Spirit, invisible but ineluctably present, would do exactly what the pillar had done: protect the people of God at the start of a perilous and precarious journey from slavery to emancipation.

▬ ▬ ▬

Another prophet, perhaps a contemporary of Haggai, recalls in still more vivid detail how the Spirit led Israel during the exodus. This prompts him to ask, to plead, even to lament:

> Where is the one who brought them up out of the sea
> with the shepherds of his flock?
> Where is the one who put within them
> his holy spirit,
> who caused his glorious arm
> to march at the right hand of Moses,
> who divided the waters before them
> to make for himself an everlasting name,
> who led them through the depths?
> Like a horse in the desert,
> they did not stumble.
> Like cattle that go down into the valley,
> the spirit of the LORD gave them rest.
> Thus you led your people,
> to make for yourself a glorious name. (Isa. 63:11–14)

This time, the Spirit does what the angel had once done: the Spirit, the *Holy* Spirit in Israel's midst, leads the people of God into the promised land. What the angel had long ago accomplished after the exodus, the prophet longs for the Spirit to undertake again.

The combination of descent and leading, as in the baptismal scene, is actually more apparent in the Greek version of Isaiah 63 than in the Hebrew. The Hebrew can be translated,

> Like a horse in the desert,
> they did not stumble.

Like cattle that go down into the valley,
  the spirit of the LORD gave them rest.
Thus you led your people,
  to make for yourself a glorious name. (Isa. 63:13–14)

According to the Hebrew, as translated by the NRSV, the cattle descended and the Spirit led. The Greek version is different; God

led them through the deep
  like a horse through a wilderness,
  and they did not become weary,
  and like cattle through a plain.
A spirit came down [*katebē*] from the Lord and guided
  [*hōdēgēsen*] them.
Thus you led your people,
  to make for yourself a glorious name.
    (Isa. 63:13–14 NETS)

In the Greek, unlike the Hebrew, a Spirit from the Lord descends and leads. The Greek was probably the version read by the Gospel writers, so at the baptism of Jesus, the Holy Spirit—it is twice called the Holy Spirit in Isaiah 63:10–11—follows the same pattern as in the Greek of Isaiah 63:13–14: the Holy Spirit descends and leads Jesus into the wilderness.

There is, of course, a subtle difference between the lament in Isaiah 63 and the baptism of Jesus in Mark's Gospel, in which the Spirit throws Jesus into the wilderness. Luke resolves the tension and softens the blow. After the Spirit descended on Jesus, Luke tells his readers that the Spirit led Jesus *in* the wilderness. This is precisely what the lament in Isaiah 63:13–14 implies: a Spirit came down from the Lord and guided Israel. Now, a Spirit comes down upon Jesus and guides him in the desert.

███   ███   ███

This much now is apparent: the story of the exodus, pressed through the sieve of Haggai 2 and Isaiah 63, provides a magnificent backdrop to the temptation of Jesus. His was not an isolated quest borne of the need for spiritual validation. His was a historic reversal. Whereas Israel had proven unfaithful during forty years in the wilderness, Jesus now would prove utterly faithful for forty days.

The impact of Haggai 2 and Isaiah 63 seeps into the telling and retelling of Jesus's baptism and temptation. All three Gospels—Matthew, Mark, and Luke—in which the Spirit descends and leads Jesus, mirror the Greek translation of Isaiah 63:14, in which the Spirit comes down from the Lord and guides Israel. In the Gospel of Mark, the Spirit descends into Jesus. In the Gospel of Matthew, the Spirit descends upon Jesus and then leads Jesus *up* to the wilderness at the start of the forty days, as at the exodus, when pillars and an angel led Israel up to Mount Sinai. In Luke's Gospel, the Spirit descends, so Jesus, "full of the Holy Spirit," returns from the Jordan River to be led by the Spirit—like Israel—in the wilderness, "where for forty days he was tempted by the devil" (Luke 4:1). Israel's baseline of leading in the wilderness has been straightforward: God led Israel with pillars and an angel. Yet in the recollection of one prophet, at least, the *Spirit* came down and led them (Isa. 63:14). The pattern is perfectly clear: the descent of the Spirit is followed by leading, both in the time-honored history of Israel and the barely launched life of Jesus.

So many themes are woven into the deceptively simple story of Jesus's temptation that they are difficult to untangle. There is, of course, the foreground of the Jewish Scriptures. Yet even the word *foreground* is misleading. Jesus is not standing in front of a backdrop of a, phony or otherwise, sunset screen or a cruise ship or puffy clouds, as in a high school graduation photo. Jesus's life is shaped by that background, governed by it, *enmeshed* in it. When he hears the words of Psalm 2 and Isaiah 42, the Jewish Scriptures become more than a background; they become a driving force that determines his destiny. The die is cast when he basks in the beauty of those words. Now it is up to him to live into that destiny, to embrace and embody the words that the angel and Zechariah and Simeon and John the Baptist have spoken of him—words deeply rooted in Israel's hopes and dreams.

Yet influence moves in more than one direction. Not only does Israel's story invest meaning in Jesus's story, but Jesus's story brings fresh meaning to Israel's story. If we watch the baptism and temptation of Jesus carefully, we can see how he wraps up the whole of Israel's Scriptures in one life. The temptation of Jesus, in the Gospel of Mark at least, takes us all the way back to the tragedy in the garden of Eden, which led inevitably to the expulsion of the first man and woman. The temptation of Jesus injects hope into that story because Jesus, expelled by the Spirit, lives peaceably with the animals and resists the devil's pressure on him. The temptation of Jesus in the Gospels of Matthew and Luke also takes us back to the story of Israel's origins, this time to the exodus. Like the pillars and the angel, which led the Israelite slaves to freedom in the land of promise, the Spirit now leads Jesus. These versions of the temptation inject hope into the story of Israel because they uncover how Jesus is able to succeed where Israel failed. Battered by an audacious opponent armed with a mastery of Scripture, Jesus reclaims the land once lost, refusing to bow or break. The Spirit leads him up to the wilderness—*in* the wilderness—in order to invest Israel's story with hope in a messianic servant who will bring light to the nations in the power of the Spirit through the nation of Israel.

The injection of hope into Israel's story may seem like a surprising dimension of the temptation story, but it is the product of a Spirit that provides a meeting point tying Israel's and Jesus's stories together so that they shed light on each other. It is not quite right to say that Jesus fulfills Israel's story. We may be better served by putting it this way: Israel's story fills Jesus's story with meaning. To know one is to know more about the other; to appreciate one is to gain greater appreciation for the other. And at the juncture of both is the Spirit, thrusting Jesus into the desert as in Mark's Gospel, leading him up to the desert as in Matthew's, or leading him in the desert as in Luke's. At the heart of the relationship between Old Testament and New, Israel and Jesus, is the Spirit.

We would do well to end this reflection with hope—an optimistic theme for the Spirit. But, as we have seen, that would be shortsighted. Whatever we make of the temptation stories, they mark the epicenter of hostility. The desert. Satan. Testing. All of this with the exclamation point of the verb *ekballein* (drive out) in Mark's Gospel. Not even Matthew and Luke dispel this hostility. The Spirit—and this is the key point—does not deliver Jesus from temptation. The Spirit may coerce him into being tested (Mark) or lead him up to that testing (Matthew) or even accompany him in it (Luke), but the Spirit never once extracts him from that fitful, fateful, forty-day test.

At the center of this imposing drama, then, from Adam to Israel to Jesus, lies the Spirit—though not a gentle dove any longer. Not by any means.

5

Spirit, Promise, Praise, and Prayer

Jesus went to Nazareth, where he had been raised. On the Sabbath he went to the synagogue as he normally did and stood up to read. The synagogue assistant gave him the scroll from the prophet Isaiah. He unrolled the scroll and found the place where it was written:

> *The Spirit of the Lord is upon me,*
> *   because the Lord has anointed me.*
> *He has sent me to preach good news to the poor,*
> *   to proclaim release to the prisoners*
> *   and recovery of sight to the blind,*
> *   to liberate the oppressed,*
> *   and to proclaim the year of the Lord's favor.*

He rolled up the scroll, gave it back to the synagogue assistant, and sat down. Every eye in the synagogue was fixed on him. He began to explain to them, "Today, this scripture has been fulfilled just as you heard it."

Everyone was raving about Jesus, so impressed were they by the gracious words flowing from his lips. They said, "This is Joseph's son, isn't it?"

Then Jesus said to them, "Undoubtedly, you will quote this saying to me: 'Doctor, heal yourself. Do here in your hometown what we've heard you did in Capernaum.'" He said, "I assure you that no prophet is welcome in the prophet's hometown. And I can assure you that there were many widows in Israel during Elijah's time, when it didn't rain for three and a half years and there was a great food shortage in the land. Yet Elijah was sent to none of them but only to a widow in the city of Zarephath in the region of Sidon. There were also many persons with skin diseases in Israel during the time of the prophet Elisha, but none of them were cleansed. Instead, Naaman the Syrian was cleansed."

When they heard this, everyone in the synagogue was filled with anger. They rose up and ran him out of town. They led him to the crest of the hill on which their town had been built so that they could throw him off the cliff. But he passed through the crowd and went on his way.

Luke 4:16–30 (CEB)

A Master Teacher

The Holy Spirit dashes here and there at the beginning of the Gospel of Luke, inspiring prophecies, powerful preaching, even pregnancy. In fact, including the stories of Mary, Elizabeth, Zechariah, Simeon, John the Baptist, and Jesus, there are ten references to the Spirit before Jesus can even take a step. In his first months in the public eye, the

Spirit descends on him in bodily form as a dove and leads him in the wilderness. Then, at the end of this ordeal, he emerges "in the power of the Spirit" (Luke 4:14).[1]

Sixteen references to the Spirit, in fact, populate Luke 1:1–4:18. The rest of the Gospel, from 4:19 until 24:53, contains a paltry four references to the Spirit (10:21; 11:13; 12:10, 12). On one occasion, at least, Matthew's Gospel refers to the Spirit where Luke's does not. Jesus claims to exorcise demons by the *Spirit* of God in Matthew (12:28); in Luke he exorcises by the *finger* of God (11:20). The references to the Spirit in Luke 4:19–24:53, then, may be paltry in number, but they are certainly not trifling in significance.

What Jesus did with "the power of the Spirit" is significant. He did not at first exorcise demons by the power of the Holy Spirit; he did not at first heal the blind, the lame, and the lepers by the power of the Holy Spirit. What did he do? *He taught.* When he returned to Galilee after his testing in the wilderness near the Dead Sea, "a report about him spread through all the surrounding country. He began to teach in their synagogues and was praised by everyone" (Luke 4:14–15).

Jesus was ever and always the inspired teacher. In the next episode, he "went down to Capernaum, a city in Galilee, and was teaching them on the sabbath" (Luke 4:31). He taught repeatedly in synagogues (6:6; 13:10) and later in the temple (19:47; 20:1). But he was not limited to the rarefied air of synagogue and temple. Once, he hopped into Simon's boat, pushed away from shore, "sat down and taught the crowds from the boat" (5:3). Fresh air, too, was a theater of learning for Jesus.

Even his miracles were an exercise in teaching. In his first miracle, an exorcism, onlookers were struck by the power of Jesus's *words*. Beforehand, notes Luke, "They were astounded at his teaching, because he spoke with authority" (Luke 4:32). After the exorcism, they asked, "What kind of utterance is this? For with authority and power he commands the unclean spirits, and out they come!" (4:36). The power of Jesus's spoken word—in teaching and exorcism alike—evoked a response of jaw-dropping amazement.

---

1. This is my translation based on the Greek, *en tē dynamei tou pneumatos*, which lacks the word *filled*.

The synergy between Spirit and teaching is essential to Luke's understanding not only of Jesus but also of believers before and after him. John the Baptist was filled with the Spirit before he was born. During his life he accomplished no recorded miracles and exorcised no demons, but he did teach in straightforward and simple ways, with clear instructions about contentment and generosity and with vivid images of axes and trees and flames. In the book of Acts, Jesus's followers at Pentecost, filled with the Holy Spirit, taught as they proclaimed God's praiseworthy acts in various languages (Acts 2:1–13). Peter, filled with the Spirit while on trial before the Jewish council (the Sanhedrin), delivered a teaching rooted in Psalm 118:22 (Acts 4:8–13). And Stephen, a man known for holy spirit and faith (6:5; 7:55),[2] antagonized his hearers with a protracted interpretation of Israelite history intended to underscore that God was not parochial, that God was not local, that God was not to be found only in the temple (7:2–53). His audience was infuriated and stoned Stephen to death (7:57–60). The Spirit, before and after Jesus, inspired powerful teaching—teaching, it seems, rooted in familiarity with the Jewish Scriptures.

It was not Jesus's exorcisms that wrenched people from their mundane existence, nor was it his miracles—not at first, at least. With the blush of his initial victory over Satan in the desert, Jesus did not begin by exorcising demons or healing lepers in the power of the Spirit. He began as a teacher. He taught like any respectable young man—in his hometown synagogue on the Sabbath. And he did so with notable success: "All spoke well of him and were amazed at the gracious words that came from his mouth. They said, 'Is not this Joseph's son?'" (Luke 4:22). Hometown boy makes good, apparently.

Yet Jesus came to his vocation as a teacher with a peculiar lens, a particular prism. He began innocently enough, among his own people, when he read from the book of Isaiah:

> The Spirit of the Lord is upon me,
>   because he has anointed me

---

2. The phrase in Acts 6:3, "full of spirit and wisdom" (*plēreis pneumatos kai sophias*), lacks a definite article. The phrase in Acts 6:5, "full of faith and holy spirit" (*plērēs pisteōs kai pneumatos hagiou*), also lacks the definite article. "Holy spirit" can, therefore, refer either to *the* Holy Spirit or to Stephen's holy spirit (*a* holy spirit).

> to bring good news to the poor.
> He has sent me to proclaim release to the captives
> and recovery of sight to the blind,
> to let the oppressed go free,
> to proclaim the year of the Lord's favor. (Luke 4:18–19)

While this looks like a simple reproduction of Isaiah 61:1–2, it is more than that. With two changes to the text of Isaiah, Jesus begins to focus his mission. First, he leaves some important words out; he ignores altogether the promise that God will comfort those who weep. That line has gone missing—and with inescapable implications. By excising the promise that God will comfort those who weep, Jesus focuses the text of Isaiah exclusively on economic, social, and physical salvation. God is not about the business of offering comfort and healing to the emotionally broken; God is about breaking the cords of injustice. Second, Jesus snatches a line from earlier in Isaiah and inserts it into his reading of Isaiah 61: "to let the oppressed go free." This is a telltale move that cements the emphasis on the economic, social, and physical dimensions of salvation that Jesus is anointed to bring. This line, which he imports into his reading of Isaiah 61, comes from Isaiah 58:6–7, which reads,

> Is not this the fast that I choose:
> to loose the bonds of injustice,
> to undo the thongs of the yoke,
> *to let the oppressed go free,*
> and to break every yoke?
> Is it not to share your bread with the hungry,
> and bring the homeless poor into your house;
> when you see the naked, to cover them,
> and not to hide yourself from your own kin? (Isa. 58:6–7, italics added)

The prophet is livid about the false piety of fasts and the misguided loyalty of festivals. Only one type of fast, one sort of festival, will satisfy God: one in which the well-fed share their bread, the well-housed welcome the homeless, the well-clothed dress the naked. By importing the line "to let the oppressed go free" from this context,

Jesus stakes a clear claim to the sort of salvation he will bring. The Spirit of the Lord is upon him, the anointed one, to bring salvation to the poor—salvation as bread, salvation as a bed, salvation as a warm cloak on a cold night.

Jesus's teaching reveals a razor-sharp awareness of his vocation: to bring good news to the poor. If we recall again the hope captured by the *Messianic Apocalypse* from the Dead Sea Scrolls, it becomes apparent that Jesus intends to fulfill the expectations on behalf of only one group of people:

> For the Lord will consider the pious, and call the righteous by name, and his spirit will hover upon the poor, and he will renew the faithful with his strength. For he will honor the pious upon the throne of an eternal kingdom, freeing prisoners, giving sight to the blind, straightening out the twisted. . . . And the Lord will perform marvelous acts such as have not existed, just as he sa[id,] [for] he will heal the badly wounded and will make the dead live, he will proclaim good news to the poor . . . and enrich the hungry.[3]

There is no dichotomy between holiness and healing, between fidelity and feeding the hungry. The Spirit is upon Jesus to do precisely this: to bring good news to the poor—news of a meal on the table, a roof over their heads, a mantle around their shoulders. Jesus teaches this not by reading rotely from Isaiah 61 but by excising the words "comfort all who mourn" and importing the words "let the oppressed go free" into his teaching.

This sermon economically communicates that the work of the Spirit is not spiritual in the sense of otherworldly. The hard labor of the Spirit is to inspire a servant-son who will reestablish equity in the earth, redistribute wealth, and release debtors from prison. This is the servant who will go on to say point-blank, "Blessed are you who are poor" and "Woe to you who are rich" (Luke 6:20, 24). There can be no vacillation about this vision, no straddling of priorities. There can be, as Simeon foresaw, only the falling and rising of many in Israel, which is exemplified in Jesus's teaching about a rich man and a poor man—only one of whom rises to eternal succor

---

3. 4Q521, fragment 2, column 2, lines 5–8, 11–13.

with Abraham while the other falls into the sweltering heat of Hades (Luke 16:19–31).

It is a masterful stroke, an inspired strategy. With this single citation and the modifications made to it, Jesus identifies himself as the inspired servant who "will bring forth justice to the nations" (Isa. 42:1). The baptismal words he heard at the Jordan River, with their echo of Isaiah 42, are already taking shape. There can be no doubt about who he is, whom he will liberate, or whom God, through this anointed servant and son, will champion. The message of Jesus, the suffering servant of Isaiah, is clear: the year of the Lord is a year of economic equity and impeccable justice, perhaps even the Year of Jubilee encoded in Torah (Lev. 25:8–55), when debts are canceled, lands are left fallow for the poor, and debt-prisoners are released.

The people seem amazed, even impressed, by this sort of teaching, but apparently the gist of his inspired teaching has not yet dawned on them. So, anointed with the Spirit, Jesus does what a masterful teacher does when students receive a teaching without understanding it: he generates a rift. Despite the positive response he has received, he accuses them of wanting to challenge him: "Doctor, cure yourself." He throws in their faces the now infamous saying "A prophet is not without honor except in a hometown." Then, just as we might expect of an inspired teacher, he digs deep into the Jewish Scriptures to come up with two examples of how God went outside of Israel to find people of faith. During an unbearable drought, the prophet Elijah went to a widow far to the north in Sidon, while his protégé, Elisha, cleansed not Israel's lepers but Naaman the Syrian.[4]

This worked: "When they heard this, all in the synagogue were filled with rage. They got up, drove him out of the town, and led him to the brow of the hill on which their town was built, so that they might hurl him off the cliff" (Luke 4:28–29). Brought to the edge of a cliff—a topographical rift comparable to the rift he had caused with his teaching—Jesus somehow slips from their grasp. And so, in this inauspicious way, the road to suffering begins. The

4. The story about Elijah in Sidon occurs in 1 Kings 17:9–24. The story about Elisha and Naaman occupies the whole of 2 Kings 5.

people of the Dead Sea Scrolls hoped for someone anointed to heal the wounded, bring good news to the poor, and enrich the hungry. Jesus's mother saw in her son the advent of a God who would fill the hungry with good things and send the rich away empty-handed (1:53). Simeon foresaw God's salvation beyond the narrow confines of Israel, "prepared in the presence of all peoples, a light for revelation to the Gentiles and for glory to your people Israel" (2:31–32). But this salvation will, as it did in the servant's own day, create a rift between those who prize salvation for themselves and those who cherish salvation for others—the debt-prisoner, the sick, the blind, the outsider. As Simeon so presciently saw, salvation for all peoples, a light for revelation to the nations, would occasion the rising and falling of many in Israel—and place a dagger in Mary's heart (Luke 2:34–35).

A True Miracle

After a flurry of references to the Spirit at Jesus's birth and the start of his public work, the Spirit goes underground until after Jesus sends seventy disciples on a mission to cure the sick and proclaim the nearness of God's reign (Luke 10:9). They return and report, "Lord, in your name even the demons submit to us!" (10:17). In an uncharacteristically unguarded moment, Jesus responds gleefully when he claims that he saw Satan fall from heaven and that he has given his closest friends authority to trample on snakes and scorpions and "over all the power of the enemy" (10:10). He continues, at that very moment, to rejoice in the Holy Spirit.

The detail that Jesus rejoices in the Holy Spirit unmistakably recalls the stories of Elizabeth and Zechariah: "Elizabeth was filled with the Holy Spirit and exclaimed with a loud cry, 'Blessed are you among women, and blessed is the fruit of your womb'" (Luke 1:41–42). Zechariah, too, "was filled with the Holy Spirit and spoke this prophecy: 'Blessed be the Lord God of Israel, for God has looked favorably on God's people and redeemed them'" (1:67–68 alt.). Like them, Jesus now "rejoices in the Holy Spirit" and, in a second, private

Matthew 11:25–30	Luke 10:21–24
At that time Jesus said, "I praise you, Father, Lord of heaven and earth, because you've hidden these things from the wise and intelligent and have shown them to babies. Indeed, Father, this brings you happiness.	At that very moment, Jesus overflowed with joy from the Holy Spirit and said, "I praise you, Father, Lord of heaven and earth, because you've hidden these things from the wise and intelligent and shown them to babies. Indeed, Father, this brings you happiness. My Father has handed all things over to me. No one knows who the Son is except the Father, or who the Father is except the Son and anyone to whom the Son wants to reveal him."
"My Father has handed all things over to me. No one knows the Son except the Father. And nobody knows the Father except the Son and anyone to whom the Son wants to reveal him.	
"Come to me, all you who are struggling hard and carrying heavy loads, and I will give you rest. Put on my yoke, and learn from me. I'm gentle and humble. And you will find rest for yourselves. My yoke is easy to bear, and my burden is light." (CEB)	
	Turning to the disciples, he said privately, "Happy are the eyes that see what you see. I assure you that many prophets and kings wanted to see what you see and hear what you hear, but they didn't." (CEB)

moment offers, not unlike Elizabeth, his own blessing: "Blessed are the eyes that see what you see!" (10:23).[5]

Jesus's inspired saying matches his mother's canticle too. In an interesting twist, Mary's words, "and my spirit rejoices in God my Savior" (Luke 1:47), which were spoken of her own soul and spirit, now become a word about inspiration: "Jesus rejoiced in the Holy Spirit" (10:21). This wrinkle in the use of words points the way to a correspondence in content. Mary rejoices because God looked with favor on "the lowliness of God's servant" and "scattered the proud in the thoughts of their hearts" (1:48, 51 alt.). In a remarkably similar vein, Jesus rejoices in the Holy Spirit because God has "hidden

5. The Greek word for "blessing" is different (*eulogein* in Luke 1:41–42, 67–68 and *makarios* in 10:23).

these things from the wise and the intelligent and . . . revealed them to infants" (10:21).

Something else lies below the surface of this story. As with so many episodes in Jesus's life, the backdrop is a story from the history of Israel—this one from the book of Numbers. As the title suggests, the book of Numbers is chock-full of mind-numbing numbers. The tribe of Gad, for instance, had 45,650 men aged twenty and up who could fight in battle. The tribe of Simeon had 59,300, Judah had 74,600, and so on. But tucked into the biblical book about numbers is a deceptively simple story of a beleaguered Moses (Num. 11:16–30). Exhausted, Moses asks God for help. God responds by taking from the spirit that was upon Moses and distributing it to seventy elders, who relieve Moses's burden by reliving their experience at Sinai— when some of the elders had, in a communal vision, celebrated together (Exod. 24:9–11).[6] Once again, then, Moses is not leading alone, because the elders join him. Yet the story has a twist toward the end, when Moses exhibits extraordinary magnanimity. When two elders who had not joined the other seventy prophesy, Moses's protégé, Joshua, is aghast. Horrified, he tells Moses to stop them, but Moses will have none of it. "Would that all the LORD's people were prophets, and that the LORD would put his spirit on them!" replies Moses, who is capable of *not* being in charge in the presence of the Spirit (Num. 11:29). The spirit outstrips even Moses's expectations.

The mission in Jesus's day is unnervingly reminiscent of the story of Moses and the seventy elders. It certainly reminded later scribes of Moses's story, for there are variants in the New Testament manuscript tradition in which Jesus sends out seventy-two rather than seventy—a clear allusion to the inclusion of Eldad and Medad, who prophesied without joining the other elders (Luke 10:1; Num. 11:26–27). The similarity is striking: like Moses's elders, Jesus's followers receive a share of his power—and to wide acclaim.

If Moses's story provides the backdrop to the mission of the seventy, then the implications are stunning. Jesus takes on the role

---

6. You will find a thorough analysis of this story in my "The Case of the Ecstatic Elders," *Catholic Biblical Quarterly* 65 (2003): 503–21. For a more accessible analysis, see chaps. 1 and 4 of *A Boundless God: The Spirit according to the Old Testament* (Grand Rapids: Baker Academic, 2020), 15–19, 78–82.

once occupied by the incomparable Moses. By doing so, he allows God to distribute to his seventy disciples a share in the Spirit, who have, to this point in his story, inspired Jesus exclusively. Ironically, the Spirit is explicit in the story of the seventy Israelite elders but only implicit in the seventy disciples' mission. The reminiscence of the prophesying elders is what creates a unique moment in the Gospels, where typically the Spirit is promised to—but not yet experienced by—Jesus's followers. The seventy disciples presumably share the Spirit that is on Jesus, just as the elders shared the Spirit that was on Moses.

Discerning the presence of the Spirit in the disciples' mission is hardly difficult, since the Spirit materializes as soon as they return, yet the Spirit materializes afterward in a different key, an altered tenor, in comparison with such an effective mission. With the rumbling of success signposting the path toward unbridled influence—imagine Jesus's power multiplied infinitely by his followers—with success ringing in their ears, "at that same hour Jesus rejoiced in the Holy Spirit" (Luke 10:21). At a moment when Jesus might have toppled into the trappings of power—even good, God-given power—the Holy Spirit draws him away from tripping over success. "At that same hour Jesus rejoiced in the Holy Spirit and said, 'I thank you, Father, Lord of heaven and earth, because you have hidden these things from the wise and the intelligent and have revealed them to infants'" (10:21). The Holy Spirit draws Jesus toward babies and not the wise, toward the weak and not the strong, and to intimacy between a father and son rather than heavy-duty miracles.

In what, then, should his followers rejoice, if not in the power of miracles? *In the revelation of God's dominion to babes rather than to the wise and understanding.* Jesus's inspired rejoicing shifts attention from miracles, even wonderful, magnificent, breathtaking miracles, to the purpose of life: to sustain an intimate relationship with God. All this talk of Father and Son is what matters. Is it good that the seventy were successful? You bet. Was it significant that Satan fell from heaven? Of course. But what matters most, what emerges from rejoicing in the Holy Spirit, is the realization that God is in the business of revelation—not to the high and mighty but to unassuming followers who learn of the Father through the Son.

The crux of Jesus's saying is not that he is Mary's son—and certainly not that he is Joseph's—but that he is *God's* Son. The word *Father* occurs five times in this prayer, and the word *Son* three times. Jesus may be awestruck by the triumph of the seventy, but he is also aware that all of this is about his intimate relationship with the Father. He is awake to the reality that he is not only David's heir and Mary's son but also uniquely his Father's Son, and the authority the seventy exercise derives exclusively from him and ultimately from his Father: "All things have been handed over to me by my Father; and no one knows who the Son is except the Father, or who the Father is except the Son and anyone to whom the Son chooses to reveal him" (Luke 10:22). Small wonder that Luke attributes this realization to the Holy Spirit, for this insight takes us straight back to Jesus's baptism, to that moment when the Spirit was especially active. After Jesus's baptism the Spirit descended in bodily form as a dove, and a divine voice confirmed the relationship of God to Jesus as father to son. "You are my Son," the words began (3:22). Then, the Holy Spirit led him in the wilderness (4:1). Shortly afterward, upon his return to Galilee, he was full of the Holy Spirit (4:14). *Father. Son. Holy Spirit.*

The reason for the appearance—the intrusion—of the Spirit following the return of the seventy may also lie in the confrontation between the Spirit and Satan. According to Luke, and Luke alone, the Spirit leads Jesus *throughout* his wilderness experience. In Luke's Gospel, the Holy Spirit is there the whole time, leading Jesus in the desert, in the presence of Satan, who tests Jesus's resolve to resist conspicuous displays of power. Now, at the return of the seventy from their triumphant mission over the demonic world, the Holy Spirit reappears, drawing Jesus's attention away from a conspicuous display of power, from the Schadenfreude evident in the plunge of Satan, and toward his relationship with the Father—that is, toward the relationship the Holy Spirit sealed when it descended on Jesus as a dove in bodily form and subsequently led him throughout his forty-day sojourn in Satan's domain.

In Luke's Gospel, then, the Holy Spirit is primarily about Jesus's relationship with the Father. Jesus may thrum with excitement over the defeat of Satan, but the Holy Spirit once again inspires him to recognize—this time with rejoicing—the fundamental relationship that draws him and the Father together. At a moment when Jesus risks becoming tangled in success, in exponential growth, in celebrity, the Holy Spirit draws him away from tripping over a second defeat of Satan. The Holy Spirit draws Jesus, simply, to the Father.

Snakes, Scorpions, and the Holy Spirit

Matthew 7:7–12	Luke 11:9–13
Ask, and you will receive. Search, and you will find. Knock, and the door will be opened to you. For everyone who asks, receives. Whoever seeks, finds. And to everyone who knocks, the door is opened. Who among you will give your children a stone when they ask for bread? Or give them a snake when they ask for fish? If you who are evil know how to give good gifts to your children, how much more will your heavenly Father give good things to those who ask him. Therefore, you should treat people in the same way that you want people to treat you; this is the Law and the Prophets. (CEB)	And I tell you: Ask and you will receive. Seek and you will find. Knock and the door will be opened to you. Everyone who asks, receives. Whoever seeks, finds. To everyone who knocks, the door is opened. Which father among you would give a snake to your child if the child asked for a fish? If a child asked for an egg, what father would give the child a scorpion? If you who are evil know how to give good gifts to your children, how much more will the heavenly Father give the Holy Spirit to those who ask him? (CEB)

We are told in the Gospel of Luke that Jesus prays. Overwhelmed by the crowds pressuring him, he prays (Luke 5:16). Confronted by a decision, such as who should accompany him, he prays (6:12). When he wants a bead on his followers' beliefs, he prays (9:18). And, of course, in anguish before his death, he prays (22:44).

But the episode after the return of the seventy is unique because it exposes the *content* of his prayer, which revolves around his relationship to God and God's relationship to the dispossessed and disenfranchised. This open window leads shortly later, and naturally, to the disciples' request, demand even, for a prayer: "Lord, teach us to pray" (Luke 11:1). So Jesus delivers to them the Lord's Prayer, the Our Father. Yet that is not all. After giving them this particular prayer—certainly part and parcel of teaching them to pray, as one of the disciples has requested—he goes further and teaches them not *what* to pray but *how* to pray. Jesus reminds his disciples to be persistent in a collection of sayings that also appear in Matthew's Gospel, though this time Luke retains a reference to the Spirit that Matthew does not. Jesus promises, "For everyone who asks receives, and everyone who searches finds, and for everyone who knocks, the door will be opened. . . . If you then, who are evil, know how to give good gifts to your children, how much more will the heavenly Father give the Holy Spirit to those who ask him!" (11:10–13).

The version in Luke's Gospel, at first blush, looks like a simple promise of the Holy Spirit—the equivalent of Matthew's more generic "good things." God answers prayer, so pray often, pray hard, and pray without ceasing to receive the Holy Spirit.

This first impression is probably wrong in light of the pairings in Luke's version. Matthew pairs bread with stone and a fish with a snake. Luke pairs a fish with a snake and an egg with a scorpion. No parent would give a snake to a child who asks for a fish, nor would a parent give a scorpion to a child who asks for an egg.

Something nags about the particular pairing of a snake and scorpion in Luke's Gospel. Commentators have noticed that a fish may look like a snake and a rolled-up scorpion like an egg. Doubtless, however, more is going on in Luke's version than a physical resemblance that causes things to be mistaken for each other during a picnic by the Sea of Galilee.

No, it is not that simple—little that Jesus says is. The strange reference to snakes and scorpions takes us back to where Luke has taken us before: the exodus from Egypt. Moses warned the Israelites not to forget God's provision following the exodus from Egypt, urging them to remember "the LORD your God, who brought you out of the land of Egypt, out of the house of slavery, who led you through the great and terrible wilderness, an arid wasteland with poisonous snakes and scorpions" (Deut. 8:14–15).

How is Jesus able to make this promise to his followers? How does he know that God will not give snakes and scorpions to people who pray? The reason is not some vacuous notion of the goodness of God; Jesus knows this because, after his baptism, he vanquished Satan in a desert teeming with snakes and scorpions. There, in an arid wasteland, a great and terrible wilderness, he took on Israel's vocation and succeeded where Israel had failed. He even resisted Satan by quoting from the portion of Deuteronomy that narrates Israel's wilderness sojourn (Luke 4:1–13). Jesus can promise that God will not give praying people snakes and scorpions, because God has already protected Israel—has protected *him*—in the wilderness.[7]

The reminiscence of Jesus's baptism and temptation may be even stronger, depending on how the phrase "from heaven" in Luke 11:13 is interpreted. The phrase "from heaven" can be associated with God and understood as "the father from heaven." Yet it can also be associated with giving the Holy Spirit and interpreted as "from heaven [God] will give the[8] Holy Spirit." In this case, the promise would read, "How much more will the Father give the Holy Spirit from heaven to those who ask?" The gift of the Holy Spirit *from heaven* would perfectly match the descent of the Holy Spirit following Jesus's baptism.

- - -

Not surprisingly, Jesus's teaching on prayer contains the same triad of prayer, Holy Spirit, and Satan that is present at his baptism and testing. It is also the same triad that appears in Luke 10:21 after the return of the seventy: Satan, rejoicing in prayer, and Holy Spirit.

Yet this saying does even more than recall Jesus's baptism and testing or the return of the seventy. The pairing of scorpions and snakes also leads seamlessly into the next episode, in which Jesus exorcises a demon. Another reason God will not give demonic gifts to people who pray is that Jesus and the seventy have already conquered those demonic powers. Satan has already fallen from the sky in defeat. Jesus's opponents cannot, then, be right to infer, "He casts out demons by Beelzebul, the ruler of the demons" (Luke 11:15).

It simply cannot be that Jesus exorcises demons by the power of Satan. After reading about the baptism and temptation, after reading about the return of the seventy, after hearing Jesus's teaching on

7. In Luke 4:4 Jesus quotes from Deut. 8:3; in Luke 4:8 he quotes from Deut. 6:13; and in Luke 4:12 he quotes from Deut. 6:16.

8. Here as elsewhere, the definite article is lacking, so the translation could read "a holy spirit," "Holy Spirit," or "the Holy Spirit."

prayer, we should find such an inference inconceivable. Two beings have already come from heaven in this Gospel: Satan fell from heaven like a bolt of lightning, and the Holy Spirit descended from heaven like a dove. Two different descents—the one a flash of violence, the other a gentle dove. Two different realities—one the epitome of evil, the other the essence of good.

In this light, Jesus's promise, "how much more will the Father from heaven give the Holy Spirit to those who ask him," is neither an all-purpose guideline to prayer nor a straightforward instruction about how to receive the Holy Spirit. By saying this, Jesus stakes his claim to the realm of God rather than the reign of Satan, to the world of a Holy Spirit rather than evil spirits. Those who learn to pray as he prays—with persistence and equanimity, with an eye toward the reign of God and the cancellation of debt (Luke 11:2–4)—will receive the Holy Spirit. They need not worry that dwelling in the realm of prayer will lead to the world of Satan, since God is not in the habit of giving scorpions or snakes to those who pray. God certainly did not give a scorpion or snake to Jesus when, after his baptism, he prayed and received the Holy Spirit, which then led him through a snake- and scorpion-infested wilderness while he vanquished Satan.

The essence of this saying is difficult to grasp because it assumes deep and enduring prayer, the sort of prayer that submerges one in a world of unpredictable spirits and evil forces. This saying is not aimed at people who pray casually, who petition God occasionally or entreat perfunctorily. Only those who wrestle in prayer, like the prophet-widow Anna, who fasted and prayed for decades on end (Luke 2:36–37); only those who pray tenaciously, as in the story of someone who knocks and knocks at midnight until the door is opened (11:5–8); and only those who ask, seek, and knock (11:9), like the widow who is so insistent that even an unjust judge relents and grants her plea (18:1–8), are deep enough in prayer to confront evil and to encounter scorpions and snakes. God is good, and those who are devoted to prayer can expect to receive only good gifts from God, only a *holy* spirit, while they wander into the realms of darkness, the domain of the prince of evil.

Jesus taught about prayer with confidence, not because he had read primers on prayer but because he had won his experience the hard way. He had encountered the Holy Spirit in the presence of Satan, in the face of animus, in a desert full of menace at the start of it all; in a nameless Samaritan village from which he gazed at the plunge of Satan as the seventy returned from their mission; and now in a desolate spot somewhere—Luke does not say exactly—where one of the disciples finally demands that he teach *them* how to pray. Jesus does just this with the confidence and conviction borne of experience. He knows the Holy Spirit, the gift that it is and even how closely it can resemble an evil spirit (as the Spirit did when it took him into the wilderness after his rapturous experience along the banks of the Jordan River).

He knows, too, that the Spirit is unconcerned with the patina of success, the allure of affluence, or the appeal of growing popularity. Whenever Jesus is on the precipice of success, the Spirit draws him away. After Jesus is blessed with untarnished clarity of vision after his baptism, the Spirit whooshes him away from the Jordan River into the isolation—the desolation—of the desert. After Jesus is blessed with untold success in mission, the Spirit whooshes him to a world within, where God is his Father and he the Father's Son, where truth is withheld from the intelligent but revealed to babies, where success is defined not by elevation but by the privation of status. So when one anonymous disciple demands that Jesus teach them to pray, he naturally and authentically teaches from hard-won experience. What he teaches is not pretty. He does not promise health or long life or prosperity in the Spirit. He promises only that the Spirit is good, a good gift, and that God will not respond to prayer with a gift of the demonic. This, too, he knows from experience. Jesus has not led an easy life, a temperate life, a balanced life—certainly not a life successful in conventional terms. But it has been a good life, springing from an elemental awareness to which the Spirit draws him back more than once from the brink of success: that he is his Father's Son, the beloved.

6

Spirit and the Threat
of Blasphemy

Matthew 12:22–32	Mark 3:20–30
They brought to Jesus a demon-possessed man who was blind and unable to speak. Jesus healed him so that he could both speak and see. All the crowds were amazed and said, "This man couldn't be the Son of David, could he?" When the Pharisees heard, they said, "This man throws out demons only by the authority of Beelzebul, the ruler of the demons." Because Jesus knew what they were thinking, he replied, "Every kingdom involved in civil war becomes a wasteland. Every city or house torn apart by divisions will collapse. If Satan throws out Satan, he is at war with himself. How then can his kingdom endure? And if I throw out demons by the authority of Beelzebul, then by whose authority do your followers throw them out? Therefore, they will be your judges. But if I throw out demons by the power of God's Spirit, then God's kingdom has already overtaken you. Can people go into a house that belongs to a strong man and steal his possessions, unless they first tie up the strong man? Then they can rob his house. Whoever isn't with me is against me, and whoever doesn't gather with me scatters. Therefore, I tell you that people will be forgiven for every sin and insult to God. But blasphemy against* [blasphēmia] the Holy Spirit won't be forgiven. And whoever speaks a word against the Human One will be forgiven. But whoever speaks against the Holy Spirit won't be forgiven, not in this age or in the age that is coming." (CEB)	Jesus entered a house. A crowd gathered again so that it was impossible for him and his followers even to eat. When his family heard what was happening, they came to take control of him. They were saying, "He's out of his mind!" The legal experts came down from Jerusalem. Over and over they charged, "He's possessed by Beelzebul. He throws out demons with the authority of the ruler of demons." When Jesus called them together he spoke to them in a parable: "How can Satan throw Satan out? A kingdom involved in civil war will collapse. And a house torn apart by divisions will collapse. If Satan rebels against himself and is divided, then he can't endure. He's done for. No one gets into the house of a strong person and steals anything without first tying up the strong person. Only then can the house be burglarized. I assure you that human beings will be forgiven for everything, for all sins and insults of every kind. But whoever blasphemes [blasphēmēsē] the Holy Spirit will never be forgiven. That person is guilty of a sin with consequences that last forever." He said this because the legal experts were saying, "He's possessed by an evil spirit." (CEB)

*I have modified the CEB translation in all three instances because the choice of "insult" in CEB, while an adequate translation, tends to blunt the hard edge of blasphemy. I have preserved, therefore, the rough transliteration, "blasphemy." Further, while CEB translates with a verb in Matt. 12:31, the Greek is actually a noun, which I have restored in the translation, "blasphemy against."

Luke 11:17–23; 12:8–12

Because Jesus knew what they were thinking, he said to them, "Every kingdom involved in civil war becomes a wasteland, and a house torn apart by divisions will collapse. If Satan is at war with himself, how will his kingdom endure? I ask this because you say that I throw out demons by the authority of Beelzebul. If I throw out demons by the authority of Beelzebul, then by whose authority do your followers throw them out? Therefore, they will be your judges. But if I throw out demons by the power of God, then God's kingdom has already overtaken you. When a strong man, fully armed, guards his own palace, his possessions are secure. But as soon as a stronger one attacks and overpowers him, the stronger one takes away the armor he had trusted and divides the stolen goods.

"Whoever isn't with me is against me, and whoever doesn't gather with me, scatters. . . ."

"I tell you, everyone who acknowledges me before humans, the Human One will acknowledge before God's angels. But the one who rejects me before others will be rejected before God's angels. Anyone who speaks a word against the Human One will be forgiven, but whoever blasphemes [*blasphēmēsanti*] the Holy Spirit won't be forgiven.

"When they bring you before the synagogues, rulers, and authorities, don't worry about how to defend yourself or what you should say. The Holy Spirit will tell you at that very moment what you must say." (CEB)

Hostility and Hard Sayings

After Jesus's death and resurrection, longer still after Jesus uttered these thorny words about blasphemy against the Holy Spirit, the Holy Spirit was hard at work in the church. Though punctuated by martyrdom, though ruptured by squabbles small and large, the inspired witness of the church went along unimpeded. No earthly command or prison or shipwreck could stall the testimony to Jesus that his followers bore on the wings of the Spirit throughout the Mediterranean world. Inspired witness began during the Jewish feast of Pentecost, when Jesus's followers were filled with the Holy Spirit and proclaimed God's praiseworthy acts in a breathtaking array of languages that hearers gathered in Jerusalem from the far corners of the Roman Empire could understand (Acts 2:1–13). Not long afterward, when opposition began to roil Jesus's followers, Peter was put on trial. The Holy Spirit filled him too so that he delivered not so much a defense as a sermon about Jesus, rooted in Psalm 118:22. The impact was immediate: "Now when they saw the boldness of Peter and John and realized that they were uneducated and ordinary men, they were amazed and recognized them as companions of Jesus" (Acts 4:13). Later still, Stephen, "full of faith and the Holy Spirit" (6:5), bore the brunt of opposition. Some men from the synagogue of the Freedmen resisted Stephen but "could not withstand the wisdom and the Spirit with which he spoke" (6:10). By all counts, Stephen spoke with unusual cogency; like Jesus's, his message of inclusion for the nations incited rage in his hearers, who went on to stone him. Even at the end, at death's door, "filled with the Holy Spirit, he gazed into heaven and saw the glory of God and Jesus standing at the right hand of God" (7:55).[1]

Into this glowing stream of inspiration tumbles the story of a prodigious miscalculation. Apparently the practice of Jesus's newfound followers was to sell their property and lay the proceeds at the feet of the apostles, who distributed the funds (Acts 4:32–37). One couple, Ananias and Sapphira, held on to a portion of the proceeds from the

---

1. While some of these references could be to a holy spirit—*Stephen's* holy spirit—they can also refer to *the* Holy Spirit, so they can correctly be included here. For a fuller discussion, see n. 2 in chap. 5.

sale of a field. That was the prodigious miscalculation. Peter susses out the situation and asks Ananias, "Why has Satan filled your heart to lie to the Holy Spirit and to keep back part of the proceeds of the land? . . . How is it that you have contrived this deed in your heart? You did not lie to us but to God!" (5:3–4).

Speechless, Ananias keels over dead. Three hours later, Sapphira enters and also lies about the price of the land, prompting Peter to ask still another question. "How is it," he challenges her, "that you have agreed together to put the Spirit of the Lord to the test? Look, the feet of those who have buried your husband are at the door, and they will carry you out." She too keels over and is buried alongside her ill-starred husband. "And great fear seized the whole church and all who heard of these things" (Acts 5:7–11).

The backdrop of Israel's story helps us to understand the church's story. Luke describes the couple's holding back with the Greek verb *nosphizein* (hold back), which occurs only once in the Greek translation of the Hebrew Bible: in the story of Achan, who hoards (*enosphisanto*) illicit spoils of war (Josh. 7:1). When confronted, Achan confesses to the crime. Nevertheless, he, his family, the spoils, his animals, and his tent—everything he is, everyone he loves, everything he has—are stoned and burned in the Valley of Achor (7:1–26). The verb *nosphizein* doubtless provides the foil against which we should understand Ananias and Sapphira's dramatic deaths, because they, like Achan, have *held back* what belongs to the community.

Much can be said about the implications of this story, not least that spirituality is economic, as in Jesus's synagogue sermon in Nazareth (Luke 4:16–30). To understand the sacred, look to the integrity of the profane. To understand the Spirit, look to fields and funds. But there is an even more disquieting dimension to this story, and this has to do with the Holy Spirit. Peter asks, "Why has Satan filled your heart to lie to the Holy Spirit and to keep back part of the proceeds of the land?" (Acts 5:3). There again is that troubling juxtaposition of Satan and the Spirit. We see it in the Dead Sea Scrolls.[2] We see it at the testing of Jesus.[3] We see it when the seventy return.[4] We even

2. The "Teaching on the Two Spirits" in the *Community Rule* (1QS), columns 3–4.
3. Matt. 4:1–11; Mark 1:12–13; Luke 4:1–13.
4. Luke 10:18.

discern it in Jesus's reference to scorpions and snakes in his teaching on prayer.[5] This disconcerting association will not go away, and it reappears in the story of the early church. When something as good, as life giving, as the Spirit is present, the potential for evil, for life quenching, lurks nearby.

Even more disconcerting is the straightforward proposition of this story: lying against the Holy Spirit is punishable by death. Twice Peter accuses Ananias of lying: he has lied to the Holy Spirit (Acts 5:3) and to God (5:4). Then, when Sapphira returns, Peter accuses her as well: "How is it that you have agreed together to put the Spirit of the Lord to the test?" (5:9).

Dealing with the Holy Spirit is serious business—dangerous business. And it is done on the level of wallets and wares. Dying in the wake of lying to the Holy Spirit is the most certain evidence that integrity matters and honesty counts, that testing the Holy Spirit occurs less in the realm of supposed spirituality—piety and prayer— than in the realm of generosity and trustworthiness. By holding back funds, Ananias and Sapphira forfeit their place in an extraordinarily equitable community that would have given them financial security. Even if they had not paid with their lives, a little more money in their pockets would have been a poor and paltry trade for a community characterized by equanimity.

We may seem to have gotten off track in our preoccupation with the ill-fated couple, but we have not. This story flows from the teachings of Jesus about blasphemy against the Holy Spirit: "Whoever blasphemes against the Holy Spirit can never have forgiveness" (Mark 3:29). This warning is as dire and devastating as the story of the star-crossed couple who leave the room feet first. In fact, the codicil that Mark adds to the saying renders it even more dreadful: whoever blasphemes against the Holy Spirit can never have forgiveness but "is guilty of an eternal sin" (3:29). Though Matthew's Gospel elsewhere tends to tone down the tenacious rhetoric of Mark's Gospel, here the author sharpens it with his own codicil: "Whoever speaks

5. Luke 11:9–13.

against the Holy Spirit will not be forgiven, either in this age or in the age to come" (Matt. 12:32). Ananias and Sapphira died; those who blaspheme against the Holy Spirit are sinful *forever*.

There is a slew of difficult sayings like this in the Gospels, many of them having to do with eternity. "You lack one thing; go, sell what you own, and give the money to the poor, and you will have treasure in heaven; then come, follow me" (Mark 10:21). "If your right eye causes you to sin, tear it out and throw it away; it is better for you to lose one of your members than for your whole body to be thrown into hell" (Matt. 5:29). "It would be better for you if a millstone were hung around your neck and you were thrown into the sea than for you to cause one of these little ones to stumble" (Luke 17:2). "Very truly, I tell you, unless you eat the flesh of the Son of Man and drink his blood, you have no life in you" (John 6:53).

These are dire sayings, but even more ominous is Jesus's warning about blasphemy against the Holy Spirit. If the saying appeared in Mark's Gospel but was effaced in the Gospels of Luke and Matthew, we might be able at least to curb its effect, if not dismiss it. It is a testimony to the integrity of memory in the early church and a witness to the authenticity of the Gospels that this terrible saying is not sidelined. It is preserved not only in all three of the Synoptic Gospels but in the gnostic Gospel of Thomas as well, where Jesus says, "Whoever blasphemes against the father will be forgiven. Whoever blasphemes against the son will be forgiven. But whoever blasphemes against the holy spirit will not be forgiven, neither on earth nor in heaven" (Gos. Thom. 44).[6] The addition of blasphemy against the Father is unique here, as is the reference to heaven and earth, but the gist of the saying remains intact: blasphemy against the Holy Spirit will not be forgiven.

The Gospel of Thomas is actually the third version of this saying preserved in various corners of the early church. The first occurs in the Gospel of Mark. Jesus, whom the scribes have just charged with blasphemy (Mark 2:7), turns the tables and warns *them* about the peril of blasphemy: "Truly I tell you, people will be forgiven for their sins and whatever blasphemies they utter; but whoever blasphemes against the

6. As translated by Stevan Davies in *The Gospel of Thomas: Annotated and Explained* (Woodstock, VT: SkyLight Paths, 2002), http://www.gnosis.org/nagham /gosthom-davies.html.

Holy Spirit can never have forgiveness, but is guilty of an eternal sin" (Mark 3:28–29). Matthew and Luke preserve this saying in a slightly different form,[7] which compares speaking against the Son of Man with blasphemy against the Holy Spirit. Luke records, "And everyone who speaks a word against the Son of Man will be forgiven; but whoever blasphemes against the Holy Spirit will not be forgiven" (Luke 12:10). Matthew's Gospel preserves the same version and adds a reference to this age and the age to come, perhaps as a nod to the words "eternal sin" in Mark's Gospel: "Whoever speaks a word against the Son of Man will be forgiven, but whoever speaks against the Holy Spirit will not be forgiven, either in this age or in the age to come" (Matt. 12:32). Various corners of the early church, then, preserved this troublesome saying in no less than three versions. Mark preserves one version; a sayings source, with slight variation in the Gospels of Matthew and Luke, preserves another; and the Gospel of Thomas preserves a third version. The early church, even different quarters of it, obviously did not shy away from safeguarding the hard sayings of Jesus.

Yet the Gospel authors did not just preserve this saying. They also wrestled with it. They did not simply insert this warning into a random context and leave it for readers or hearers to interpret it. All three Synoptic Gospels—and the Gospel of Thomas—contain this saying, and each does something different with it, presumably in an effort to make sense of such an unfathomable saying. The marks of wrestling with this warning about blasphemy are everywhere to be seen, leaving the indisputable impression that the Gospel writers were keen to preserve the harshest of Jesus's sayings, even if it demanded some serious grappling with how to situate the saying so as to provide a clear key to its interpretation.

Blasphemy and the Demonic

In the heat of controversy early in the Gospel of Mark, when Jesus forgives the sins of a paralyzed man whom he heals, the scribes in-

---

7. This is typically identified as the Q source. According to the hypothesis, Q is composed of sayings Matthew and Luke have in common that do not originate with Mark's Gospel.

quire, "Why does this fellow speak this way? It is blasphemy! Who can forgive sins but God alone?" (Mark 2:7). Not long after, Jesus's family thinks he is out of his mind (3:21), and the scribes from Jerusalem somewhat less sympathetically charge, "He has Beelzebul, and by the ruler of the demons he casts out demons" (3:22). Jesus reverses their charge and aims it at them: "Truly I tell you, people will be forgiven for their sins and whatever blasphemies they utter; but whoever blasphemes against the Holy Spirit can never have forgiveness, but is guilty of an eternal sin" (3:28–29).

Jesus's warning in the Gospel of Mark is embedded in a context scarred by scathing but confused and conflicted accusations. The first, with which the episode begins and ends, is the allegation that Jesus "has gone out of his mind" or, in other words, "has an unclean spirit." The first accusation leveled against Jesus, then, is that he is demon possessed. The second accusation is that Jesus casts out demons because he has the authority of Beelzebul, the ruler of demons.

These accusations are not the same; they are inconsistent. Both cannot be the case. In the first, the scribes contend that Jesus "has an unclean spirit." Jesus is out of control, like the Gerasene man possessed by an unclean spirit, who cannot be shackled even with chains (Mark 5:3–5), or the boy whom a spirit throws to the ground and causes to foam at the mouth, grind his teeth, and become rigid (9:17–18). Even Jesus's own family believes that "he has gone out of his mind" (3:21).

In the second offensive, the scribes accuse Jesus of harnessing the power of Satan, perhaps through magical incantations. Jesus is accused of being an exorcist, like those who later in the Gospel are able to drive out demons in Jesus's name (Mark 9:38–41). In this accusation—Jesus casts out demons by the ruler of demons—Jesus is in control, albeit by the power of Satan.

One accusation characterizes Jesus as *out of control*, dominated by Beelzebul; the other characterizes Jesus as being *in control*, dispensing the power of Beelzebul. It is essential to distinguish between these accusations in the Gospel of Mark.

The coexistence of these allegations reveals that nearly everyone around Jesus is flummoxed. This realization leads to the statement regarding blasphemy against the Holy Spirit. In Mark's Gospel, Jesus's warning is a response to a jumbled set of allegations that have arisen because Jesus makes outlandish claims backed by astounding miracles. Confused by his extraordinary abilities, some charge him with demon possession, while others accuse him of collusion with Satan. Some may even charge him with both at the same time.

But Jesus? Jesus dismisses both charges. If he is demon possessed—the first accusation—how has he had the power to do all that he has done? Jesus has done nothing to suggest that he has lost control to an unholy spirit. None of Jesus's teachings, none of his healings, not even his exorcisms, have the slightest hint of powerlessness.

Nor is he in cahoots—the second accusation—with the powers of darkness. It may be true that the Spirit drove him—cast him out like a demon—into the desert following his baptism. In the eyes of many in Jesus's day, including members of the community at Qumran, who left behind the Dead Sea Scrolls, this initial expulsion may have aligned Jesus with the Prince of Darkness. Jesus's ability now to exorcise demons would, then, be due to his inevitable alignment with the Angel of Darkness. Yet if he is in collusion with Satan, retorts Jesus, why would he exorcise Satan's demons? A house divided against itself cannot stand.

Whether the claim is that Jesus is possessed by or possesses the appalling power of the devil, blasphemy against the Holy Spirit amounts to this: a failure to acknowledge the *Holy* Spirit that descended into him at baptism, a failure to recognize the *Holy* Spirit that drove him into the wilderness to do battle with Satan, a failure to concede that Jesus's abilities are due to the *Holy* Spirit within him. Blasphemy against the Holy Spirit, in the Gospel of Mark, is less about the false charges against Jesus, which are muddled and confused, than about the fundamental inability of his opponents to acknowledge the true source of Jesus's power.

Strangely, blasphemy against the Holy Spirit in the Gospel of Mark is related to claims about both the *source* of Jesus's power (he is in Beelzebul's camp) and the *absence* of Jesus's power (he is possessed). People have missed the vitality within Jesus to the extent that they are irredeemable, irredeemably wrong, and ultimately so misguided that they can no longer even acknowledge the authority within him. They refuse to acknowledge how deftly he controls the evil powers around him, how effectively he unravels the cords of sickness, how daringly he tailors traditions to human need.

Enter Jesus's family. There is powerful irony in the return of Jesus's family at the end of this scene. Mark describes Jesus's mother and brothers as "standing outside." Then the crowd tells Jesus that his family is "outside." Mark invests this simple word, *outside*, with sad irony in this tragic scene. Even those closest to Jesus stand in danger of blaspheming the Holy Spirit and being found as outsiders rather than followers. Why? Because they mistake the remarkable and remarkably iconoclastic authority of Jesus for either madness or collusion—but not inspiration.

Before dismissing the scribes and Pharisees as inept and Jesus's family as calloused—and both as utterly misguided—we should recall again the current that runs beneath the surface of the Gospels. So often when the Spirit is present, Satan lingers there as well. The attribution of Jesus's power to Satan rather than the Spirit is not the residue of an obsolete apocalyptic perspective during the first century. It reflects a depth of experience that sees the potential for good intertwined with the capacity for evil. The great gains Jesus makes and the startling claims that accompany them create a miasma of confusion about the ultimate source of his power. Were he to live superficially, void of power and absent of conviction, he would raise no questions—and certainly no hackles. It is the intensity of his living—his healing, his exorcising, his teaching—that precipitates a crisis. Is this man an inspired emissary of God or a misguided emissary of Satan? The answer to this question can be given only in retrospect, in the wake of Jesus's resurrection. Until then, it remains an open—and unsettling—question.

Blasphemy and Authority

If Mark sets Jesus's warning about blasphemy against the Holy Spirit in the context of crisis, Matthew situates it in a context that accentuates the relationship between Jesus's inspiration by the Holy Spirit and his authority. Matthew does this by including no fewer than three references to the Spirit in relatively close succession.

Before Matthew lands Jesus in the thick of controversy (where Jesus launches into his warning about blasphemy in the Gospel of Mark), Matthew includes a summary of Jesus's healing and the mysterious command to keep those healings a secret (Matt. 12:15–16). This command of secrecy, Matthew claims, fulfills the prophecy of Isaiah 42:1–4, which details the quiet character of God's inspired servant:

> Here is my servant, whom I have chosen,
>   my beloved, with whom my soul is well pleased.
> *I will put my Spirit upon him,*
>   and he will proclaim justice to the Gentiles.
> He will not wrangle or cry aloud,
>   nor will anyone hear his voice in the streets.
> He will not break a bruised reed
>   or quench a smoldering wick
> until he brings justice to victory.
>   And in his name the Gentiles will hope. (Matt. 12:18–21,
>   italics added)

In the prior scene, just before this quotation, Jesus heals a man who has a withered hand (Matt. 12:9–14). In the next scene, just after this quotation, Jesus cures a demon-possessed man who is blind and mute (12:22). Before Jesus engages his opponents, then, Matthew identifies him as the servant of Isaiah 42, whose quiet strength is bracketed by a healing and an exorcism. Jesus's enormous power may be nearly inaudible, but it is enormous power nonetheless.

Not long after, Matthew includes a second saying about the Spirit: "But if it is by the Spirit of God that I cast out demons, then the kingdom of God has come to you" (Matt. 12:28). This connection between Spirit and kingdom makes perfect sense in this context. Matthew's quotation of Isaiah 42 has just identified Jesus as the inspired servant, a quiet but unremitting light to the nations. Now Jesus identifies himself as the harbinger of the kingdom of God. The focal point of both the quotation and the saying is the Spirit.

The link between servant, kingdom, and Spirit transports readers full circle to the baptism of Jesus. When the Spirit descends on him, Jesus hears snippets from Psalm 2 (declaring him to be king) and

Isaiah 42 (declaring him to be servant) in what the voice from heaven says: "This is my Son, the Beloved, with whom I am well pleased" (Matt. 3:17). Whether in the quiet of a cool river or on the brink of heated controversy, the core of who Jesus is remains the same, and the glue that makes this two-sided vocation stick is the Spirit of God.

In the third reference to the Spirit in close succession, it is not only what Matthew quotes or Jesus says but what Matthew *omits* that provides a clue about Jesus's dreadful warning about blasphemy against the Holy Spirit. The claim in Mark's Gospel that Jesus is beside himself is gone. The allegation that Jesus is possessed by a demon is gone. There is no reason to suppose, in Matthew's Gospel, that blasphemy against the Holy Spirit has anything to do with Jesus being demon possessed. There is no basis for believing that Jesus is powerless, out of control, or in the grip of demonic power.

Blasphemy in Matthew's Gospel has to do with the Spirit as the source of Jesus's authority, which is by now well established through the Sermon on the Mount (Matt. 5–7), a string of healings that Matthew has artfully drawn together (Matt. 8–9), a successful mission to Israel (Matt. 10), a testy series of indictments against those in Galilee (11:20–24), and a lengthy quotation of Isaiah 42 bracketed by a healing and an exorcism (12:9–22). The kingdom of God touches those around Jesus because he is more than just a trained exorcist, more than just a charismatic healer, more than just an exceptional teacher. Jesus is all three at once—inspired healer, inspired teacher, inspired exorcist—because he is God's beloved servant and God's Son, upon whom God's Spirit rests.

Everything in Matthew's Gospel, in other words, is directed toward what is the second accusation in Mark's Gospel: that Jesus's authority derives from Satan. The first—that Jesus is possessed—has gone missing. So Jesus tells a little parable—the strong man (Satan) must be bound (by exorcisms) before his house can be plundered (by Jesus)—to underscore that he is not Satan's minion (Matt. 12:29). He then lays down the gauntlet, drawing a clear dividing line of devotion, and says point blank, "Whoever is not with me is against me, and whoever does not gather with me scatters" (12:30). This line in the sand leads to one of the most difficult sayings in the Gospels: "Therefore I tell you, people will be forgiven for every sin and blasphemy, but blasphemy against the Spirit will not be forgiven. Whoever speaks a word against the Son of Man will be forgiven, but whoever speaks against the Holy Spirit will not be forgiven, either in this age or in the age to come" (12:31). In these, the third and fourth references to the Spirit in a remarkably short span, Matthew twice underscores that opposition to the Spirit, the source of Jesus's authority, is unforgivable.

Often Luke's Gospel is thought to be the Gospel of the Holy Spirit, no doubt because of the more than a dozen references to *pneuma* in its early chapters, as well as its association with the book of Acts. But it is the Gospel of Matthew that anchors the heart of Jesus's story in the presence and power of the Holy Spirit. A brief outline of Matthew 12, with its dual emphases on authority and the Spirit, makes this inescapably clear:

- 12:1–8: plucking grain on the Sabbath—*the Son of Man is Lord of the Sabbath*
- 12:9–14: healing on the Sabbath—*the Pharisees conspire to destroy the Lord of the Sabbath*
- 12:15–21: healing the crowds and demanding silence—*Jesus is the Spirit-anointed servant of Isaiah 42*
- 12:22–28: casting out a demon—*if Jesus does this by the Spirit, the kingdom of God has come upon his hearers*
- 12:29–32: plundering a strong man's house—*Jesus's warning against blasphemy against the Holy Spirit*

The authority of Jesus and the authorization of Jesus by the Holy Spirit fuse at this tipping point in the Gospel, where controversy heats up and conflict bubbles to the surface.

The centrality of the Spirit as the source of Jesus's authority in Matthew's Gospel, compared to Luke's Gospel, is also evident in Jesus's claim, "But if it is by the Spirit of God that I cast out demons, then the kingdom of God has come to you" (Matt. 12:28). Luke's version of Jesus's saying reads "finger" instead of "Spirit": "But if it is by the finger of God that I cast out the demons, then the kingdom of God has come to you" (Luke 11:20). The word *finger* introduces a powerful allusion to the story of the exodus. During the ten plagues, Pharaoh's magicians say, "This is the finger of God!" (Exod. 8:19; 8:15 MT). Later at Mount Sinai God gives Moses "the two tablets of the covenant, tablets of stone, written with the finger of God" (Exod. 31:18). Still later Moses recalls how "the LORD gave me the two stone tablets written with the finger of God" (Deut. 9:10). While the authority to exorcise demons in Luke's version is due to the finger of God, which subdued Egypt and inscribed the ten words on tablets of stone, this authority is not traced, as in Matthew's Gospel, to the Holy Spirit.

With Jesus's final warnings about blasphemy against the Holy Spirit in Matthew 12:31–32, the debate between Jesus and the scribes and Pharisees ends abruptly, only to resurface later. Jesus has argued on their terms in many respects: *their* accusation that he exorcises with the power of Beelzebul, *their* company of exorcists, and *their* conception of this age and the age to come. But they cannot win the argument—not because Jesus's logic is airtight but because these are the sayings of the one who is authorized by the Holy Spirit to be both servant and king.

Dire Consequences

This conflict between Jesus and his opponents began earlier on, along the shores of the Jordan River, where Jesus stood dripping wet and absorbed the divine words he heard, watching the Holy Spirit descend like a dove toward him. Then, in an abrupt shift, the Spirit threw him or led him—depending on which Gospel you read—into the wilderness to be tested by Satan. The story lying behind this series of events is Israel's experience of the exodus interpreted not in the book of Exodus or Psalms but in a lament folded unobtrusively into the waning chapters of the book of Isaiah (see chap. 4 above). The lament in Isaiah 63:7–14 refers three times to the Spirit:

> An angel of his [God's] presence saved them[8]
> in his love and in his pity he redeemed them;
>   he lifted them up and carried them all the days of old.

8. My translation is based upon the Hebrew. The NRSV translates the Greek, which reads "It was no ambassador or angel but the Lord himself that saved them" (my translation).

> But they rebelled
>   and grieved his holy spirit;
> therefore he became their enemy;
>   he himself fought against them.
> . . . .
> Where is the one who put within them
>   his holy spirit,
> who caused his glorious arm
>   to march at the right hand of Moses,
> . . . .
> Like cattle that go down into the valley,
>   the spirit of the LORD gave them rest.[9] (Isa. 63:9–14 alt.)

In this unique poem, references to the Spirit—the *Holy* Spirit—occur in rapid succession:

- "But they rebelled and grieved his holy spirit."
- "Where is the one who put within them his holy spirit?"
- "Like cattle that go down into the valley, the spirit of the LORD gave them rest" (Greek: a spirit came down from the Lord and guided them).

The first mention of the Spirit in this lament—"but they rebelled and grieved his holy spirit"—is the one that braces Jesus's threat about blasphemy against the Holy Spirit. This line in the lament is actually rooted in a still earlier promise of an angel that would guide Israel from Egypt to the promised land. Shortly after a recitation of the Ten Commandments, and in the context of various laws intended to regulate Israel's new life, God promises, "I am going to send an angel in front of you, to guard you on the way and to bring you to the place that I have prepared. Be attentive to him and listen to his voice; *do not rebel against him*, for he will not pardon your transgression; for my name is in him. But if you listen attentively to his voice and do all that I say, then I will be an enemy to your enemies and a foe to your foes" (Exod. 23:20–22, italics added). In the lament, this warning about the angel is transferred to the Holy Spirit (see chap. 1):

9. The Greek reads, "A spirit came down from the Lord and guided them" (NETS).

But they rebelled
and grieved his holy spirit;
therefore he became their enemy;
he himself fought against them. (Isa. 63:10)

In Exodus, there is no pardon for those who rebel against the angel. In Isaiah, God becomes the enemy of those who rebel against God's Holy Spirit.[10]

The warning about the angel of the exodus, transferred to the Spirit in the prophetic lament, provides the backdrop for Jesus's warning about the Holy Spirit in his own day. As harsh as his warning is, it is no more harsh than the warnings in the Old Testament. The threat—and it is a threat—issued at Mount Sinai contains stern words. If Israel does not rebel, God will be an enemy to their enemies, yet if Israel does rebel, God warns that the angel "will not pardon your transgression." No loopholes. No caveats. No escape clauses. When the prophet of lament grabs hold of this warning and transfers it to the Holy Spirit, he sets God squarely against Israel, who had "rebelled and grieved his holy spirit; therefore he became their enemy; he himself fought against them." God fought, not against Israel's enemies but against Israel itself, according to this prophet. When Jesus takes hold of the initial warning about the angel, refracted through the lens of the lament as a word about the Spirit, he is not *less* harsh—but neither is he *more* harsh—than his Scriptures. A failure to acknowledge the source of Jesus's authority, to attribute it to Satan rather than the Spirit, is to go unforgiven, to live unpardoned, to proceed with inexcusable and inexorable ignorance.

In Matthew's Gospel, the weight of Jesus's warning falls heavily on his opponents. The Pharisees in particular demonstrate that they are enemies of Jesus because they attribute his exorcisms to Satan rather than the Holy Spirit. In this way, they rebel against God's Holy Spirit, with the result that, as in Isaiah 63, God becomes their enemy. They

---

10. You can find a more detailed analysis of Hag. 2:5 and Isa. 63:7–14 in chap. 8 of my *A Boundless God: The Spirit according to the Old Testament* (Grand Rapids: Baker Academic, 2020), 139–55. For a full analysis of these texts, see my *The Holy Spirit before Christianity* (Waco: Baylor University Press, 2019), the entirety of which deals with this interpretation of Hag. 2:5 and Isa. 63:7–14 and the implications of this interpretation for Christian theology.

can be forgiven for their rejection of Jesus's Sabbath practices (Matt. 12:1–8), for their dismissal of his healings on the Sabbath (12:9–14), for their refusal to acknowledge that Jesus is David's son (12:23), even for speaking against the Son of Man (12:32). They cannot be forgiven, however, for their failure to reckon with the Holy Spirit, for attributing Jesus's exorcisms to the prince of demons rather than the Holy Spirit. They cannot be forgiven for this precisely because of what their own tradition says, that God becomes the enemy of those who rebel against the Holy Spirit. They are indicted by their own Scriptures.

We noted at the outset how the Gospel writers grappled with this saying, difficult as it was, without discarding it. Mark saw it as a response to two conflicting accusations: Jesus was demon possessed and Jesus possessed power over demons. Matthew turned it into a fulcrum for the relationship between Spirit and authority, which Jesus's opponents refused to grasp. Luke, we will see in the next chapter, turned it against Jesus's own followers. The gist of blasphemy is, in Luke's scenario, a failure of Jesus's followers to wait upon the Spirit for faithful witness.

However this difficult saying is interpreted, whatever context it is inserted into, whomever it indicts, we have come a long way from the bliss of the Holy Spirit, from Zechariah's prophecies and Elizabeth's blessings, from the descent of the dove, from spiritual gifts that pepper the letters of Paul, from the kind and loving and peaceable fruits of the Spirit. Jesus's teaching about blasphemy in the Gospels lies in a thicket of controversy and against an Old Testament foreground that notches up the consequences of being mistaken about the source of Jesus's authority. The stakes are high and the message ominous. But saving someone from an egregious error can be as significant, as essential, as offering them a word of encouragement. And God knows, there are many egregious errors from which everyone—the people of God, too—needs to be saved. None of them, by Jesus's own reckoning, is more crucial than a failure to acknowledge the Holy Spirit as the source of his authority.

7

Spirit and the Hazard
of Hostility

Matthew 10:16–23	Mark 13:9–13
Look, I'm sending you as sheep among wolves. Therefore, be wise as snakes and innocent as doves. Watch out for people—because they will hand you over to councils and they will beat you in their synagogues. They will haul you in front of governors and even kings because of me so that you may give your testimony to them and to the Gentiles.	Watch out for yourselves. People will hand you over to the councils. You will be beaten in the synagogues. You will stand before governors and kings because of me so that you can testify before them. First, the good news must be proclaimed to all the nations.
Whenever they hand you over, don't worry about how to speak or what you will say, because what you can say will be given to you at that moment. You aren't doing the talking, but the Spirit of my Father is doing the talking through you. Brothers and sisters will hand each other over to be executed. A father will turn his child in. Children will defy their parents and have them executed. Everyone will hate you on account of my name. But whoever stands firm until the end will be saved. Whenever they harass you in one city, escape to the next, because I assure that you will not go through all the cities of Israel before the Human One comes. (CEB)	When they haul you in and hand you over, don't worry ahead of time about what to answer or say. Instead, say whatever is given to you at that moment, for you aren't doing the speaking but the Holy Spirit is. Brothers and sisters will hand each other over to death. A father will turn in his children. Children will rise up against their parents and have them executed. Everyone will hate you because of my name. But whoever stands firm until the end will be saved. (CEB)

Pearls on a String

Beginning in the early 1900s, many New Testament form critics began to describe the Gospel saying as pearls on a string. Here is how the logic goes: Jesus delivered many sayings, and in the course of time, the church preserved these sayings but not their original contexts. When it came time for the Gospel writers to situate these sayings into the narrative of Jesus, they occasionally had to invent contexts. That is why, for instance, the Lord's Prayer or Our Father is set in the Sermon on the Mount in Matthew's Gospel (Matt. 6:9–13) but in a desolate district where Jesus is praying in Luke's Gospel (Luke 11:1–4). Different sayings follow the prayer, too, as if each writer

Luke 12:4–12

I tell you, my friends, don't be terrified by those who can kill the body but after that can do nothing more. I'll show you whom you should fear: fear the one who, after you have been killed, has the authority to throw you into hell. Indeed, I tell you, that's the one you should fear. Aren't five sparrows sold for two small coins? Yet not one of them is overlooked by God. Even the hairs on your head are all counted. Don't be afraid. You are worth more than many sparrows.

I tell you, everyone who acknowledges me before humans, the Human One will acknowledge before God's angels. But the one who rejects me before others will be rejected before God's angels. Anyone who speaks a word against the Human One will be forgiven, but whoever insults the Holy Spirit won't be forgiven.

When they bring you before the synagogues, rulers, and authorities, don't worry about how to defend yourself or what you should say. The Holy Spirit will tell you at that very moment what you must say. (CEB)

strung a different pearl after it. After the prayer in Matthew's Gospel come sayings about forgiveness and fasting (Matt. 6:14–18), while after the prayer in Luke's Gospel come sayings about being persistent in prayer (Luke 11:5–8). Since the Gospel writers apparently did not have the original context, they set the prayer into unique contexts. In other words, they both received the prayer—the pearl—but chose to string it differently.

This logic serves to explain why so many of Jesus's sayings occur in different contexts in different Gospels. It also serves to explain why Jesus's promise of the Holy Spirit is set in different contexts in each of the Synoptic Gospels.

In the Gospel of Mark—probably the earliest of the Gospels—the promise of the Holy Spirit during persecution occurs in a context that imagines the destruction of the temple in Jerusalem at the hands of Roman soldiers, which in turn is set in a context of apocalyptic, cosmic chaos. The saying is set, in essence, among other sayings that look ahead forty years or so after Jesus's death to the tragedy of 70 CE, when Rome would destroy the temple.

In the Gospel of Matthew, the promise of the Holy Spirit occurs in a different context: the sending out of the twelve disciples on a mission to Israel while Jesus is still alive. Matthew's version of Mark's apocalyptic chapter (Mark 13) occurs much later, in Matthew 24—fourteen chapters after the mission of the seventy. If Matthew used Mark as a literary source, then he saw fit to detach this saying from its original context in a discourse about the destruction of Jerusalem (Mark 13; Matt. 24) and transpose it to a more local setting (Matt. 10), in which the disciples perform miracles and teach while Jesus is still alive. They will have notable success, he promises, but with the possibility of maltreatment, too, from their countrymen and countrywomen.

In the Gospel of Luke, something altogether different happens to this saying. Luke includes it in 12:4–12—at a point that is concerned neither with the mission of the disciples (Matt. 10) nor with the destruction of Jerusalem (Mark 13 and Matt. 24). The mission of the seventy (the context in Matthew's Gospel) is over and done by the time Jesus promises the Spirit in Luke's Gospel. That mission occurred two chapters earlier, and in that context, Jesus delivered no saying about the Spirit. The destruction of Jerusalem (the context in Mark's Gospel) will not occur until much later in Luke's Gospel, in chapter 21, and Jesus will not deliver a saying about the Spirit in that context either. Luke's designs on this promise are different from Matthew and Luke; Luke sets it near other sayings about public witness—not the limited mission of Matthew 10 or the destruction of the temple in Mark 13. Luke is keen to have Jesus communicate about the power and perils of public witness, plain and simple, rather than public witness during an actual mission (Matt. 10) or an eventual cataclysm (Mark 13).

This single pearl is strung differently in all three Gospels. In the Gospel of Matthew, it lies in the past. In the Gospel of Mark, it lies in the future. In the Gospel of Luke, the saying is timeless. The same saying, in other words, is set in three different contexts, with variations in wording each time. Yet the sense of urgency, the intensity expressed here, does not dissolve in the amalgam of differences. The resolve Jesus expresses about faithful witness cannot be tamped down by the placement of this saying in disparate contexts. Through a variety of means, all three Gospels portend the inescapability of persecution, the indispensability of faithful witness, and the inevitability of divine accompaniment.

- "For it is not you who speak, but the Holy Spirit" (Mark 13:11).
- "For it is not you who speak, but the Spirit of your Father speaking through you" (Matt. 10:20).
- "For the Holy Spirit will teach you at that very hour what you ought to say" (Luke 12:12).

Three contexts and three slightly different versions—but one cogent promise. This is what Jesus delivers. The singularity of this promise, the awareness of where Jesus's commitments lie, actually *increases* when we recognize how deftly and carefully each Gospel author has tended to this saying. Perhaps the early form critics were right: the Gospel writers treat the sayings of Jesus like pearls—pearls of great price.

Testimony rather than Rescue

Tensions run high in the Gospels, where even a promise of the Spirit's presence can become ominous. In all three Synoptic Gospels, Jesus says that the Spirit will deliver words to believers who are under the heat of harassment. As with Jesus's warning against blasphemy, then, we encounter another tough saying of Jesus that the earliest followers of Jesus opted to preserve rather than purge. And as with the saying about blasphemy, each Gospel writer was compelled to set this saying in a different context, which may be an indication of just how thorny it is.

The context of the saying in the Gospel of Mark begins simply enough, with someone admiring the temple: "As he came out of the temple, one of his disciples said to him, 'Look, Teacher, what large stones and what large buildings!'" (Mark 13:1). Jesus will have none of this unblinking admiration for human endeavors, even sacred ones.

"Do you see these great buildings?" he probes. "Not one stone will be left here upon another; all will be thrown down" (13:2).

When the disciples pull him aside privately to ask for a sign of when this will happen, Jesus falls into an apocalyptic miasma. "For nation will rise against nation, and kingdom against kingdom," he predicts. "There will be earthquakes in various places; there will be famines. This is but the beginning of the birth pangs" (Mark 13:8). This saying has two horizons—the fall of Jerusalem to the Romans in 70 CE and the end of the world—though for those in fields and on housetops in Judea, for pregnant and nursing women forced to flee, the Roman attack on Jerusalem just forty years hence would eclipse the distant apocalyptic horizon at the end of the age.

Into this gush of apocalyptic imagery—wars, famines, the desolating sacrilege, untold suffering, false messiahs, false prophets, a darkened sun, a dimmed moon, stars falling from heaven, the coming of the Son of Man on heaven's clouds—Jesus inserts a word peculiarly aimed at his disciples:

> As for yourselves, beware; for they will hand you over to councils; and you will be beaten in synagogues; and you will stand before governors and kings because of me, as a testimony to them. And the gospel must first be proclaimed to all nations. When they bring you to trial and hand you over, do not worry beforehand about what you are to say; but say whatever is given you at that time, for it is not you who speak, but the Holy Spirit. Brother and sister will betray each other to death, and a father his child, and children will rise against parents and have them put to death; and you will be hated by all because of my name. But the one who endures to the end will be saved. (Mark 13:9–13 alt.)

When Jesus turns his attention in the Gospel of Mark to the impending destruction of the temple and the apocalyptic events that will usher in the end of the age—these actually overlap in his sayings—he includes a harrowing promise that the Holy Spirit will give the earliest martyrs what they need to say.

If there is a method of world evangelization Jesus can be said to proffer in this context, this is it. He says that his disciples—the word is exclusively for them—will stand before rulers and kings "as a testimony [*martyrion*] to them." Their martyrdom becomes *martyrion* (testimony). This point is so important, so crucial, so readily lost on the path to security and success, that Jesus, in the Gospel of Mark, interrupts the flow of thought with an aside, "and the gospel must first be proclaimed to all nations." Jesus's words read more smoothly without this reference to the gospel:

> You will be beaten in synagogues;
> and you will stand before governors and kings because of me, as a
> testimony to them.

> *And the gospel must first be proclaimed to all nations.*

> When they bring you to trial and hand you over,
> do not worry beforehand about what you are to say.

The words "and the gospel must first be proclaimed to all nations" create an interruption, a disturbance—a portentous one at that—that expresses the global influence the gospel will exercise through the testimony of the persecuted.[1]

In chapter 10, we will pause over the Great Commission in Matthew's Gospel: "Go therefore and make disciples of all nations" (Matt. 28:19). Mark has his own great commission too, right here, where it may be obscured by the swirl of imperial politics and apocalyptic annihilation: the gospel must first be proclaimed to all nations. The gospel will be proclaimed not by the popular but by the persecuted, not by the wise but by the wretched.

Here is where we discover the only promise of the Spirit in the Gospel of Mark. There is no promise of the Holy Spirit to someone who asks, seeks, and knocks at midnight, as in the Gospel of Luke (11:9–13). There is no claim that Jesus's exorcisms take place by the Spirit of God, as in the Gospel of Matthew (12:28). There is no talk in the Gospel of Mark of the Spirit gushing up, as in the Gospel of John (7:37–39). In Mark's Gospel, we encounter only three clear references to the Spirit apart from Jesus's baptism and testing: a warning about

---

1. Willi Marxsen makes this important point in *Mark the Evangelist: Studies on the Redaction History of the Gospel*, trans. James Boyce, Donald Juel, and William Poehlmann, with Roy A. Harrisville (Nashville: Abingdon, 1969), 120–21, 174–75, 201–2.

blasphemy against the Holy Spirit (3:28–29), an aside that David wrote Psalm 110:1 by the Holy Spirit (12:36),[2] and this promise of the Holy Spirit during persecution (13:11). Of those three, only the third is a promise—or is it a warning?

The truth—the tragedy—is that the Holy Spirit will not give believers words of successful self-defense. The Spirit is not an escape clause or a defense attorney. The Spirit will speak only a word of testimony, of witness, of *martyrion*. From where Jesus sits at this point, surveying the destruction of the temple years hence and the apocalyptic end of the age, the Spirit will not titillate and impress, compelling synagogue rulers, procurators, and kings to fall on their faces in repentance and release their charges. No, Jesus promises only that the Spirit will testify, speaking the gospel truth to the earth's ends.

With this simple observation about the Spirit, Mark subtly returns his readers to the debut of the Spirit, or nearly so. After descending gently like a dove, the Spirit drives Jesus into battle with Satan in a world filled with wild animals. Jesus is able to plumb the depths of his vocation, his sonship, and his servanthood only in the face of hatred and hostility; there, and not along the bucolic shores of the Jordan River, he begins to grasp the scope of his power to battle evil. Why should it be different for Jesus's followers? They too plumb the depths of their commitment in the face of hostility and hatred. The Spirit does not drive them to this hostility and hatred, as it drove Jesus into the desert, but it does meet them there, speaking when they cannot, talking when they must.

As if this were not enough, under the surface of harsh geopolitical realities lies a more personal threat for Jesus's disciples: the breakup of the family, the tragedy of betrayal. Jesus warns that even families will be the source of hatred for the faithful. Earlier, Jesus's family tried to restrain him (Mark 3:21). Now Jesus projects this hostility into the future, where it comes into the open as betrayal—brothers and sisters betraying one another, fathers betraying children to death, and children betraying their parents. This will be a horrific time, when "you will be hated by all because of my name" (13:13). This

---

2. On David's composition of the psalms, see 11Q5 in the Dead Sea Scrolls. 11Q5 column 27, line 4, refers to a spirit of discernment (*rûaḥ nəbônâ*) God gave to David. The precise meaning is difficult to determine. Was this spirit given at birth or at a particular point in time (i.e., in order to compose the psalms)?

will also be the moment when the Holy Spirit delivers the message of the gospel to all nations.

This word of testimony need not be prepared and polished beforehand. Jesus commands his followers not to "worry beforehand" about what to say. No need to fuss over words; no need to plot what to say. What Jesus's followers are to say will be given "at that hour" (Mark 13:11, author's translation). This is a precise moment, a single point, not a span of time. Mark uses this word, *hour*, in only one other context, when he describes the "ninth hour," at which time Jesus cries out with a loud voice, "Eloi, Eloi, lema sabachthani?" (Mark 15:34). At the hour of trial, and not a moment beforehand, what the disciples are to say will be given to them. There is even a pun here: when they are "given over" (*paradidontes*), what they are to say will be "given" (*dothē*) to them—the Greek root of both is the verb *didōmi*. And how so? The Holy Spirit will speak—and not a moment too soon.

This is not a universal promise that undercuts preparation or eschews deliberation, as if no one should ever work to prepare what they will say about God. This is not that sort of universal message. It is a promise aimed at a specific occasion of political persecution that is apocalyptic in scope. It is a promise aimed at a world in which nursing women are forced to flee. It is not a promise aimed at people of leisure, people plying trades, or people enjoying the small, good life. It is a promise aimed at people under extraordinary duress because of their faith.

What the Spirit does, according to Jesus, may be a small comfort to those who look to the Spirit as the source of inner peace, guidance, joy, kindness, or self-control. This Spirit alleviates the need for fuss and bother beforehand—and this may be comforting. But before what? Before beatings, trials, and prison stays. And what does this Spirit offer when it speaks? Testimony. Proclamation of the good news. *This* is the comfort proffered by the gospel, by *Jesus* in the Gospels: the disciples' final breath will be with a word of the Spirit.

Cold Comfort

If in Mark's Gospel Jesus speaks of the Holy Spirit in a prediction of a dire future marred by imperial destruction and apocalyptic chaos, in Matthew's Gospel he speaks of the Holy Spirit in the context of a well-planned mission of the twelve disciples to Israel. Mark's chaos yields, as we have learned to expect, to Matthew's penchant for order. Jesus prepares his disciples with clear instructions about what not to take: no gold or silver or copper, no bag, no spare tunics or sandals or staff (Matt. 10:9–10). He gives specific directions on exactly how to enter a village, whom to stay with, and how to "shake off the dust from your feet" as they leave the homes of the inhospitable (10:11–15). Mission in Matthew's Gospel is terribly well organized.

Though the contexts of the Gospels of Mark and Matthew could hardly be more different, Jesus's promises in the two Gospels thrum with the same note. Both pinpoint the reception of the Holy Spirit in a context of mission. Both straddle the border between faith and politics—whether the politics of Israel or the politics of Rome—and a crumbling world order. Both are directed to people who occupy the liminal space between safety and vulnerability. Both anticipate the opportunity disciples will have to imitate Jesus, whether in the near (Matthew) or distant (Mark) future. So Jesus urges them, "When they hand you over, do not worry about how you are to speak or what you are to say; for what you are to say will be given to you at that time; for it is not you who speak, but the Spirit of your Father speaking through you" (Matt. 10:19–20). The words of Jesus in both Gospels are chilling; both of them portend the inevitability of hardship, the inescapability of fierce opposition from those in positions of power.

And this mission, in both Gospels, will tear families apart. Immediately following this harrowing promise of the Spirit, Jesus, in the Gospel of Matthew, as in Mark, shifts to the shattering of families. Brother will betray brother to death, children will have their parents put to death, and they will be hated by all for Jesus's name. But those who endure to the end will be saved (Mark 13:12–13; Matt. 10:21–22). The Spirit will show up at a time of vicious and vitriolic hatred by both everyone outside and anyone inside the family. This will be a time of remarkable testimony and amazing witness, even if it is a time that costs believers the comfort of home.

Yet in the Gospel of Matthew, discomfort is not just the by-product of persecution. Later, Jesus states that the tearing apart of families is not just collateral damage; it is his *purpose*. This claim takes us beyond the Gospel of Mark, in which Jesus foresees the shattering consequences of following him but does not say he came to catalyze those consequences. In the Gospel of Matthew, it looks like Jesus has spun out of control when he returns to the theme of shattered families:

> Do not think that I have come to bring peace to the earth; I have not come to bring peace, but a sword.
>> For I have come to set a man against his father,
>> and a daughter against her mother,
>> and a daughter-in-law against her mother-in-law;
>> and one's foes will be members of one's own household.
> Whoever loves father or mother more than me is not worthy of me; and whoever loves son or daughter more than me is not worthy of me. (Matt. 10:34–37)

This depiction of treachery in Matthew's Gospel may go further than Jesus in Mark's Gospel, but both pick up on the vivid words of the eighth-century-BCE southern prophet Micah, who imagines the horrors of a time when "the devout has perished from the land, and there is none among people who is upright" (Mic. 7:2 NETS).[3] "Put no trust in friends," cautions Micah,

>> and do not hope in leaders;
> guard yourself against your bedmate,
>> so as to communicate anything to her;
> for a son dishonors a father,
>> a daughter shall rise up against her mother,
> a daughter-in-law against her mother-in-law;
>> the enemies of a man are the men in his house.
> But as for me, I will look to the Lord;
>> I will wait for God my savior;
>> my God will hear me. (Mic. 7:5–7 NETS)

In the Gospel of Matthew in particular, Jesus is hell-bent on driving precisely this sort of wedge between family members without offering

---

3. I cite the Greek translation of the Hebrew here because the Gospel writers probably used the Scriptures in this language.

a single word of encouragement—except for the promise that "the Spirit of your Father" (rather than "the Holy Spirit," as in Mark's Gospel) will tell them what to say, what to speak. These words blunt, at least slightly, the sharpness of the conflict and its consequences. Earthly fathers may be driven away by an all-encompassing drive to follow Jesus, but there will be another Father who will breathe life into the faithful. This is Jesus's own Father, who identified Jesus as God's own Son at the precise moment when Jesus received the Spirit (Matt. 3:16). Now Jesus's Father will be the disciples' Father as well and give them the Spirit as they, too, enter a time of trial.

Jesus's advice is no less applicable to the church that will carry on his mission after his death and resurrection than it is to the Twelve, who head into their mission with Israel. To put it succinctly: the sending of the Twelve anticipates the mission of the church to the end of the world. "But the one who endures to the end," promises Jesus, "will be saved" (Matt. 10:22). What Jesus has to say is relevant not only to the Twelve but also to the church in the throes of persecution. *Ecclesiology* and *eschatology*, to use technical terms, merge in the promise of the Holy Spirit to followers threatened with violent death. Though it applies to the Twelve, the promise of the Spirit in Matthew 10:20 retains the more global edge of Jesus's teaching about the end of the age, which permeates the source of this saying in Mark 13. There is an urgency of mission here, the realization that Jesus has set in motion—with the relatively small mission of the Twelve to Israel—events that will result in an earthquake of persecution, an eruption of violence against the followers of Jesus.

What must not be lost in Matthew's Gospel, as in Mark's, is that *this promise of the Spirit to Jesus's disciples occurs in the setting of vicious, official persecution that arises in the context of mission.* The Spirit is not promised in the usual to and fro of life. The Spirit is promised to disciples in mission who are handed over against their will to Jewish councils, who are flogged in synagogues, who are dragged before governors and kings, who lose the love and support of family. More significant still, the Spirit will speak only a word of testimony, of witness—of *martyrion*. In the Gospels of Matthew and Mark, Jesus promises only that the Spirit will testify to Israel and the nations—not shield believers from desolation and death. This may not be a sustainable model for world mission, but it appears to be Jesus's vision of mission. For this demanding—*devastating* might be a better word—task, they will receive the Holy Spirit, the Spirit of their Father, *his* Father. Cold comfort perhaps, but comfort nonetheless.

Blasphemy and Belief

In the Gospel of Mark, the section containing the promise of the Spirit for the persecuted began with admiration for the temple (Mark 13:1). In the Gospel of Matthew, the section began with Jesus summoning the disciples to a mission of exorcism and healing (Matt. 10:1). In the Gospel of Luke, it begins with crushing crowds: "When the crowd gathered by the thousands, so that they trampled on one another, he began to speak first to his disciples, 'Beware of the yeast of the Pharisees, that is, their hypocrisy'" (Luke 12:1). This seems like a strange way to begin teaching the disciples amid immense crowds, but Jesus actually anticipates a time when integrity—the polar opposite of hypocrisy—will be put to the test. Luke strings sayings together like pearls to communicate that his disciples must remain faithful witnesses: what is done in the dark will be brought to light (12:2–3); do not be afraid of death (12:4–5); God's eye is on the sparrow (12:6); God has counted the hairs on our heads (12:7); and to acknowledge God now is to be acknowledged later by the Son of Man, and to deny God now is to be denied later (12:8–9). These sayings occur in other contexts in Matthew's Gospel, but Luke has gathered them together to create a series of sayings about witnessing to the faith in times of terror.

In this scenario, Jesus introduces his final teaching about the Spirit—actually a combination of two sayings that occur in separate contexts in both Mark's and Matthew's Gospels. In the Gospel of Mark, the warning about blasphemy against the Holy Spirit (Mark 3:28–30) is separated by ten chapters from the promise of the Spirit to the persecuted (13:11). In the Gospel of Matthew, the warning about blasphemy (Matt. 12:31–32) is separated by two chapters from the promise of the Spirit (10:20). In the Gospel of Luke, these two independent sayings fuse in quick succession: "And everyone who speaks a word against the Son of Man will be forgiven; but whoever blasphemes against the Holy Spirit will not be forgiven. When they bring you before the synagogues, the rulers, and the authorities, do not worry about how you are to defend yourselves or what you are to say; for the Holy Spirit will teach you at that very hour what you ought to say" (Luke 12:10–12). Mark and Matthew undoubtedly interpret the warning about blasphemy against the Holy Spirit as an indictment of Jesus's opponents. Mark and Matthew clearly interpret the promise of the Spirit as a guarantee to besieged disciples. The warning is for his opponents, the promise for his followers.

It is possible that Luke understands this word about blasphemy as an indictment of Jesus's opponents. Although he fuses the two sayings, he may still have two separate audiences in mind: Jesus's opponents and his followers. The warning against blasphemy, from this perspective, would be directed at the Pharisees, while the promise of the Spirit would be directed at his followers. This reading is possible because, at this point in Luke's Gospel, Jesus has just railed against his opponents for murdering Israel's inspired prophets (Luke 11:49–51). With this charge, Jesus follows in the footsteps of the Israelite prophet Zechariah, who says, "They made their hearts adamant in order not to hear the law and the words that the LORD of hosts had sent by his spirit through the former prophets. Therefore great wrath came from the LORD of hosts" (Zech. 7:12). The opponents, in short, have resisted the Spirit—which is precisely what Jesus warns against in his admonition against blasphemy.

The book of Acts, which completes the Gospel of Luke, provides examples of just such resistance to the Holy Spirit, especially in the story of Stephen. We have seen already that Stephen was a man "full of faith and the Holy Spirit" (Acts 6:5), whose opponents "could not withstand the wisdom and the Spirit with which he spoke" (6:10).

Stephen's speech came to a head with an acerbic accusation: "You stiff-necked people, uncircumcised in heart and ears, you are forever opposing the Holy Spirit, just as your ancestors used to do. Which of the prophets did your ancestors not persecute? They killed those who foretold the coming of the Righteous One, and now you have become his betrayers and murderers" (Acts 7:51–52). The crowd's response was immediate and malicious—and in line with the Israelites, who had betrayed and murdered the prophets—for "when they heard these things, they became enraged and ground their teeth at Stephen," whom they proceeded to stone to death (7:54–60).

Their reaction is vehement, their opposition relentless. Enraged, they close their ears again and again. Their blasphemy is particularly egregious because, when opponents rage and grind their teeth, like they do here in the book of Acts, they oppose not mere human beings—even devout and dedicated ones—but inspired people, those whom "the Holy Spirit will teach" at that very hour what they ought to say (Luke 12:12). Those who stone Stephen blaspheme the Holy Spirit, for Stephen, like Jesus, is "filled with the Holy Spirit" (Acts 7:55). For people such as these, there is no forgiveness, because they are enraged at—and cut off from—the inspired testimony Jesus's followers offer.

While it is plausible that the Pharisees are those whom Jesus warns about blasphemy in Luke's Gospel, especially since Matthew and Mark interpret the saying in this way, this is probably not the most judicious reading of Luke's Gospel. The intractable difficulty with this understanding is that Luke has moved the saying about blasphemy to another context altogether and, even more telling, fused it with the promise of the Holy Spirit to those under severe persecution. The synthesis of warning and promise that occurs only in the Gospel of Luke lends a new and menacing tenor to Jesus's stern word of caution against blasphemy. The warning now has to do with the public acknowledgment of Jesus *by his followers*. Blasphemy seems to be, in short, a matter not for Jesus's opponents but for believers who fail to give testimony to Jesus under fire because they also fail to receive the teaching of the Holy Spirit at that particular moment of intimidation and terror.

From this perspective, the sayings of Jesus that Luke gathered earlier crescendo in his dual sayings about the Holy Spirit. First come the warnings that what happens in the dark or behind closed doors will become known. And so the disciples should not fear those who kill bodies; they should fear those with authority over hell (Luke 12:2–5). Next come the assurances of the disciples' worth in light of the worth of sparrows and the hairs on a head (12:6–7). Last come the alternatives, the possibilities, the *decision* followers must make under the pressure of persecution not to deny the Son of Man, not to blaspheme against the Holy Spirit, and not to worry about what to say, "for the Holy Spirit will teach you at that very hour what you ought to say" (12:10–12). Together these sayings signal that there is a higher loyalty and a more enduring destiny for those who, taught by the Holy Spirit, acknowledge the Son of Man when their backs are against the wall.

The Gospel of Luke dispels any notion that the Spirit will be given in an automatic way—to mindless automatons, unreflective vessels of the Spirit—since Jesus's promise contains the word *teach*. The Spirit follows the practice of Jesus, who in the Gospel of Luke is a teacher from beginning (Luke 4:14–15), when he teaches in a synagogue in Nazareth (4:16–30), to end, when he teaches daily in the temple (19:47; 21:37). At Jesus's trial before Pilate, Jesus's detractors even accuse him of stirring up people from Galilee to Judea *with his teaching* (23:5). The Holy Spirit, too, will teach, promises Jesus, and will teach when it is most needed, when Jesus's followers are brought to trial in synagogues, before rulers, and before authorities.

In the book of Acts, we have seen that Luke offers vivid examples of the Holy Spirit's ability to teach followers in the throes of trial. For instance, after Peter and John are arrested, Peter, *filled with the Holy Spirit*, preaches a sermon rooted in Psalm 118:22–23 that ends climactically: "There is salvation in no one else, for there is no other name under heaven given among mortals by which we must be saved" (Acts 4:12). The impact is immediate: "Now when they saw the boldness of Peter and John and realized that they were uneducated and ordinary men, they were amazed and recognized them as companions of Jesus" (4:13). No doubt a measure of that realization is due to the fact that Peter has quoted a section of the psalm that Jesus himself quoted in his parable about the evil tenants who kill the landowner's son (Luke 20:9–19). As Jesus has taught them, so his disciples teach others. And so the audience realizes that Peter and John are Jesus's disciples because they ably communicate *his* teaching. Apparently, Peter experiences exactly what Jesus promised: the teaching of the Holy Spirit.

Not surprisingly, the inspiration of Peter under duress looks a good deal like the inspiration of the old man Simeon (Luke 2:25–35). Simeon gathered what he had learned from the Scriptures into an inspired word to Jesus's receptive parents; Peter gathers what he has learned from Jesus's interpretation of the Scriptures into an inspired word to a hostile gathering of leaders. The Holy Spirit teaches Peter precisely what he needs to say when he is brought before rulers and priests (Acts 4:1–21) but teaches him by incorporating what he has learned from Jesus about Psalm 118. Like Simeon's song, Peter's sermon is a combination of inspiration and education.[4]

What Peter says is delivered entirely as *testimony* to Jesus, yet it functions too as *defense*—which is the gist of the promise and the genius of the Holy Spirit in the Gospel of Luke. Of course, testimony does not automatically bring release. Stephen, who spoke with untold boldness, did not survive a stoning, though he did survive into eternity because he experienced exactly what Jesus promised that faithful disciples would experience: "But filled with the Holy Spirit, he gazed into heaven and saw the glory of God and Jesus standing at the right hand of God. 'Look,' he said, 'I see the heavens opened and the Son of Man standing at the right hand of God!'" (Acts 7:55–56). Stephen, filled with the Spirit, publicly and powerfully acknowledged the Son of Man. Stephen, in one fell and devastating swoop, experienced firsthand the fulfillment of the promise of Jesus.

Met by a Bear, Bit by a Snake

The Israelite prophet Amos once criticized his people for their facile hope of deliverance on the day of the Lord: "Alas for you who desire the day of the LORD!" he would rail,

> Why do you want the day of the LORD?
> It is darkness, not light;
> > as if someone fled from a lion,
> > and was met by a bear;
> or went into the house and rested a hand against the wall,
> > and was bitten by a snake. (Amos 5:18–19)

---

4. The same can be said of Stephen's speech in Acts 7, which is a combination of erudition and inspiration.

Finishing the last chapter, which contains the barbed saying on blasphemy against the Holy Spirit, might have felt like escaping a lion. Then we turned to Jesus's promise of the Holy Spirit, which seems benign at first blush and, well, *promising*. In reality, we fled from a lion to be met by a bear; we rested our hand on the wall of our home only to be bitten by a snake. We went from a saying about the Spirit and blasphemy to a saying about the Spirit and hostile persecution. This sequence of sayings makes it hard to catch our breath, to regain our equilibrium. Where is the Spirit of love? Where is the Spirit of joy? Of grace?

We have lost the assurance—the *false* assurance, at least from the perspective of the Synoptic Gospels—that the Spirit exists to comfort and encourage followers of Jesus. But we have gained insight into Jesus too. He was relentless and focused, intense and passionate, keen to prepare his disciples for the hazards ahead: the risk of testimony, the cost of discipleship. Jesus refused to surrender to a soppy and sloppy spirituality. He recognized that a sentimental religiosity would fail to sustain his disciples in the days ahead, not only the foreseeable persecution spawned by their faithful witness but the inevitable torment from which the whole of Israel would fail to escape, when Rome would bring its imperial hammerblow down on Jerusalem. This world, this challenging, occasionally grim, and invariably forbidding world demanded—demands—of Jesus's disciples veneration, trepidation perhaps, even terror in the face of a Holy Spirit that shows up with an essential word in the toughest of circumstances.

8

Spirit, New Birth, and Living Water

He came to Jesus at night and said to him, "Rabbi, we know that you are a teacher who has come from God, for no one could do these miraculous signs that you do unless God is with him."

Jesus answered, "I assure you, unless someone is born anew, it's not possible to see God's kingdom."

Nicodemus asked, "How is it possible for an adult to be born? It's impossible to enter the mother's womb for a second time and be born, isn't it?"

Jesus answered, "I assure you, unless someone is born of water and the Spirit, it's not possible to enter God's kingdom. Whatever is born of the flesh is flesh, and whatever is born of the Spirit is spirit. Don't be surprised that I said to you, 'You must be born anew.' God's Spirit blows wherever it wishes. You hear its sound, but you don't know where it comes from or where it is going. It's the same with everyone who is born of the Spirit."

Nicodemus said, "How are these things possible?" Jesus answered, "You are a teacher of Israel and you don't know these things?" . . .

. . . "The one whom God sent speaks God's words because God gives the Spirit generously. The Father loves the Son and gives everything into his hands."

John 3:2–10, 34–35 (CEB)

Jesus answered, "Everyone who drinks this water will be thirsty again, but whoever drinks from the water that I will give will never be thirsty again. The water that I give will become in those who drink it a spring of water that bubbles up into eternal life." . . .

. . . "But the time is coming—and is here!—when true worshippers will worship in spirit and truth. The Father looks for those who worship him this way. God is spirit, and it is necessary to worship God in spirit and truth."

The woman said, "I know that the Messiah is coming, the one who is called the Christ. When he comes, he will teach everything to us."

John 4:13–14, 23–25 (CEB)

Many of his disciples who heard this said, "This message is harsh. Who can hear it?"

Jesus knew that the disciples were grumbling about this and he said to them, "Does this offend you? What if you were to see the Human One going up where he was before? The Spirit is the one who gives life and the flesh doesn't help at all. The words I have spoken to you are spirit and life. Yet some of you don't believe." Jesus knew from the beginning who wouldn't believe and the one who would betray him.

John 6:60–64 (CEB)

On the last and most important day of the festival, Jesus stood up and shouted,

> "All who are thirsty should come to me!
> All who believe in me should drink!
> As the scriptures said concerning me,
>   *Rivers of living water* will flow out from within him."
>
> Jesus said this concerning the Spirit. Those who believed in him would soon receive the Spirit, but they hadn't experienced the Spirit yet since Jesus hadn't yet been glorified.
>
> John 7:37–39 (CEB)

New Lands and Fresh Insights

When my wife, Priscilla, and I lived in Germany for the first time, we decided to visit the Loire Valley in France. We began our trip in the evening, stopped in the dark of night, and holed up in a roadside motel. The next morning, we hopped in our car and headed west. We had left behind the German villages of the Black Forest, with their perfectly painted facades, dark wooden balconies, and window boxes full of flowers. As we passed through our first French town, we noticed shabby exteriors that were gray and unwashed, but the daintiest lace was inside the windows. Everything seemed different, yet we were only a few hours from Tübingen, where we had lived for the year.

When we travel from the Synoptic Gospels—Matthew, Mark, and Luke—to the Gospel of John, everything seems different, even geography. In the Synoptic Gospels, Jesus travels only once to Jerusalem, when he is prepared to face death. In fact, the core of Luke's Gospel, Luke 9:51–19:11, is a single journey from Galilee through Samaria to Jerusalem. But in the Fourth Gospel, Jesus goes back and forth between Galilee and Jerusalem a few times.

Miracles differ too. In the Synoptic Gospels, the signal miracle of Jesus is the exorcism ("If it is by the Spirit of God that I cast out demons, then the kingdom of God has come to you," Matt. 12:28), but not a single exorcism can be found in the Fourth Gospel. Miracles are even identified differently; the author of the Fourth Gospel uses the signature word *signs* to describe Jesus's miracles.

Jesus's method of teaching differs dramatically as well. In the Synoptic Gospels, Jesus tends to utter short sayings and parables and riddles in the form of stories, many of them strung together like pearls on a string, as we noted in the last chapter. For example, in Mark 9:47–50 Jesus says,

> And if your eye causes you to stumble, tear it out; it is better for you to enter the kingdom of God with one eye than to have two eyes and to be thrown into hell, where their worm never dies, and the fire is never quenched.
>
> For everyone will be salted with fire. Salt is good; but if salt has lost its saltiness, how can you season it? Have salt in yourselves, and be at peace with one another.

These seem like four unrelated sayings—one about avoiding hell, one about being salted with fire, one about staying salty, one about salt and peace—connected by catchwords. Mention of *fire* in the first connects it to the second, in which people are salted with fire; mention of *salt* in the second, in turn, connects it to a third saying about salt; and even a final command to live peacefully is connected to the prior sayings by a reference to salt. But in the Fourth Gospel, Jesus teaches differently, with long conversations and protracted, winding speeches that cannot be reduced to simple sayings connected like pearls on a string.

Even the content of Jesus's teaching takes us to new terrain. In the Gospels of Matthew, Mark, and Luke, Jesus rarely divulges much about himself and teaches instead about the kingdom of God. In the Fourth Gospel, Jesus mentions the kingdom of God only in a single conversation with a Jewish teacher, Nicodemus (John 3:3, 5); otherwise, he remains mum on a topic that pervades the Synoptic Gospels. Yet, so unlike his persona in the Synoptic Gospels, he readily reveals himself in the Fourth Gospel. We catch him often saying "I am": I am the bread of life (John 6:48), the light of the world (8:12), the good shepherd (10:11), the resurrection and the life (11:25), the living and true way (14:6), and the true vine (15:1). In the Fourth Gospel, Jesus is more than willing to talk about himself at length.

When we move from the Synoptic Gospels to the Fourth Gospel, we find ourselves in unusually altered terrain—thankfully, we might admit. We leave behind the grim tones of the Synoptic Gospels regarding the Holy Spirit. In the Fourth Gospel, the Holy Spirit plays absolutely no role in Jesus's encounter with Satan in the desert. Not a whiff of this ordeal remains in the Fourth Gospel; instead, the Spirit simply descends and *remains* on Jesus (John 1:32–33). Nor is there a trace of Jesus's forbidding saying on the unpardonable sin of blasphemy against the Holy Spirit, even though it appears in all three Synoptic Gospels, as well as the gnostic Gospel of Thomas. And the saying that the Holy Spirit will supply words to martyrs on the verge of death? That, too, has vanished from the pages of the Fourth Gospel.

The Fourth Gospel offers a fresh understanding of the Holy Spirit. Jesus even introduces a new word for the Holy Spirit, *paraklētos.* Fresh as this understanding is, no one in the Fourth Gospel, except Jesus, seems to grasp much about this Spirit—not a male Jewish teacher who comes to Jesus in the dark of night, not a Samaritan woman who meets him in the light of day, and not even Jesus's own disciples, who seem to skate along with a superficial grasp of most realities Jesus wants to plumb. But how could they know? The Spirit gives understanding, and this Spirit, according to the Fourth Gospel, is not given until Jesus is crucified and raised from the dead. Still, the disciples' failure to understand in this mysterious Gospel mirrors ours. Thank goodness for the Jewish teacher, the Samaritan woman, and the disciples in the dark, who help us, too, to find our way.

The Spirit and Birth

The drama of the Spirit begins in the Fourth Gospel with a burst of metaphor when, under the cover of darkness, a Jewish teacher approaches. Jesus toys with him by playing on the ambiguity of the words *anōthen* and *pneuma.*

The word *anōthen* can mean either "again" or "from above." Jesus says to Nicodemus ambiguously, "Very truly, I tell you, no one can see the kingdom of God without being born *anōthen*" (John 3:3 alt.). Nicodemus understands the word *anōthen* in preposterously carnal terms as "again," as rebirth, as reentry into a mother's womb, when he responds, "How can anyone be born after having grown old? Can one enter a second time into the mother's womb and be born?" (3:4). For his part, Jesus understands the word to mean "from above." Later in this episode, this is precisely its meaning: "The one who comes from above [*anōthen*] is above all; the one who is of the earth belongs to the earth" (3:31).

The word *pneuma* connotes both Spirit and wind; Jesus draws an analogy between the wind, which is heard but not seen, and the Spirit, which is also heard but not seen: "The wind blows where it chooses, and you hear the sound of it, but you do not know where it comes from or where it goes. So it is with everyone who is born of the Spirit" (John 3:8).

The Spirit (*pneuma*) belongs to the world above—better yet, the world that comes *from* above (*anōthen*). Nicodemus does not quite grasp this, but Jesus, on this point at least, is unambiguous: "What is born of the flesh is flesh," he asserts unmistakably, "and what is born of the Spirit is spirit. Do not be astonished that I said to you, 'You must be born *anōthen*'" (John 3:6–7 alt.).

Nicodemus can hardly be blamed for his failure to comprehend what Jesus says about the Spirit, because the Spirit has not yet been given to prompt him to understand. Later in the Gospel, Jesus cries, "Let anyone who is thirsty come to me, and let the one who believes in me drink. As the scripture has said, 'Out of his heart shall flow rivers of living water'" (John 7:37–38 alt.). We will come to this perplexing saying soon enough. Of particular interest for now is the aside the author inserts after this saying: "Now he said this about the Spirit, which believers in him were to receive; for as yet there was no Spirit, because Jesus was not yet glorified" (7:39). Nicodemus did not understand Jesus because he *could not* understand him.

The church, the community that cherished and perhaps composed the Fourth Gospel, does understand, unlike Nicodemus. We know this because the community, like a chorus in a Greek tragedy, chimes into the conversation between Nicodemus and Jesus in the first person *plural*: "Very truly, I tell you, *we* speak of what *we* know and testify to what *we* have seen; yet *you* [plural] do not receive *our* testimony" (John 3:11, italics added). This community understands because it exists after the death and resurrection of Jesus, after he was glorified. They are the ones the Spirit, the "paraclete" in the Fourth Gospel, has reminded of all that Jesus said and did (14:26).[1] The paraclete has guided *them*, though not yet Nicodemus, into the truth (16:13).

From the standpoint of life after the death and resurrection of Jesus, this community doubtlessly understood Jesus's words about being born from water and Spirit, at least in part, as an expression of the essential character of baptism. Jesus had said, in emphatic parallelism:

> Very truly, I tell you, no one can see the kingdom of God without being born from above. (John 3:3)

> Very truly, I tell you, no one can enter the kingdom of God without being born of water and Spirit. (John 3:5)

The triad of birth *anōthen*, birth of water, and birth of Spirit evokes the mystery of baptism in the early church. The Letter to Titus, for example, with its penchant for preserving sure sayings and traditional belief, contains this short and stellar summary of salvation:

> But when the goodness and loving kindness of God our Savior appeared, he saved us, not because of any works of righteousness that we had done, but according to his mercy, *through the washing of regeneration*[2] and renewal by the Holy Spirit. This Spirit he poured out on us richly through Jesus Christ our Savior, so that, having been justified by his grace, we might become heirs according to the hope of eternal life. (Titus 3:4–7 alt.)

This association of water and Spirit with baptism suits the Fourth Gospel beautifully. In the Synoptic Gospels, John the Baptist, we saw, tends to avoid the unequivocal association of his baptism with water and Jesus's baptism with the Holy Spirit. In the Gospel of

---

1. For a discussion of this "paraclete," see chap. 9.
2. The NRSV translation reads, "through the water of rebirth," which sounds more like the Fourth Gospel than I think it should, since the Greek reads *dia loutrou palingenesias*.

Mark, John the Baptist announces, "The one who is more powerful than I is coming after me; I am not worthy to stoop down and untie the thong of his sandals. I have baptized you with water; but he will baptize you with the Holy Spirit" (Mark 1:7–8). In the Fourth Gospel, the Baptist says only, "I baptize with water. Among you stands one whom you do not know, the one who is coming after me; I am not worthy to untie the thong of his sandal" (John 1:26–27). Gone is the apparent contrast of baptisms. Then, the next day, John the Baptist expresses himself again in a way that avoids this contrast: "I myself did not know him; but I came baptizing with water for this reason, that he might be revealed to Israel. . . . I saw the Spirit descending from heaven like a dove, and it remained on him. I myself did not know him, but the one who sent me to baptize with water said to me, 'He on whom you see the Spirit descend and remain is the one who baptizes with the Holy Spirit.' And I myself have seen and have testified that this is the Son of God" (John 1:31–34). While John the Baptist draws a distinction between himself and Jesus, he does not draw a contrast between his water baptism and Jesus's Spirit baptism. There is rather a keen sense of continuity between water and Spirit.

Even the preposition Jesus adopts, *ex*, occurs only once in the statement "Very truly, I tell you, no one can enter the kingdom of God without being born of water and Spirit" (John 3:5). Jesus does not say "from water and from Spirit," (*ex hydatos kai ek pneumatos*); he says, with a single preposition governing both words, "from water and Spirit" (*ex hydatos kai pneumatos*).

The symbiosis of water and Spirit grew easily in the soil of first-century Judaism. In their charter document, the community at Qumran expresses the conviction that a participant among the people of faith has to be cleansed by both water and Spirit: "And it is by the holy spirit of the community, in its truth, that he is cleansed of all his iniquities. And by the spirit of uprightness and of humility his sin is atoned. And by the compliance of his soul with all the laws of God his flesh is cleansed by being sprinkled with cleansing waters and being made holy with the waters of repentance."[3]

3. 1QS column 3, lines 6–9.

Water and Spirit are tandem realities, realities understood as a single experience of baptism, in which one is plunged simultaneously into water *and* Spirit to emerge in a birth from above. *Tandem*, however, is by no means tame. Spirit *anōthen*, from above, is rich with memories of inventive prophetic promises of God's Spirit outpoured.[4]

The prophet Isaiah cajoles insolent and indulgent women in the 700s BCE to tremble, shudder, strip, put on sackcloth, and beat their breasts in mourning

> for the palace will be forsaken,
>> the populous city deserted;
> the hill and the watchtower
>> will become dens forever,
> the joy of wild asses,
>> a pasture for flocks. (Isa. 32:14)

But Isaiah urges that they should do this only

> until a spirit from on high is poured out on us,
>> and the wilderness becomes a fruitful field,
>> and the fruitful field is deemed a forest.
> Then good judgment will dwell in the wilderness,
>> and justice abide in the fruitful field.
> The effect of righteousness will be peace,
>> and the result of righteousness, quietness and trust
>>> forever.
> My people will abide in a peaceful habitation,
>> in secure dwellings, and in quiet resting places.
>>> (Isa. 32:15–18 alt.)

Both wilderness and cultivated fields, Isaiah imagines, will be the locus of the Spirit's deluge. This is the impact of the Spirit from above.

More than a century later, as Babylonian exile strangles what remains of the Southern Kingdom of Israel, Ezekiel springs into motion

---

4. You will find a thorough study of these texts in my *A Boundless God: The Spirit according to the Old Testament* (Grand Rapids: Baker Academic, 2020), 89–103.

with a quick succession of promises. He pledges the gift of a new heart and spirit: "I will *splatter*[5] clean water upon you, and you shall be clean from all your uncleannesses, and from all your idols I will cleanse you. A new heart I will give you, and a new spirit I will put within you; and I will remove from your body the heart of stone and give you a heart of flesh. I will put my spirit within you, and make you follow my statutes and be careful to observe my ordinances" (Ezek. 36:25–27 alt.). He promises, through a magnificent vision, that God will breathe new life into very many, very dry bones (37:1–14). And he predicts that the restored nation will "know that I am the LORD their God because I sent them into exile among the nations, and then gathered them into their own land. I will leave none of them behind; and I will never again hide my face from them, when I pour out my spirit upon the house of Israel, says the Lord GOD" (39:28–29). This is the impact of the Spirit from above.

Decades after Ezekiel issues this remarkable series of promises in a context of utter despair, another prophet faces both the harsh reality of Babylonian exile and the expectation of its end, with the defeat of Babylon at the hands of Persia. Hope burgeons, at least for this seer, who claims a bright future for those languishing in exile. "For I will pour water on the thirsty land," promises the prophet's God,

> and streams on the dry ground;
> I will pour my spirit upon your descendants,
> and my blessing on your offspring.
> They shall spring up like a green tamarisk,
> like willows by flowing streams.
> This one will say, "I am the LORD's,"
> another will be called by the name of Jacob,
> yet another will write on the hand, "The LORD's,"
> and adopt the name of Israel. (Isa. 44:3–5)

Israel has suffered enough; they are now in desperate need of hope. This promise, therefore, is framed to allay fear. From insignificance

---

5. This is my translation; the Hebrew word typically translated as "sprinkled" depicts a more kinetic *splattering* of blood on the altar. I make this case in *A Boundless God*, 136–37.

arises a great people. From an exilic few rises a robust nation. This is the impact of the Spirit from above.

Finally, the prophet Joel delivers a promise that bursts the wineskins of his prophetic predecessors:

> Then afterward
>> I will pour out my spirit on all flesh;
> your sons and your daughters shall prophesy,
>> your old men shall dream dreams,
>> and your young men shall see visions.
> Even on the male and female slaves,
>> in those days, I will pour out my spirit.

> I will show portents in the heavens and on the earth, blood and fire and columns of smoke. The sun shall be turned to darkness, and the moon to blood, before the great and terrible day of the LORD comes. (Joel 2:28–31; 3:1–4 MT)

This unbridled promise of an outpouring of the Spirit on all flesh outstrips all other Israelite conceptions of outpouring. In other prophetic texts, the Spirit restores Israel. Joel imagines the scope of the Spirit to include *all* flesh. This, too, is the impact of the Spirit from above.

If baptism lies in the background of Jesus's conversation with Nicodemus, it does not lie there dormant. This is no paltry act of sprinkling that leaves the participant apparently unchanged. It is no symbolic soul washing, no mere assumption that the Spirit is present but unseen and unheard. The Spirit is no trickle; it is a full, lavish gush, like a downpour during the dog days of August or a mountain waterfall when the snow melts. It is a gift beyond measure (John 3:34). It is something *out of* which a believer emerges, drenched. It is children born not by human lust but by divine desire (John 1:12–13).

Perhaps Nicodemus is not so far off after all. No, a grown man does not reenter his mother's womb. Still, are the images of gush and flow, birth from above, and the penchant of a divine father to produce children any less jarring, any less disquieting, or any less unsettling than being shoved again into a mother's womb? The absurdity of his misperception is no more outlandish than what Jesus demands: people must be born from a different sphere altogether, from above—from the divine father's urge to have children, to make the word flesh, and to establish a colony, a corner of the world that is full of grace and truth.

The Spirit and Truth

The man and woman are a study in contrasts. A Jew and a Samaritan. A Pharisee and a divorcée. A leader and an outcast. A person with a name and one without. Not in the cloak of darkness but in the harsh light of midday, Jesus talks with a Samaritan woman about running, living water. This brief conversation offers still another point of contrast—something in common too—between the twin stories of Nicodemus and the Samaritan woman. The Spirit, Jesus told the man, comes *anōthen*, "from above," in a burst of new birth. The water, he tells the woman, is "a spring of water gushing up to eternal life" (John 4:14). It "gushes up" (*hallomenou*)—a word used in Acts 3:8 (*hallomenos*) to describe the impulsive bounding of the lame man healed by Peter, who walked and *leaped* and praised God. The Spirit's downpour from above is perfectly matched by the water gushing up from below. Like the endless spring, the Spirit is a lavish gift, "the Spirit without measure" (John 3:34), endless and ample, rife with vitality, rich with vigor. Think of Noah and that fateful day, when "all the fountains of the great deep burst forth, and the windows of the heavens were opened" (Gen. 7:11). Torrents from above and a surge from below, gushing and pouring, the Spirit immeasurable—*un*measurable—a flood of life, a life-giving deluge.

The gush of Spirit-water is boundless, and for that reason, it is not mindless. On the contrary, the Spirit, which is amply given, is intimately related to the truth. As the conversation unfolds, the woman brings up the age-old rivalry between Samaritans and Jews, the wedge driven between two communities that worship on different mountains. Jesus, who will have none of this trivialization of divine presence, responds by promising this woman that "the hour is coming, and is now here, when truthful worshipers will worship the Father in spirit and truth, for the Father seeks such as these to worship him.

God is spirit, and those who worship him must worship in spirit and truth" (John 4:23–24 alt.). In the short measure of this promise, Jesus refers no fewer than three times to "the truth." Even more to the point, Jesus refers twice to "spirit and truth." Once again, a preposition tells the story: the preposition *in* occurs only once in relation to both words. It is not "in spirit and in truth" that is demanded but worship "in spirit and truth," *en pneumati kai alētheia.*

This telling association between Spirit and truth means that content matters in an experience of worship; substance is integral to the presence of the Spirit. Jesus does not say, "God is spirit, and those who worship him must worship in spirit." He does say, "God is spirit, and those who worship him must worship in spirit *and truth*"—in a truthful Spirit or a Spirit-inspired truth. Truth and Spirit are tandem realities; the absence of one voids the validity of the other.

A penchant for Spirit and truth permeates the Fourth Gospel. On his last night with the disciples, Jesus twice identifies the Spirit as the Spirit of truth (John 14:17; 16:13), which will "teach you everything, and remind you of all that I have said to you" (14:26); "guide you into[6] all the truth"; and "take what is mine and declare it to you" (16:13–14). Clearly, content matters. Truth is an essential dimension of the Spirit.

Later still, in an unexpected turn, it is not the Spirit that sanctifies. *Truth* sanctifies believers. Jesus prays, "Sanctify them in [by] the truth; your word is truth. As you have sent me into the world, so I have sent them into the world. And for their sakes I sanctify myself, so that they also may be sanctified in [by] truth" (John 17:17–19). We might expect sanctification by the Spirit. Instead, Jesus offers sanctification by the truth. Clearly, knowledge of that truth matters. Truth is essential to Spirit-filled worship.

It is no coincidence that, in the Fourth Gospel, the Holy Spirit is the "Spirit of truth." Experience, even enthusiastic experience, is simply not enough. Worship, Spirit-inspired worship, must be fed from the wells of knowledge, knowledge that leads through the living and true way (John 14:6) to God, the embodiment of truthfulness (8:26). Jesus underscores this association slightly later when his disciples

6. Or, in some ancient manuscripts, "in."

question his teaching: "The words that I have spoken to you are spirit and life" (John 6:63). These are not the emotions you feel, not the experience you have, and not the well-being you possess. Spirit and truth come together—along with life, *challenging* life—in the disquieting teachings of Jesus.

In the Fourth Gospel, neither truth nor Spirit has priority; to privilege one without the other is to forfeit both. Jesus's early conversations in the Fourth Gospel signal that those who claim to know the truth *and* to have received the Spirit are on a relentless quest to uncover the teaching of Jesus in order to exhibit that rare combination of Spirit and truth that enlivens, like rivers of living water, and illumines, like the inescapably difficult but defining words of Jesus.

The Spirit and Guts

Only three times in the Fourth Gospel does Jesus cry out, and each time he has something of particular significance to say. On the first occasion, he cries, "You know me, and you know where I am from. I have not come on my own. But the one who sent me is true, and you do not know him" (John 7:28). On the last, he cries, "Whoever believes in me believes not in me but in the one who sent me" (12:44 alt.). On the second occasion, on the last day of Sukkoth, the Feast of Tabernacles, he stands and cries, "Let anyone who is thirsty come to me, and let the one who believes in me drink. As the scripture has said, 'Out of his[7] belly shall flow rivers of living water'" (7:37–38 alt.). To this bewildering word the author of the Gospel is compelled to add an explanation: "Now he said this about the Spirit, which believers in him were to receive; for as yet there was no Spirit, because Jesus was not yet glorified" (7:39).

The importance of this announcement is enormous. In a bald-faced invitation, Jesus takes on the role of God in the grand prophetic summons of Isaiah 55:1:

7. While I would prefer the gender-neutral pronoun *their*, I have preserved *his* because many ancient interpreters interpreted this passage as referring to Jesus.

Ho, everyone who thirsts,
    come to the waters;
and you that have no money,
    come, buy and eat!
Come, buy wine and milk
    without money and without price.

An iteration of this utterly gratuitous and sumptuous offer is extended to the impoverished, closing the book of Revelation—and the New Testament as a whole:

The Spirit and the bride say, "Come."
And let everyone who hears say, "Come."
And let everyone who is thirsty come.
Let anyone who wishes take the water of life as a gift. (Rev. 22:17)

Jesus's summons is also noteworthy because, in a Gospel that often eschews the commonplace, Jesus adopts an outright traditional word, "receive" (*lambanein*), which routinely refers to the Holy Spirit in the letters of the apostle Paul. Paul writes, for instance, "Now we have received not the spirit of the world, but the Spirit that is from God, so that we may understand the gifts bestowed on us by God" (1 Cor. 2:12).[8] For all that is novel in this Gospel, this word anchors Jesus's invitation to the earliest communities of faith.

No less salient is this narrative aside: there was as yet no Spirit. This is a principal dividing line in the Fourth Gospel. Even those who believe during the lifetime of Jesus cannot receive the Spirit because being filled with the Spirit cannot occur prior to the death of Jesus. Not for Nicodemus. Not for the Samaritan woman. Not even for the disciples.

This saying is salient for yet another reason: its ambiguity. *Whose* belly? Will rivers of living water flow from the belly of Jesus or a believer?[9]

8. Paul adopts the same word in Rom. 8:15 and Gal. 3:2 to describe reception of the Spirit.

9. You will find further details in Raymond Brown, *The Gospel according to John*, 2nd ed., 2 vols., Anchor Bible 29A–B (Garden City, NY: Doubleday, 1977), 1:320–23.

Many early Christian writers, such as Justin, Hippolytus, Cyprian, and Tertullian, saw Jesus as the source of living water. They identified Jesus with the rock that produced water in the Sinai wilderness when Moses struck it (Exod. 17:1–7; Pss. 78:16; 105:41; cf. 1 Cor. 10:4), and they believed that Jesus's prediction of the Spirit's gushing was fulfilled in John 19:34, when water and blood flowed from Jesus's wounded side at his crucifixion. The problem with interpreting this saying as a reference to Jesus's death is that John 19:34 reduces the promised *flow* of water to little more than a *trickle*. John 19:34 states, understates really, that the water and blood simply went out, without the slightest sense of a flowing or gushing of water-spirit.

Other Christian writers understood the source of these waters to be the bellies of believers: Origen, Athanasius, and Cyril, all from Alexandria; Eusebius of Caesarea and Cyril of Jerusalem, from Palestine; Basil, Gregory of Nyssa, and Gregory of Naziansus, from Cappadocia; Chrysostom from Antioch; and Ambrose, Jerome, and Augustine, from the Roman West. These authors tied this cryptic saying to Jesus's conversation with the Samaritan woman, when Jesus promised, "Everyone who drinks of this water will be thirsty again, but those who drink of the water that I will give them will never be thirsty. The water that I will give will become in them a spring of water gushing up to eternal life" (John 4:13–14).

The question of whose belly (Jesus's or believers') is the source of the waters may never be settled, but the significance of the saying lies less in the particular source of the water—certainly the author of the Fourth Gospel is content to leave the pronoun ambiguous—than in the imagery of the Feast of Tabernacles, which is when Jesus delivered this brief speech. Tabernacles, or Sukkoth, was the third of the great Jewish harvest festivals, which first-century Jewish historian Josephus called particularly sacred and significant.[10] According to the rabbis, during each of the seven mornings of the feast there was a procession to the Gihon Spring, which supplied the pool of Siloam. Upon arrival, a priest would fill a golden pitcher with water while a choir repeated Isaiah 12:3: "With joy you will draw water from the wells of salvation." The procession would then head to the temple

---

10. Josephus, *Ant.* 8.100.

via the Water Gate while singing the Hallel psalms (Pss. 113–18) and holding signs of the harvest, including a lulab—willow twigs and myrtle tied with a palm, which were used to construct booths—and a lemon or citron, which symbolized the harvest. Upon reaching the sacrificial altar in front of the temple, they would circle it, waving their lulabim and singing Psalm 18:25: "With the loyal you show yourself loyal; with the blameless you show yourself blameless." On the last day, the *great* day in the Fourth Gospel, they would circle the altar seven times. These magnificent processions, songs, and symbolic activities then culminated in the priest's ascent to the altar, where he would pour water into a silver funnel, through which it flowed onto the ground.[11]

The image of water gushing out of a cavity in the earth—the Gihon Spring—fuses with the image of the priest's pouring water during the Feast of Tabernacles. We have seen this dual flow, from above and below, before, in the conversations Jesus has with Nicodemus and the Samaritan woman. The Spirit, Jesus tells Nicodemus, comes from above; living waters, Jesus tells the woman, gush from below. The image is one of surfeit, excess, the Spirit given beyond measure.

The impact of Jesus's words in the context of this feast is difficult to overlook. The water that flows from the Gihon Spring and the water that the priest pours out—water from above, water from below—will now flow from a new temple. If the source is Jesus, then living water will flow from Jesus's temple, the body that his opponents will destroy (John 2:19–21). If the source is the believer, then living water will flow from believers in a living temple, a temple perhaps analogous to the members of the community at Qumran, who regarded themselves as a living temple,[12] or analogous to the church as a temple of believers depicted by Paul in a letter to the Corinthians (1 Cor. 3:16–17). In either case, this magnificent river, full of life, will no longer flow from the Temple Mount, which, built of stone, was

---

11. You will find details of this procession in Brown, *Gospel according to John,* 1:326–27; Gary T. Manning discusses rabbinic sources in *Echoes of a Prophet: The Use of Ezekiel in the Gospel of John and in Literature of the Second Temple Period* (New York: T&T Clark, 2004), 176.

12. 1QS column 8, lines 5–6.

vulnerable to Roman ramparts. It will flow from within believers or Jesus himself—both of them living and breathing beings.

This image of water flowing from a cavity deep within a human body is hardly tidy; it is visceral. The *koilia* (belly) could be any cavity in the body, including the heart or womb or lungs. The word may have been selected because, unlike the heart—where believers, according to Paul, receive the Spirit (e.g., 2 Cor. 1:22)—it provides an exact counterpart to the Gihon Spring, which comes from a cavity in the earth. Not from the *cave* of Gihon, says Jesus, but from a *cavity* in the human body will flow living water, the Spirit that is not yet given. This signals a visceral—*gut-wrenching* might be a better word—experience. It would be shortsighted to overlook the force of this saying about the Spirit: "Out of his or her *guts* shall flow rivers of living water."

Jesus makes remarkable claims about the Spirit in the Fourth Gospel in what he says to Nicodemus, the Samaritan woman, and the throngs swarming the temple during Sukkoth. The ambiguity of his words, his use of metaphor, even the playfulness of his conversations, render these claims elusive. Still, at the heart of these claims lies the reality that Jesus, and Jesus alone, is the source of the Spirit, the spring of living waters, whether or not it eventually will flow from his dying torso or from the lungs and livers and colons of believers. At stake is the vital and vibrant presence of Jesus, who says, "It is the spirit that gives life; the flesh is useless. The words that I have spoken to you are spirit and life" (John 6:63). These are not benign words—vacuous or vapid. They are decisive words. They are the language of costly discipleship. That is why the Spirit and life inherent in Jesus's words do not yield uniformly robust harvests. That is why so many refuse to follow. In fact, just a few moments later, with his disciples ready to jump ship (John 6:66–67), this otherwise resolute teacher is left to ask, in one of the few questions that leave him looking lost, "Do you also wish to go away?"

9

Spirit and Inspired Memories

> I will ask the Father, and he will send another paraclete,[1] who will be with you forever. This paraclete is the Spirit of Truth, whom the world can't receive because it neither sees him nor recognizes him. You know him, because he lives with you and will be with you.
>
> John 14:16–17 (CEB)

> The paraclete, the Holy Spirit, whom the Father will send in my name, will teach you everything and will remind you of everything I told you.
>
> John 14:26

> I assure you that it is better for you that I go away. If I don't go away, the paraclete won't come to you. But if I go, I will send him to you. When he comes, he will show the world it was wrong about sin, righteousness, and judgment. He will show the world it was wrong about sin because they don't believe in me. He will show the world it was wrong about righteousness because I'm going to the Father and you won't see me anymore. He will show the world it was wrong about judgment because this world's ruler stands condemned.
>
> John 16:7–11

> However, when the Spirit of Truth comes, he will guide you in all truth. He won't speak on his own, but will say whatever he hears and will proclaim to you what is to come. He will glorify me, because he will take what is mine and proclaim it to you. Everything that the Father has is mine. That's why I said that the Spirit takes what is mine and will proclaim it to you.
>
> John 16:13–15

Two Teachers

More than two hundred years before the death of Jesus, a man named Ben Sira led an academy—an early yeshiva, we might say—for boys in Jerusalem. He demanded of his protégés an intense commitment to learning. Wisdom, he believed, was concentrated in Torah, and Torah deserved all the devotion in the world. The attainment

---

1. In these passages, I have modified the CEB by substituting an anglicized transliteration, *paraclete*, for "Companion" (CEB); NRSV translates "Advocate."

of wisdom demanded apprenticeship too. Therefore, Ben Sira encouraged his boys,

> If you are willing, my child, you can be disciplined,
>   and if you apply yourself you will become clever.
> If you love to listen you will gain knowledge,
>   and if you pay attention you will become wise.
> Stand in the company of the elders.
>   Who is wise? Attach yourself to such a one.
> Be ready to listen to every godly discourse,
>   and let no wise proverbs escape you.
> If you see an intelligent person, rise early to visit him;
>   let your foot wear out his doorstep. (Sir. 6:32–36)

Two centuries later, according to the Fourth Gospel, Nicodemus comes to Jesus by night. *By night* could signify that Nicodemus does not want to be found out and so comes under the cover of darkness. Yet the phrase may mean something else: that Nicodemus comes between sunset and sunrise because he is rising early or staying up late, around the edges of his workday, to meet an intelligent person. When he approaches Jesus, he addresses him as "rabbi" and adds, "We know that you are a teacher who has come from God" (3:2). Ben Sira advises, "If you see an intelligent person, rise early to visit him; let your foot wear out his doorstep." Perhaps Nicodemus is doing just that, since he has discovered someone wise, someone intelligent, someone worth rising early or staying up late to meet.

In the Synoptic Gospels, Peter twice calls Jesus "rabbi" (Mark 9:5; 11:21), and in an ironic and poignant twist, Judas calls Jesus "rabbi" during their last meal together and just before betraying him with a kiss (Matt. 26:25, 49). Jesus is called "rabbi" often in the Fourth Gospel (John 1:38, 49; 3:2; 4:31; 6:25; 9:2; 11:8). When, early on, the author of the Fourth Gospel translated the word "rabbi" for readers unfamiliar with Hebrew (1:38), he had a range of alternatives. He might aptly have chosen the word "lord," *kyrios*, especially in light of Jesus's resurrection; this would certainly have been a natural translation. He chose instead to translate the word "rabbi" as "teacher," *didaskalos*—certainly a title of honor but far less laudatory than *kyrios*. Still, to describe Jesus as a teacher in the Fourth Gospel, even if it is a less vaunted translation than *kyrios*, is fitting. Jesus delivers extended discourses in the Fourth Gospel. He even begins his final, intimate hours with the disciples with this brief remark: "You call me *teacher* and lord—and you are right, for that is what I am. So if I, your lord and *teacher*, have washed your feet, you also ought to wash one another's feet. For I have set you an example" (13:13–15 alt.). Jesus is indeed a rabbi—a *teaching* rabbi.

That is why he offers his students, his disciples, one final, protracted stint of teaching, which spans chapters 13–16 (plus a lengthy prayer in chap. 17 that provides clear teaching about unity), on his final night with them. In the course of this stretch, Jesus delivers four distinctive blocks of teaching on the Spirit (John 14:16–17; 14:26; 16:7–11; 16:13–15). He promises the presence of the Spirit of truth, another paraclete, whose vocation will mirror what Jesus's own vocation has been throughout the Fourth Gospel—to *teach*: "But the paraclete, the Holy Spirit, whom the father will send in my name, will teach you everything" (John 14:26 alt.). In a final saying about the Spirit, Jesus promises that "when the Spirit of truth comes," that Spirit "will guide you into [in] all the truth" (16:13).[2] Such promises are reminiscent of the psalmists' prayers:

> Teach me to do your will,
>> for you are my God.
> Let your good spirit lead me
>> on a level path. (Ps. 143:10)

> Lead me in your truth, and teach me,
>> for you are the God of my salvation. (Ps. 25:5)

What sort of truth lies at the heart of the Fourth Gospel? Jesus has told his disciples precisely what sort of truth lies there—and in his final hours he divulges more than once, in terms that are fresh and fascinating, that its source is the Holy Spirit.

---

2. As I noted in chap. 8, textual uncertainty makes it difficult to determine whether the Spirit in the original text is said to lead "in" or "into" truth. Of the major codices, Alexandrinus and Vaticanus read "into," while Sinaiticus and Bezae read "in."

Two Paracletes

Much of what the Spirit will become for believers is neatly summed up in the first of Jesus's sayings about a figure called the paraclete:[3] "If you love me, you will keep my commandments. And I will ask the Father, and he will give you another paraclete, to be with you forever. This is the Spirit of truth, whom the world cannot receive, because it neither sees it nor knows it. You know it, because it remains with you, and it will be in you" (John 14:15–17 alt.).[4] This is a pivotal statement. For starters, it is the *first* promise of the Spirit in the farewell discourses; as such it provides the perspective from which the following three promises must, by dint of sequence alone, be viewed.

From a literary standpoint, as well, this initial block of teaching comprises the most original promise of the Spirit in the Fourth Gospel. John 14:1–27, in which this saying is situated, concludes, "Rise, let us be on our way" (14:31). Originally this was probably followed by their departure in 18:1: "After Jesus had spoken these words, he went out with his disciples across the Kidron valley to a place where there was a garden, which he and his disciples entered." Chapters 15–17 interrupt this simple sequence by creating a lengthy pause between Jesus's command to be on their way in 14:31 and their actual departure in 18:1. Chapters 15–17 ought, therefore, to be seen as a commentary on chapter 14. What this means is that the *original* promise of the Spirit is situated in the original farewell discourse in chapter 14. In this light, the others, which are situated in chapters 15–16, are expansions of the original promise in John 14:15–17.

This initial teaching is important as well because in it Jesus introduces the Spirit, not in the traditional language of Holy Spirit but as the paraclete and the Spirit of truth. In the Fourth Gospel, Jesus is both an innovator (when he describes the Spirit as another

3. Marianne Meye Thompson offers an excellent discussion of this background in *The God of the Gospel of John* (Grand Rapids: Eerdmans, 2001), 145–88.

4. It is difficult to know what pronoun to adopt in reference to the Spirit here. The Greek *pneuma* is neuter—hence, "it." Yet the paraclete is masculine. In either case, the pronoun is not rooted solely in the gender of the noun. In this instance, I will adopt the neuter, though with a strong measure of dissatisfaction. For a brief discussion of the gender of the Spirit, see my *A Boundless God: The Spirit according to the Old Testament* (Grand Rapids: Baker Academic, 2020), 160–62.

paraclete) and someone willing to adopt recognized categories (when he uses the term *Spirit of truth*, an early Jewish term familiar from the Dead Sea Scrolls).

■ ■ ■

Paraclete is a designation that, at base, means "one called alongside," though this definition communicates images as different as the Comforter of the King James Version and a courtroom attorney. Both are called alongside but in different ways and for different purposes.

This elusive word, *paraklētos*, occurs in the Greek Old Testament only in Job 16:2, in which Job criticizes his friends for being worthless comforters. "I have heard many such things; comforters of what's worthless are you all," retorts Job. "What? Is there any rhyme or reason to windy words [words of *pneuma*]?" (Job 16:2–3 NETS). These words suggest comfort, though in Job's case it is false comfort—a function that lies far afield of the paraclete's teaching, reminding, guiding, and convicting of sin.

Another possible foreground for the paraclete of the Fourth Gospel may consist of the many mediator figures, such as preeminent angels (including Michael and Gabriel), who populated the world of early Judaism. These figures functioned in four roles that the paraclete also occupies: revealing knowledge, mediating, defending followers, and prosecuting opponents. Michael, for example, in the *War Scroll* from Qumran, leads the sons of light in a battle against the forces of darkness, led by the evil Belial.[5] In the Fourth Gospel, of course, there is no actual battle, though the paraclete becomes an advocate for believers in a hostile world.

Still another possibility is that the paraclete is a prophet like Israel's prophets, who mediated God's words to Israel. There is an appealing element to this foreground because it helps to explain why the Fourth Gospel is so different from the Synoptics, with its lengthy speeches and descriptions of healing. It is possible that prophets in the early church spun short sayings and healing stories, such as those found typically in the Synoptic Gospels, into long monologues and miracles, as in the Fourth Gospel. From this vantage point, the

5. 1QM column 13, lines 9–12; column 17, lines 6–8.

paraclete sayings reveal the source of prophetic inspiration in the early church. The paraclete, the Holy Spirit, the Spirit of truth, was believed to teach the community *through prophets* who under inspiration reminded them, guided them, and led them into the fullness of truth about what Jesus said and did.

■ ■ ■

Whatever the foreground, Jesus identifies the paraclete as *another* paraclete, which is an incontestable indication that the paraclete occupies a role parallel to Jesus. The role is borne out by the overlap in functions between Jesus and the paraclete.

- Both are *given* (John 3:16; 14:16) and *sent* (chaps. 5; 7; 8; 12; 14:26) by the Father.
- Both are *not received* (1:11; 14:17), *not known* (8:19; 10:14; 14:17; 16:3), and *not seen* (14:19; 16:16–17) by the world.
- Both *testify* (5:31–47; 8:13–20; 15:26).
- Both are preoccupied by *the truth* (14:6; 16:13; 18:37).

These correspondences pinpoint the indispensable link between understanding Jesus and understanding the Spirit. The ability to understand—and experience—*Jesus* demands an experience of the paraclete. The ability to understand—and experience—*the Spirit* demands an intimate knowledge of Jesus.

This is a cautionary note rung by the Fourth Gospel for anyone who believes that the ability to understand Jesus is possible without the Spirit, and it equally cautions those who claim to experience the Spirit without an enduring and nearly unendurable thirst to learn about the Jesus of the Gospels. Both are essential elements of inspiration. Study void of the Spirit and experience void of learning are equally invalid. The end, the goal, the purpose of the paraclete is to inspire followers to know Jesus—Jesus come in the flesh—intimately. That is why the verbs attributed to the paraclete—*teach, remain, remind, convince, guide* into truth, *speak* what is heard, *declare* what will come, *glorify, take* what is Jesus's and *declare* it to the disciples— have little to do with sentiment or sensation and everything to do with learning and living and worshiping. As if to underscore the intimate and essential relationship the paraclete has with the Jesus whose life is narrated in the Gospels, Jesus repeats the last verbs twice (John 16:14–15):

> "It will glorify me, because it will take what is mine and declare it to you." (alt.)
>
> "For this reason I said that it will take what is mine and declare it to you." (alt.)

It is difficult to overemphasize the taut relationship between Jesus and the Spirit. A spirituality of the Spirit, the Spirit of *truth*, must be one that is determined to delve deeply into the teachings of Jesus. Spirit and truth are joined at the hip, just as they were early in the Fourth Gospel, when Jesus championed this pair—this *fusion* of Spirit and truth—in his conversation with the Samaritan woman.

███   ███   ███

The tapestry of the Fourth Gospel is beautifully woven so that the paraclete is also tautly bound not solely with the Son but also with the Father. Much of what the paraclete will accomplish is what the Father has already accomplished.

- Both *testify* to Jesus (John 5:37; 8:18; 15:26–27).
- Both *glorify* Jesus (5:44; 8:54; 12:23; 13:31–32; 16:14; 17:1, 5).
- Both will *be with* the disciples (14:17, 23; 17:11, 26).
- Both *teach* (6:45; 14:26; 16:13).

The fundamental tasks of Father, Son, and Spirit are richly and irrevocably intertwined in the Fourth Gospel. To learn of one is to learn about the others.

At the heart of these tasks is Jesus. The Father and the Spirit both testify to Jesus and glorify him. Both teach, and the topic of that teaching is Jesus. Jesus himself claims in the Fourth Gospel, "It is written in the prophets, 'And they shall all be taught by God.' Everyone who has heard and learned from the Father comes to me" (6:45). Jesus in the Fourth Gospel is rabbi, teacher. He is nothing if not committed to a lifetime of learning, as is the Father and the other paraclete about whom Jesus teaches so appreciatively in his final—and arguably finest—hour with his disciples, as he washes their feet and prepares them for the steep learning curve that lies ahead.

The Spirit of Truth

This teaching does not take place in the relatively safe and rarefied air of an academy, such as Ben Sira's in Jerusalem. Jesus was not a rabbi in the sort of yeshiva that was led by first-century luminaries such as Hillel and Shammai. An air of hostility intrudes into the private discourse between teacher and friends when Jesus identifies the paraclete as "the Spirit of truth, whom the world cannot receive, because it neither sees it nor knows it" (14:17 alt.). Jesus precipitated conflict between dark and light, religious leaders and himself, superficial followers and true disciples. This scenario would survive Jesus's absence, because the paraclete, the Spirit of truth, would not reside in the portion of the human race that refused to receive Jesus (1:13–14; 14:17).

This essential insight links the Fourth Gospel to the Gospels of Matthew, Mark, and Luke. The war between light and darkness, ignorance and wisdom, does not draw to a peaceful close with the advent of the Spirit. Although the sayings in the Synoptic Gospels are not quite like this one, the gist is the same. Jesus in those Gospels also connects the promise of the Spirit to a warning of hostility. In a horrifying context that portends persecution, Jesus promises the Spirit: "When they bring you to trial and hand you over, do not worry beforehand about what you are to say; but say whatever is given you at that time, for it is not you who speak, but the Holy Spirit" (Mark 13:11). In Matthew's Gospel, Jesus substitutes the fatherhood of God for hostile fathers who betray their children to death when he promises, "For it is not you who speak, but the Spirit of your Father speaking through you" (Matt. 10:20). For Luke, virulent opposition will be the crucible in which the Spirit, as in the Fourth Gospel, teaches believers: "The Holy Spirit will teach you at that very hour what you ought to say" (Luke 12:12).

Jesus's promise in all four Gospels does not offer a gentle presence that aids the war weary, but it does offer assurance to the faithful. Jesus's heartbroken friends will soon be graced with the privilege of friendship (John 15:12–17), and even now they may bask in the prospect of adoption (14:18–24). They are promised the accompaniment and inner presence of the Spirit (14:17). When the Spirit arrives, it will teach the disciples, remind them about Jesus (14:26), and guide them into all the truth of Jesus's life, death, and resurrection (16:13). There is closeness, intimacy in these promises; there is the anticipation of memories, of minds alert and awakened that are drawn back to the meaning of what their cherished teacher taught them.

For those outside, there awaits a cosmic court drama in which the Spirit of truth will take sides. Whatever the foreground of the word *paraclete*, its function, at least in part, is judicial. The Spirit of truth will testify on Jesus's behalf (John 15:26) and against the world with respect to sin, justice, and judgment. There is no benevolent judge in this scene—only a paraclete who will defend Jesus's disciples and prosecute the world. The paraclete "will convince the world about sin and righteousness and judgment: about sin, because they do not believe in me; about righteousness, because I am going to the Father and you will see me no longer; and about judgment, because the ruler of this world has been condemned" (16:8–11 alt.).

This promise of a judicial standoff is reminiscent of a particularly vitriolic exchange in which Jesus identified his opponents as the children of the devil. "Which of you convicts me concerning sin?" (John 8:46 alt.), he asked them. The work of the paraclete mirrors this exquisitely; the paraclete will "convict [*elenxei*] the world concerning sin" (16:8 alt.). And as God has testified on Jesus's behalf while Jesus has been alive, the Spirit of truth, who comes from the Father, will testify on Jesus's behalf (5:37; 15:26). In the grand law court of truth, Jesus knows that no one can convict him of sin; in that same grand law court, the paraclete will put the world on the defensive by convicting it of sin and defending Jesus from its contempt.

The drama of a cosmic court battle between truth and deceit, between the children of the devil and the children of God, between darkness and light, which underlies the entire span of Jesus's life in the Fourth Gospel, may explain the barbed introduction of seemingly superfluous clauses that describe the paraclete, the Spirit of truth, in its first appearance in the Gospel: "whom the world cannot receive because it neither sees it nor knows it" (John 14:17). This is no mere fumarole in a dormant volcano but a fresh eruption that promises long-standing consequences. It is a redrawing of the battle lines— battle lines that were familiar to those who occupied various corners of Judaism in Jesus's day, including the fragmented community that received the New Testament letter of 1 John and the community at Qumran.

A segment of the *Community Rule* known as "The Teaching on the Two Spirits" instructs the "sons of light" about "the nature of all the sons of *adam*."[6] This teaching is tricky and ambiguous. At its base lies an interpretation of the divine breathing of Genesis 2:7, in which God

> created *humanity* to rule the world and placed within him two spirits so that he would walk with them until the moment of his visitation: they are the spirits of truth and of deceit. From the spring of light stem the generations of truth, and from the source of darkness the generations of deceit. And in the hand of the Prince of Lights is dominion over all the sons of justice; they walk in paths of light. And in the hand of the Angel of Darkness is total dominion over the sons of deceit; they walk on paths of darkness. (1QS column 3, lines 17–21)

The two spirits represent two spheres in conflict. The spirit of truth brings "intelligence, understanding, potent wisdom, . . . a spirit of knowledge in all the plans of action, . . . careful behaviour in wisdom concerning everything . . ." The spirit of deceit brings "greed, sluggishness in the service of justice, wickedness, falsehood, pride . . ."[7]

Those who follow these two spirits do so "until the moment of his [God's] visitation." At that moment, the sons of truth will inherit "healing, plentiful peace in a long life, fruitful offspring with all everlasting blessings, eternal enjoyment with endless life, and a crown of glory with majestic raiment in eternal light."[8] The sons of deceit

---

6. Technically, this word should be transliterated *'ādām*, but I have left it *adam* for easier reading.

7. 1QS column 4, lines 2–6.

8. 1QS column 4, lines 6–8.

will inherit "an abundance of afflictions at the hands of all the angels of destruction, for eternal damnation by the scorching wrath of the God of revenges, for permanent terror and shame without end with the humiliation of destruction by the fire of the dark regions. And all the ages of their generations (they shall spend) in bitter weeping and harsh evils in the abysses of darkness until their destruction, without there being a remnant or a survivor for them."[9]

In the broken church represented by the short letter known as 1 John, battle lines have been drawn between the community of the letter and those who have left, those who "went out from us," those who "did not belong to us" (1 John 2:19). The author claims they are liars, deceivers, and even the antichrist (1 John 2:22; 4:1–6; cf. 2 John 7). In the drawing of these communal battle lines, the Spirit plays an invaluable role, a role that reflects the tenor of the letter, a letter that espouses a contrast between the spirits of truth and error.

This preoccupation with drawing lines demands a principle of differentiation; the author of the letter meets this demand by providing a precise principle of discrimination. "Beloved, do not believe every spirit, but test the spirits to see whether they are from God; for many false prophets have gone out into the world. By this you know the Spirit of God: every spirit that confesses that Jesus Christ has come in the flesh is from God, and every spirit that does not confess Jesus is not from God. And this is the spirit of the antichrist, of which you have heard that it is coming; and now it is already in the world" (1 John 4:1–3). Though minimal, this is an irrefutable, verifiable criterion of faith that is related to the confession that Jesus Christ came in the flesh. Its function is similar to the confession "Jesus is Lord" in Paul's contention that "no one can say 'Jesus is Lord' except by the Holy Spirit" (1 Cor. 12:3). Amid a variety of itinerant prophets and prophetic messages, and the spirits that allegedly inspire them, it proves difficult to discern the truth, and so this is the dividing line, the test of truth: Jesus is from God and in the flesh.

In a tenuous but decisive way, this criterion drives us back to Jesus's teaching on the paraclete, whose vocation lies in leading people back to Jesus—the authentic Jesus of the Gospels. The community

9. 1QS column 4, lines 12–14.

refuses to forfeit the fundamental belief that Jesus has come in the flesh. Apparently others, whom we know only through the vitriol of this letter—and so we know them poorly—are willing to believe in a Jesus who has *not* come in the flesh. This is the line the author of 1 John will not—cannot—cross, a line that the paraclete, too, will never cross, given its vocation of teaching all that Jesus has said in the flesh.

This criterion is clear evidence of a deep divide in the church: "We are from God. Whoever knows God listens to us, and whoever is not from God does not listen to us. From this we know the spirit of truth and the spirit of error" (1 John 4:6). Here there are two spirits, two realms, two communities. This is a tidily divided world; to the one side belongs a community of the spirit of truth, to the other those who do not listen to the teachers of this community and therefore situate themselves in the world of the spirit of error.

In the letter of 1 John, the two spirits look like they are viewed the same way as in the *Community Rule*. Whether the author of 1 John has been influenced by this teaching, or whether both inhabit the same conceptual universe, the *Community Rule* offers at length what appear only as catchphrases in 1 John 4:6. Between those who have left and the faithful believers in the author's charge, there is utter incompatibility, even conflict. Although the author does not frame this in the potentially violent terms of the *Community Rule*, there exists nevertheless a harsh disjuncture between the beloved community and those who have left (whom the author identifies as liars, deceivers, and the antichrist).

The edgy introduction of the Spirit of truth in the Fourth Gospel, with the wedge that is drawn between the disciples and the world, may reflect a similar perspective to that of the letter of 1 John and the *Community Rule*, though it is muted by comparison. There are even important mismatches as well. In particular, the symmetry of the *Community Rule* has no exact match in the Fourth Gospel. There is no battle within the human heart occasioned by two spirits from birth, nor is there a neat division of humankind into the children of light and the children of darkness. In a particularly heated moment, Jesus does excoriate children of the devil: "You are from your father the devil, and you choose to do your father's desires" (John 8:44). Yet there is no corresponding group; the children of light apparently do not yet exist. Jesus refers only once to children of light—in his final words following the crowd's stubborn refusal to believe. In such a context, he is especially intent on making clear that the refractory crowd does *not* belong to this group, even if they may think they do. His warning, in fact, is a thinly veiled threat. Jesus himself is the light, and they had best learn to walk in it: "The light is with you for a little longer. Walk while you have the light, so that the darkness may not overtake you. If you walk in the darkness, you do not know where you are going. While you have the light, believe in the light, so that you may become children of light" (12:35–36). Jesus is clear: they do not belong among the children of light. Not yet.

Human existence is divided, therefore, in the Fourth Gospel as it is in the *Community Rule*, but not symmetrically so. In the *Community Rule*, although the spirit of truth within is tempered by the spirit of deceit, with which it battles, it is nonetheless present within as the source of a life of virtue. The scenario seems to be darker, more pessimistic, in the Fourth Gospel, in which Jesus enters a world that is darkened by deceit, a world in which Jesus's enemies are children of the devil and the crowds are not yet children of light. There is no community—not yet anyway—with the Spirit of truth infusing it with truth. For the time being, one person alone stands in the light. His opponents reject him. The crowd waffles over him. The disciples remain fretful about him—so grief stricken that Jesus cannot, even in his final moments alone with them, prepare them adequately for the appalling events that inevitably lie ahead.

Inspired Memories

In his final hours alone with the disciples, Jesus promises more than a vague sensation of his presence or an oblique assurance of guidance and teaching. He is more definite, more certain than that. Jesus promises that the Spirit will teach the disciples *all* things and will guide them into (or in) *all* the truth. This appears to be a fantastic promise, a voyage into the unknown realms of the future. Notwithstanding the blank check Jesus appears to offer the disciples, there is a more pedestrian but also more essential strain to the promise, the scope of which is constrained by the rationale Jesus gives: "I still have many things to say to you, but you cannot bear them now. When the Spirit of truth comes, he will guide you into [in] all the truth" (John 16:12–13). The "many things" that Jesus has yet to say consist of what he did not say when he was with the disciples: "I did not say these things to you from the beginning, because I was with you" (16:4). He did not say them because he did not need to; he himself was with them.

Now, on his last night with them, he begins to discuss his impending death, but his disciples have become despondent because of what he has said: "But because I have said these things to you, sorrow has filled your hearts" (John 16:6). As a result, admits Jesus, the disciples "cannot bear them now" (16:12). What is it they cannot bear? *Teachings that have to do exclusively with Jesus's imminent departure.* This poses a conundrum: Jesus wants to tell the disciples, his friends, about his death, but they simply cannot bear it.

This is where the Spirit of truth enters the picture: what Jesus cannot now say about his impending death (because of the disciples' heavyheartedness), the Spirit of truth will say on his behalf *after* his death. Because the disciples cannot accept any more of Jesus's teaching prior to his death, the Spirit of truth will lead the disciples in retrospect into all the truth about his departure.

Within the perspective of the farewell discourses—and this is the indispensable perspective we have for the interpretation of this saying—the "things to come" are not events that lie in the disciples' future after they receive the Spirit; those are not teachings that the disciples cannot bear because of the sorrow they generate. The "things to come" are those events that lie in Jesus's *immediate* future, events that, from Jesus's perspective at this moment in the narrative of the Fourth Gospel, are still to come: his death, departure, and glorification. Because the disciples cannot endure such teaching, the paraclete, when it is given, will teach them *afterward* the meaning of Jesus's glorification—what Jesus would have taught were they not now so heavyhearted—in precisely the way that Jesus would have because the paraclete "will take what is mine and declare it to you" (John 16:14).

To construe the paraclete's vocation as unrestrained prophetic prediction, therefore, is to misunderstand Jesus's promise and to neglect the constraints that the narrative context places on it within the Fourth Gospel. The "all things" that the paraclete will guide the disciples into do not lie in our, the readers', future; the "all things" lie, in the context of the Fourth Gospel, in the *disciples'* immediate future. The focus of the paraclete's vocation is not to predict all things in general but to recollect all things related to Jesus, who will soon be glorified on the cross. The Spirit within will faithfully draw the disciples back to Jesus, particularly to those events that take place following their last night together. The nature of this peculiar vocation of recollection is clear in what Jesus says in the second promise about the paraclete in the farewell discourses: "The paraclete, the Holy Spirit, whom the Father will send in my name, will teach you all, and remind you of all that I have said to you" (John 14:26 alt.). This saying of Jesus draws together two essential bits of content the paraclete will teach—"everything" and "all" that Jesus has said to them. The "all" that the Holy Spirit will teach is the *all* that Jesus himself has said and accomplished. Teaching, in short, is a matter of inspired reminding.

What, then, is to be made of the promise "When the Spirit of truth comes, it will guide you into all the truth; for it will not speak on its own, but will speak whatever it hears, and it will declare to you the things that are to come. It will glorify me, because it will take what is mine and declare it to you" (John 16:13–14 alt.)?[10] While this looks at first blush like the promise of boundless revelation, it is not. *The things that are to come are those events that lie in Jesus's immediate future.*

Unfortunately, the verb *declare* in English suggests the revelation, even prediction, of things to come, while the Greek verb *anangellein* more fundamentally points backward, to reporting or narrating

10. Throughout this chapter, I have had difficulty trying to avoid exclusively male language for the paraclete, especially given the male language employed in translations. In this instance, I substitute "it" and "its" for "he" and "his" in the NRSV. Neuter language can be said to blunt the personal character of the paraclete, but exclusively male language may suggest too unequivocally that the paraclete was considered to be male.

something from the past. In his letter to the Corinthians, Paul tells his readers that Titus "reported" (*anangellōn*) to Paul how the Corinthians longed for him (2 Cor. 7:7). In the book of Acts, Paul and Barnabas "*related* [*anēngellon*] all that God had done with them" during their first journey to the church in Antioch, which had launched their mission (Acts 14:27). In the Fourth Gospel, the man healed at the pool of Siloam "*told* [*anēngeilen*] the Jews that it was Jesus who had made him well" (John 5:15).[11] In all of these instances, someone narrates what has already taken place—not something that will take place. This is not a matter of prediction; it is a matter of recollection. It is a declaration of the meaning of what has taken place.

The conversation between Jesus and the Samaritan woman illuminates this distinction between prediction and remembrance. In the course of the conversation, she ventures, "I know that Messiah is coming," and "when he comes, he will proclaim all things to us" (John 4:25). The verb *anangellein*, translated as "proclaim," may suggest that the Messiah will reveal what is going to happen. But the verb in this context actually suggests that the Messiah will explain the meaning of everything that has happened. Everything, in short, will become clear in the presence of the Messiah. Jesus responds, "I am he, the one who is speaking to you" (4:26). What happens next confirms that declaration, *anangellein*, is, in the Fourth Gospel, less about prediction than about meaningful narration of the past. The woman returns to her people and says, "Come and see a man who told me everything I have ever done! He cannot be the Messiah, can he?" (4:29). Jesus did not predict what would happen to her; he *narrated* her life, telling her everything that she had done. He did not forecast; he reported. The verb *anangellein* in this story suggests that Jesus was about the business that would eventually preoccupy the paraclete in the days ahead. He explained to the woman not what *would* happen but what *had* happened.

For the disciples, the glorification of Jesus through death and resurrection will soon occur. The meaning of those events the paraclete will reveal, declare, explain, disclose, uncover—*anangellein*.

11. Similarly, in the Gospel of Mark swineherds "narrated" (*apēngeilan*) what had happened: that Jesus cast demons into their pigs (Mark 5:14).

Twice in the Fourth Gospel the curtain is drawn back on the content of inspired remembrance, of revelation-as-reminiscence. After Jesus raises his protest against the temple, he says, "Destroy this temple, and in three days I will raise it up" (John 2:19). His Jewish colleagues misunderstand and are, as a consequence, baffled, since the Herodian temple took forty-six years to build. John ventures, by way of aside, "But he was speaking of the temple of his body. After he was raised from the dead, his disciples remembered that he had said this; and they believed the scripture and the word that Jesus had spoken" (2:21–22). This aside illuminates the process of teaching as reminding; such teaching is not mere memory work but recollection that brings deeper understanding.

Much later, Jesus enters Jerusalem on a young donkey to the resounding praise of the crowd. As in the Synoptic Gospels, John sees this triumphal entrance as the fulfillment of Zechariah's words. However, unlike the authors of the Synoptic Gospels, he explains in a unique and fascinating aside how the disciples came to see this event in relation to Zechariah: "His disciples *did not understand* these things at first; but when Jesus was glorified, then *they remembered* that these things had been written of him and had been done to him" (John 12:16, italics added). The fingerprints of the paraclete are detectable on this aside because the association between understanding and remembrance is so like the connection drawn between teaching and reminding, which Jesus attributes to the Spirit in his final discourses (14:26).

Even while teaching his disciples on their last night together, when he has so much to say about the paraclete, Jesus takes off his robe, ties a towel around his waist, pours water into a basin, begins to wash the disciples' feet, and says to an incredulous Peter, who puts up resistance, "You do not know now what I am doing, but later you will understand" (John 13:4–7). They will understand later, they are soon to learn, because "the paraclete, the Holy Spirit, whom the Father will send in my name, will teach you everything, and remind you of all that I have said to you" (14:26 alt.).

The Spirit's principal vocation, therefore, is to lead the disciples, in the aftermath of the glorification of Jesus in death and resurrection, into the truth of what they have already heard and experienced—into the truth of his life and death. Yet there is more to the process of inspired recollection. In these two examples—the destruction of the temple, Jesus's body, and the triumphant entry into Jerusalem—full recollection includes Israel's Scriptures. A full understanding of the temple saying leads the disciples to believe both the Scripture and the word that Jesus spoke. A full comprehension of Jesus's entry on a colt hinges on their remembrance that these things have been *written of him* and have been *done to him*. Both narrative asides draw a taut correlation between particular Scriptures and a particular word or event in Jesus's life.

In a Gospel that begins with an overture in which Jesus is the *logos*, in a Gospel that is rife with an appreciation for knowledge, in a Gospel where Jesus expresses his rabbinic vocation through teaching, it comes as no surprise that the paraclete, the Holy Spirit, the Spirit of truth, teaches about Jesus by setting his words and actions in the context of Israelite Scripture (John 2:22; 12:16; 14:26). The irony of the Fourth Gospel is that the paraclete's task of drawing people back to Jesus, teaching through reminding, and saying only what originates with Jesus actually brings in its train a rich measure of ingenuity. Miracles become signs. Teaching about the kingdom of God is supplanted largely by Jesus's self-revelation. Exorcisms disappear. Crucifixion becomes glorification. What the Spirit teaches and recollects and receives from Jesus is not rote, repetitive, or routine.

As marvelous as this knowledge may be, it arrives only with the Spirit of truth. There is no provision for the crowd or the disciples that enables them to understand the truth of Jesus's teaching while he is alive. Such insight will come to bloom only in retrospect, when the paraclete leads the disciples in all the truth, when it teaches and reminds them of all that Jesus said, and when it prompts the recollection of scriptural texts that illumine his otherwise inscrutable actions and sayings. For all its embrace of learning and knowledge and wisdom, then, the perspective of the Fourth Gospel is that understanding was unavailable, insight inaccessible, wisdom unattainable before the crucifixion of Jesus. The paraclete, it seems, would interpret the crucifixion by way of inspired remembrance, not as a death at all, at least not finally a death, but in a development of inspired proportions, as a lifting up, an elevation, a moment not of defeat but of intense glory.

10

Spirit and Our Future

Jesus came near and spoke to them, "I've received all authority in heaven and on earth. Therefore, go and make disciples of all nations, baptizing them in the name of the Father and of the Son and of the Holy Spirit, teaching them to obey everything that I've commanded you. Look, I myself will be with you every day until the end of this present age."

Matthew 28:18–20 CEB

These signs will be associated with those who believe: they will throw out demons in my name. They will speak in new languages. They will pick up snakes with their hands. If they drink anything poisonous, it will not hurt them. They will place their hands on the sick, and they will get well.

Mark 16:17–18 CEB

Jesus said to them, "These are my words that I spoke to you while I was still with you—that everything written about me in the Law from Moses, the Prophets, and the Psalms must be fulfilled." Then he opened their minds to understand the scriptures. He said to them, "This is what is written: the Christ will suffer and rise from the dead on the third day, and a change of heart and life for the forgiveness of sins must be preached in his name to all nations, beginning from Jerusalem. You are witnesses of these things. Look, I'm sending to you what my Father promised, but you are to stay in the city until you have been furnished with heavenly power."

Luke 24:44–49 CEB

It was still the first day of the week. That evening, while the disciples were behind closed doors because they were afraid of the Jewish authorities, Jesus came and stood among them. He said, "Peace be with you." After he said this, he showed them his hands and his side. When the disciples saw the Lord, they were filled with joy. Jesus said to them again, "Peace be with you. As the Father sent me, so I am sending you." Then he breathed on them and said, "Receive the Holy Spirit. If you forgive anyone's sins, they are forgiven; if you don't forgive them, they aren't forgiven."

John 20:19–23 CEB

Back to the Future

We began with a birth but not only a birth—a beginning, a *genesis*. The *rûaḥ* brooded over the watery abyss at the beginning of the world; now *rûaḥ*, a holy spirit, broods over the belly of a young Galilean peasant, overshadowing her with power in a damaged world.

That is how the Spirit enters the story in the Gospel of Matthew. The Gospel of Luke begins with another birth—not Jesus but John the Baptist—but with no less a ring of hope, a peal of promise: "Even before his birth he will be filled with the Holy Spirit" (Luke 1:15) and "With the spirit and power of Elijah he will go before him, to turn the hearts of parents to their children, and the disobedient to the wisdom of the righteous, to make ready a people prepared for the Lord" (1:17). This assurance also transports us back not with Matthew to the seventeenth word of the Jewish Scriptures but to the prophet Elijah, who would defy the likes of Jezebel and her tepid husband-king, Ahab. But John is also meant to look ahead "to make ready a people prepared for the Lord." The harbinger of the consolation of Isaiah 40, John will remove the rubble and roll the stones away so that Jesus can walk the way of deliverance.

The birth stories in the Gospels of Matthew and Luke are rife with anticipation despite their differences—exotic astrologers rather than shepherds, a guiding star rather than singing angels in the sky, five stories intended to fulfill the Jewish Scriptures rather than a mishmash of praise and blessing gushing up from thankful and nearly nameless people. This is not surprising. Birth, especially miraculous birth, marks the opening of a vista and not just a womb.

What is surprising is that the Gospels *end* with anticipation. You will find no eulogy here, no obituary at the tail end of Jesus's life. There is no final line, such as "His was a life well lived," nor do the Gospels end with an epitaph, such as "Devoted son. Beloved cousin." The Gospels are not biographies that wrap up the loose ends of Jesus's life in a seamless narrative. They end with anticipation, expectation, the prospect of more highways to be cleared and shipping lanes along the horizon to be plowed by itinerant apostles bearing the good news to far-flung Roman lands.

Knowing what we know now, it may not surprise us that the Holy Spirit lies at the center of this frisson. The Holy Spirit was central to that first outburst of anticipation surrounding the baby born to be king. The Holy Spirit filled John the Baptist before birth to prepare the way for Jesus. The Holy Spirit descended like a dove, then drove, led up, or simply led Jesus in the desert as Satan tested Jesus's mettle against the allure of ambition and personal comfort. The Holy Spirit inspired Jesus to teach constantly and once to rejoice but always to possess the durable sense that he was his Father's Son, which was the only assurance that mattered. Jesus occasionally promised the Holy Spirit to his followers, though not without the prospect of testing—he knew from experience that Satan lingered wherever the Spirit flourished—and the inevitability of maltreatment at the hands of family and politicians alike.

It will not surprise us, knowing what we now know, that the Spirit is central not just to the drama that unfolds in the Gospels but to the drama yet to unfold. Not now a *genesis* but a new *genesis*, a "new creation," as the apostle Paul so memorably phrases it (2 Cor. 5:17). The praise and prophesying not now of a select few—Elizabeth, Zechariah, Mary, Simeon, and Anna—but of swaths of people and unexpected people, like women and men in Caesarea, non-Jews who, when the Holy Spirit poured over them, found themselves praising God (Acts 10:44–45).[1] The Holy Spirit is no less essential at the tail end of the Gospels than at their beginning.

Five Signs

Three women arrive at the tomb early Sunday morning, where they discover the stone rolled away and a young man in white telling them, of all things, not to be afraid but to take this news back to the men (especially Peter), who are not there. Their response, which marks the end of the Gospel of Mark, is odd: "So they went out and fled from the tomb, for terror and amazement had seized them; and they said nothing to anyone, for they were afraid" (Mark 16:8). The English translation offers a puzzling ending. There is an empty tomb but no risen Jesus, unlike what we find in the other Gospels.

The situation is even more baffling in the original Greek text, which ends abruptly with the odd word *gar*. Translated in English as "for

---

1. I omitted "spoke in tongues" here because of how much interpretation it requires to understand correctly. This story suggests, in my opinion, that these people spoke in other languages as at Pentecost. If you would like to explore this interpretation further, you will find a discussion in my *Inspired: The Holy Spirit and the Mind of Faith* (Grand Rapids: Eerdmans, 2013), 91–97.

they were afraid," the Greek reads, "They were afraid, for." *Gar* is a conjunction, like *and* or *but*. Imagine, "They were afraid, and" or "They were afraid, but"—an odd conclusion to an entire Gospel. The construction simply does not work.

Coupled with the need for an appearance of the resurrected Jesus, as in the other three Gospels, this awkward sentence led to the addition of various longer endings to the Gospel of Mark.[2] One reads rather magnificently: "And all that had been commanded them they told briefly to those around Peter. And afterward Jesus himself sent out through them, from east to west, the sacred and imperishable proclamation of eternal salvation" (Mark 16:8).[3]

Following a series of resurrection appearances (Mark 16:9–14), Jesus appears to the Eleven and scolds them for not believing those who testified to his resurrection; what he says sounds like a brief summary of Matthew 28:16–20: "And he said to them, 'Go into all the world and proclaim the good news to the whole creation'" (Mark 16:15). Then several other sayings of Jesus or narrative snippets follow, each of which looks like an embellishment of this one, whether they originated with a single author or several authors:

The one who believes and is baptized will be saved; but the one who does not believe will be condemned. (Mark 16:16)

And these signs will accompany those who believe: by using my name they will cast out demons; they will speak in new tongues; they will pick up snakes in their hands, and if they drink any deadly thing, it will not hurt them; they will lay their hands on the sick, and they will recover. (Mark 16:17–18)

So then the Lord Jesus, after he had spoken to them, was taken up into heaven and sat down at the right hand of God. (Mark 16:19)

2. The value of these longer endings is debatable—and debated. They do not belong to the earliest manuscripts and are, consequently, not part of the original Gospel in Greek. Yet for many Christians, these endings still belong to the Bible. Therefore, they should be not merely dismissed but interpreted as part of the Christian Bible, even if they offer less insight than earlier—and shorter—manuscripts of the Gospel of Mark.

3. This occurs in a longer version of Mark 16:8 than is usually found in translations.

> And they went out and proclaimed the good news everywhere, while the Lord worked with them and confirmed the message by the signs that accompanied it. (Mark 16:20)

If the references to baptism (Mark 16:16) and the ascension of Jesus (16:19) are deleted, this ending reads smoothly. Jesus gives a commission to go and proclaim the good news to the whole creation (16:15), Jesus authorizes five signs that accompany faith (16:17–18), and the disciples go out and proclaim the good news with signs accompanying them (16:20).

The five signs Jesus promises are nothing short of stratospheric, brimming with the extraordinary and bordering on the bizarre; they are signs intended to leave no doubt about the authenticity of the proclamation. This assertion, of course, begs the question of Jesus's life. Signs similar to some of these accompanied Jesus's proclamation, but they did not inevitably confirm his claims. In fact, they often had the opposite effect of precipitating antagonism. Still, the five signs Jesus authorizes in Mark 16:17–18 include exorcism, speaking in new tongues, snake handling, poison drinking, and healing through the laying on of hands.

Snakes and Poison

Two of these signs, protection from snakes and poison, are nowhere to be found among New Testament signs of the Holy Spirit. In the Gospel of Luke, the disciples have authority to tread on snakes (Luke 10:19), but this authority is not attributed to the Holy Spirit, not even by extension from Jesus, who himself does not tread on snakes. More likely, this is an allusion to Israel's wilderness wanderings. Moses warned his people not to become complacent once they settled the promised land; they were instead to remember what God did for them. *God* is the one who "brought you out of the land of Egypt, out of the house of slavery, who led you through the great and terrible wilderness, an arid wasteland with poisonous snakes and scorpions. He made water flow for you from flint rock, and fed you in the wilderness with manna that your ancestors did not know, to humble you and to test you, and in the end to do you good" (Deut.

8:14–16). If the saying in Luke 10:19 offers a clue to the meaning of the sign at the tail end of the Gospel of Mark, then the saying of Jesus in the Gospel of Mark is also less about miraculous signs than about divine provision in treacherous situations.

The matter of snakes comes up again in Luke's Gospel in Jesus's instructions about prayer. Jesus tells those who pray that God will give them the Holy Spirit rather than snakes and scorpions (Luke 11:9–13). This teaching has nothing to say about *protection* from snakes. On the contrary, Jesus assures people that no demonic darkness, no satanic evil, no snakes or scorpions will be theirs in the depths of prayer. It is not that they will handle snakes safely; there will be *no* snakes—no deep, dark evil—for people of intense prayer to handle at all.[4]

There are, then, no corresponding references to snakes in the Gospels. Mark 16:18 stands alone—as does the reference to drinking poison unharmed. There is certainly no connection between these signs and the Holy Spirit anywhere else in the four Gospels.

Exorcisms

The three other signs may be associated with the Holy Spirit elsewhere in the New Testament. In the Gospel of Matthew, the connection to exorcisms, for example, is explicit: Jesus casts out demons by the Holy Spirit (Matt. 12:28). In the Gospel of Mark, this association is implicit. While Jesus does not draw an explicit connection as in the Gospel of Matthew, Jesus does deliver a dire warning about blasphemy against the Holy Spirit in response to his opponents' reaction to his exorcisms (Mark 3:21–35). Exorcism becomes, then, a natural sign of the Spirit for Jesus's followers.

New Tongues

The next sign of the Spirit listed at the end of Mark's Gospel, "new tongues" (*glōssais kainais*), may also be related to other experiences of the Holy Spirit found in the New Testament, though these are

---

4. I have already interpreted this passage in chap. 5, "Spirit, Promise, Praise, and Prayer," in the section "Snakes, Scorpions, and the Holy Spirit."

altogether different experiences. On the one hand, "new tongues" may be related to glossolalia, or speaking in tongues—a spiritual gift Paul describes in a letter to the Corinthians (1 Cor. 12:10). More than one form of glossolalia seems to have existed in the churches Paul helped to found. It could refer to a private prayer language, to which Paul himself laid claim (14:18–19), or to an incomprehensible public worship language, which Paul limited to no more than three occurrences per worship service (he also advised that this gift should be practiced only when someone with the spiritual gift of interpretation was present; 14:1–28).

The expression "new tongues," on the other hand, may be related to speaking in *known* languages—a phenomenon that occurs in the story of Pentecost, when Jesus's followers "were filled with the Holy Spirit and began to speak in *other* languages" (Acts 2:4, italics added). Some of those in the audience asked, "Are not all these who are speaking Galileans? And how is it that we hear, each of us, in our own native language?" (2:7–8). From this perspective, the longer ending of the Gospel of Mark contains Jesus's command to proclaim the Gospel in new languages. This interpretation of the sign of new tongues fits the context of global mission. In order to execute that mission, Jesus's followers will need to speak in new languages.

Laying On of Hands

The fifth sign, healing, occurs in one of Paul's lists of spiritual gifts (1 Cor. 12:9).[5] The rub comes with the connection between healing and the laying on of hands in the longer ending of Mark's Gospel. Paul does not make this connection. In the Gospels, especially the Gospel of Mark, Jesus heals people by laying hands on them (e.g., Mark 5:23; 6:5; 7:32; 8:23; Luke 4:40; 13:13). Later, in the book of Acts, Ananias lays his hands on Paul, who has gone blind during his Damascus Road experience (Acts 9:12, 17), and Paul himself cures the father of Publius, the leading man on the island of Malta, by laying hands on him (Acts 28:8). In none of these stories, however, is healing by the laying on of hands traced explicitly to the Holy Spirit.

5. He does not include this gift in another list in Rom. 12:4–8.

The association of healing with the Holy Spirit—though not the laying on of hands—occurs in the Gospel of Matthew, which contains a quotation describing the Spirit-inspired servant of Isaiah 42 (Matt. 8:17). The most salient connection between healing and the Holy Spirit occurs in the book of Acts, when Peter offers a terse summary, perhaps an early confession or creed, about Jesus: "That message spread throughout Judea, beginning in Galilee after the baptism that John announced: how God anointed Jesus of Nazareth with the Holy Spirit and with power; how he went about doing good and healing all who were oppressed by the devil, for God was with him" (Acts 10:37–38). Still, neither of these references suggests the practice of laying on of hands.

The relationship, then, between healing, the laying on of hands, and the Holy Spirit is nowhere to be found in the New Testament.[6] Strange as it may seem, this connection is not found in the longer ending of Mark's Gospel either—and this brings us to one of the more puzzling aspects of Mark's longer ending: *the absence of the Holy Spirit.*

The Spirit Gone Missing

Drinking poison and handling snakes are not mentioned elsewhere in the New Testament. Yet exorcism, speaking in new tongues, and healing (though not necessarily through the laying on of hands) can be associated with the Holy Spirit. Since three of the five signs may be associated with the Spirit to varying degrees elsewhere in the New Testament, and since each of the other three Gospels ends with a promise of the Holy Spirit (Matt. 28:18–20; Luke 24:49; John 20:20–23), then something about the longer ending of the Gospel of Mark is curious, even amiss, and this is simply that Mark does not attribute these signs to the Holy Spirit. Jesus lists them clearly and promises them unconditionally, but he attributes them to "my name"

6. Deut. 34:9 does refer to the passing of the spirit of wisdom from Moses to Joshua by the laying on of hands: "Joshua son of Nun was full of the spirit of wisdom, because Moses had laid his hands on him; and the Israelites obeyed him, doing as the Lord had commanded Moses." You will find an analysis of Deut. 34:9 in chap. 4 of my *A Boundless God: The Spirit according to the Old Testament* (Grand Rapids: Baker Academic, 2020), 84–85.

rather than the Holy Spirit. This text is an oddity, therefore, not only because it was a later addition to the original Gospel of Mark—not even because it contains some signs (arguably somewhat unusual signs) that occur nowhere else in the New Testament—but because the author of this ending did not attribute these five signs to the Holy Spirit, though everything we know suggests that, for three of them at least, he should have done so.

The Great Commission

The Spirit in the Gospel of Matthew, we saw, is an essential ingredient in the birth of Jesus, either in the form of Mary's holy spirit or the Holy Spirit. Recall the uncharacteristic imprecision of an expression that could be translated as either "the child conceived in her is from the Holy Spirit" or "the child conceived in her is from *a* holy spirit" (Matt. 1:20).

No such imprecision characterizes the two clusters of references to the Spirit that punctuate Matthew's Gospel. The first cluster occurs at the start of Jesus's public life, with John the Baptist's prediction of Spirit and fire (Matt. 3:11), Jesus's baptism (3:16), and Jesus's testing in the desert (4:1). The second cluster gathers around the question of Jesus's authority, with the citation of Isaiah 42:1–4 (Matt. 12:18–21), Jesus's claim to exorcise demons by the Spirit of God (12:28), and Jesus's warning about blasphemy against the Holy Spirit (12:31–32). Jesus refers twice more to the Spirit prior to his crucifixion—in the promise that the Spirit will speak through persecuted believers (10:20) and the assumption that David composed the psalms under inspiration (22:43).

Once more, at the very end of the Gospel, the Spirit appears, this time in association with the Father and the Son. The command to baptize in the name of Father, Son, and Holy Spirit shimmers with the reminiscence of Jesus's own baptism, when the Spirit descended and the Father said, "You are my Son." This is more a close-knit trio than a Trinity. It is like some of the apostle Paul's statements, which refer to this trio without necessarily suggesting a fully formed Trinity. In 1 Corinthians 12:4–6, for example, Paul writes, "Now there are varieties of gifts, but the same Spirit; and there are varieties of services, but the same Lord; and there are varieties of activities, but it is the same God who activates all of them in everyone." He concludes a later letter to the same church with this benediction: "The grace of the Lord Jesus Christ, the love of God, and the communion of the Holy Spirit be with all of you" (2 Cor. 13:13).

Jesus's final words in Matthew's Gospel resonate as well with instructions about baptism in an early Christian compendium of practices and instruction known as the *Didache* (*The Teaching of the Twelve*):

> Now concerning baptism, baptize as follows: after you have reviewed all these things, baptize in the name of the Father and of the Son and of the Holy Spirit in running water. But if you have no running water, then baptize in some other water; and if you are not able to baptize in cold water, then do so in warm. But if you have neither, then pour water on the head three times in the name of Father and Son and Holy Spirit. And before the baptism let the one baptizing and the one who is to be baptized fast, as well as any others who are able. Also, you must instruct the one who is to be baptized to fast for one or two days beforehand. (*Didache* 7.1–4)[7]

The *Didache* is far more fastidious in its understanding of how to baptize than Jesus is at the finale of Matthew's Gospel, but the same community of Father, Son, and Holy Spirit is essential to both.

The inclusion of the Holy Spirit alongside Father and Son in the Gospel of Matthew suggests that the Spirit is other than an impersonal power or a fiery wind of judgment, as in John the Baptist's prediction. This sense of a personality suits a Gospel in which the Spirit leads Jesus up into the wilderness after his baptism, like the angelic Spirit of Isaiah 63:7–14, who led Israel from Egypt to the promised land (Matt. 4:1–2). It fits a Gospel that pits the Holy Spirit against Beelzebul, the personal embodiment of evil (12:25–28). Both are powerful rulers over their respective dominions, like the Prince of Lights and the Angel of Darkness in the Dead Sea Scrolls.

7. This quotation is from Michael W. Holmes, trans., *The Apostolic Fathers: Greek Texts and English Translations*, 3rd ed. (Grand Rapids: Baker Academic, 2007), 355.

The Spirit is now an enduring partner with the Father and the Son in the primary rite of initiation. Not every disciple will see the heavens opened, hear a fatherly voice, or experience the Spirit's descent like a dove, but every disciple can experience baptism in the name of the Father, the Son, and the Holy Spirit.

Jesus does not say in the Great Commission how disciples experience the Spirit, at least not explicitly. Still, one aspect of this experience is certain: the Great Commission does not associate the Spirit with the spectacular, despite the association of the Spirit with Jesus's healing, preaching, and exorcisms earlier in the Gospel. Installed with all authority, Jesus now confronts his disciples with a more prosaic commission, more menial acts, more tedious activities. They must, simply put, go, make disciples, baptize, and teach. Nothing here is acutely captivating or stirring. Nothing is especially magnetic. Nothing is particularly alluring.

And that is the point. Disciple making involves teaching without the promise of charisma or revelation or incontrovertible inspiration. No signs, as in the addition to the Gospel of Mark, accompany proclamation of the gospel.

In fact, proclamation has no place in the Great Commission; *teaching* does. Earlier in the Gospel, Jesus does proclaim the kingdom of heaven (Matt. 4:17) and the good news of the kingdom (9:35), and Jesus orders his disciples to proclaim the kingdom of heaven (10:7; 10:27). Jesus both preaches and teaches in tandem (4:23; 11:1). Jesus even speaks in global terms about the proclamation of the gospel. In his description of the future, he predicts that "this good news of the kingdom will be proclaimed throughout the world, as a testimony to all the nations; and then the end will come" (24:14). When a woman anoints him, he vows, "Truly I tell you, wherever this good news is proclaimed in the whole world, what she has done will be told in remembrance of her" (26:13). Yet now, invested at the end with all authority in heaven and on earth, Jesus does not command his followers to *proclaim* the gospel of the kingdom. He mentions neither proclamation nor the now familiar message about the kingdom of heaven. Instead, he tells them to teach—teaching as he did when he delivered the Sermon on the Mount (5:2), as he did with authority (7:29), as he did in the synagogue (13:54), as he did in Jerusalem (21:23), and as he did in the temple (26:55).

And the content of this teaching? It is as severe as it is simple: *all* that Jesus commanded them. Here is Jesus nearly enthroned, invested with all of the heavenly and earthly authority there is to be had, standing once again like Moses on a mountaintop. And what does he tell his disciples to do?

Perform grand signs, such as trampling snakes and drinking poison, as in the longer ending of Mark's Gospel? No.

Deliver spellbinding discourses, as in the book of Acts? No.

Forgive sins, as in the Fourth Gospel? No.

Jesus's commands are simple—and perilously inescapable. The Eleven must go. They must make disciples. They must baptize them. And they must teach, not in a way that impresses with ingenuity or astonishes with oratorical flourish or attracts with winsome promises. The Eleven must teach them to obey *everything* Jesus commanded. The Eleven must teach in a way that *makes disciples* of hearers.

This sort of teaching, of disciple making, rests not on charismatic revelation or miraculous signs but on *knowledge*—intimate and exhaustive knowledge of *everything* Jesus commanded. The sort of teaching Jesus demands is the product of memory—memorization—rather than revelation: *teaching them to obey everything that I have commanded you.* The commands are there already. Now they must be taught, every last one of them. That sort of meticulous attention to detail lies at the heart of the Great Commission.

This is a daunting and dogged task that demands impeccable integrity and a gritty commitment to study. It is a matter of unswerving allegiance to every single command of Jesus, who had dotted his i's and crossed his t's, fulfilling every jot and tittle of Torah (Matt. 5:17–20—not just select commands, certainly not comfortable ones, and definitely not commands interpreted for convenience.

There is no need in this Great Commission for the charisma of healing, exorcism, or inspired speech. Such drama would only distract from the formidable and forthright task of disciplined learning that equips teachers to make disciples of all nations, bar none, by holding *everything* dear, without exception, as Jesus himself had taught.

The Promise of Power

In the bustle of birth and the hustle of Jesus's early days after his baptism, the Holy Spirit pulses, inspiring and guiding, it seems, nearly everyone who comes into contact with the servant Son of God. Then the Spirit goes underground like a mountain spring, only to bubble up in a rare glimpse of Jesus's rejoicing in the Holy Spirit (Luke 10:21), followed by a few scattered sayings in the early days of his journey to Jerusalem (11:13; 12:10–12). Then the Spirit disappears altogether from the Gospel of Luke only to reemerge toward the beginning of the book of Acts, when "suddenly from heaven there came a sound like the rush of a violent wind, and it filled the entire house where they were sitting. Divided tongues, as of fire, appeared among them, and a tongue rested on each of them. All of them were filled with the Holy Spirit and began to speak in other languages, as the Spirit gave them ability" (Acts 2:2–4).

Even Jesus's last words are veiled in promise rather than presence, although there is ample opportunity for the Spirit to emerge in the wake of resurrection along the road to Emmaus, where an anonymous Jesus, as yet unrecognized, "beginning with Moses and all the prophets," explains to two disconsolate disciples "the things about himself in all the scriptures" (Luke 24:27). After he has left them, they reflect, "Were not our hearts burning within us while he was talking to us on the road, while he was opening the scriptures to us?" (Luke 24:32). This scenario is so like the inspiration of Simeon—the old man in the temple whose inspired recognition of Jesus gathered shards of Isaiah into a single, solitary vision of salvation—that it is surprising that the Holy Spirit does *not* show up on the road to Emmaus. But the Spirit does not descend, does not fill, does not inspire, at least not overtly, on this propitious road.

Nor does the Spirit fall on the rest of the disciples. Instead, Jesus, raised from the dead, "opened their minds to understand the scriptures, and he said to them, 'Thus it is written, that the Messiah is to suffer and to rise from the dead on the third day, and that repentance and forgiveness of sins is to be proclaimed in his name to all nations, beginning from Jerusalem'" (Luke 24:45–47). In essence, John the Baptist's blunt message about contentment and integrity is here made universal; the Baptist had gone "into all the region around the Jordan, proclaiming a baptism of repentance for the forgiveness of sins" (Luke 3:3). That message was to be proclaimed worldwide, not least because, as Peter and the apostles would claim, when told not to speak, "We must obey God rather than any human authority. The God of our ancestors raised up Jesus, whom you had killed by hanging him on a tree. *God exalted him at his right hand as Leader and Savior that he might give repentance to Israel and forgiveness of sins.* And we are witnesses to these things, and so is the Holy Spirit whom God has given to those who obey him" (Acts 5:29–32, italics added). The testimony for this coalescence of repentance and forgiveness comes from Jesus's followers *and the Holy Spirit.*

Yet all of this lies in the future. For now, at the end of Luke's Gospel, the Holy Spirit, promised through the word *power*, is not yet a reality. This delay is surprising. The opportunity for the Holy Spirit to appear, to inspire praise or prophecy, as at the start of it all, is perfect. And the promise of proclamation, of a global mission—could there be a better place than the road to Emmaus for the Holy Spirit to descend on the disciples of Jesus? But the Spirit, again, does not descend upon or fill or guide or inspire, at least not overtly, Jesus's followers, who are told simply to wait in Jerusalem.

The last recorded words of Jesus in the Gospel of Luke, therefore, continue along the vein of promise rather than presence: "I am sending upon you what my Father promised," he forecasts, "so stay here in the city until you have been clothed with power from on high" (Luke 24:49). There is work left to be done, waiting left to endure.

In retrospect, through the lens of their experience at Pentecost, it is clear that Jesus is promising the Holy Spirit. But at this point in the story, it is not. The promise is vague, the prediction covert, with the chief clue lying in the single verb *clothe*. They are to wait until they have been "clothed with power from on high."

Clothing evokes two figures from the Old Testament. Gideon went on to defeat the Midianites after being clothed with the Spirit (Judg. 6:34). Amasai, a leader of warriors, when clothed with the Spirit, delivered such a persuasive speech to King David that "David received them [Amasai and his warriors], and made them officers of his troops" (1 Chron. 12:16–18). Centuries later, Jesus tells his own disciples to wait to be clothed with power. Does he mean military power suited to a kingdom or rhetorical power suited to a mission? The book of Acts is testimony to the right answer, as followers of Jesus, one after another, testify on his behalf. But at this point, from the perspective of the Old Testament, the answer remains elusive, as if Jesus is being purposefully obscure.

If avoidance of the word *pneuma* and the ambiguity of the verb *clothe* suggest that there is indeed an element of purpose in the indistinctness of this promise, the word *power* may allow us to pierce the fog, if only tentatively. It is barely a step from power to Spirit in the Gospel of Luke and the book of Acts. To refer to one is to imply the presence of the other. Early on in Luke, Gabriel promises Mary that "the Holy Spirit will come upon you, and the power of the Most High will overshadow you" (Luke 1:35). Spirit and power are joined at the hip.

Typically, Spirit and power inspire speech. John the Baptist comes in "(the) spirit and power of Elijah" (Luke 1:17), not with the miracles of Elisha but with compelling speech. After his test in the wilderness, Jesus returns to Galilee, "filled with the power of the Spirit." With this power, "he began to teach in their synagogues and was praised by everyone" (Luke 4:14–15). Miracles are nowhere yet in sight; inspired teaching is. The association of Spirit with the power of effective speech extends into the book of Acts, including the foundational promise, "But you will receive *power* when the *Holy Spirit* has come upon you; and you will be my *witnesses* in Jerusalem, in all Judea and Samaria, and to the ends of the earth" (Acts 1:8, italics added).

The scenario is not so simple that we can draw a direct line from power to Spirit to inspired speech. Later in the book of Acts, in a summary of Jesus's words and work that we mentioned earlier, Peter—for the first time in Luke's writings—draws a clear line between the Holy Spirit, power, and miracles: "God anointed Jesus of Nazareth with (the) Holy Spirit and with power; how he went about doing good and healing all who were oppressed by the devil, for God was with him" (Acts 10:38 alt.). This association between a Holy Spirit, power, and Jesus's miracles appears to be an article of faith in the early church; this summary has all the marks of a traditional confession. In fact, though Luke does not associate the Spirit with miracles until here in the tenth chapter of Acts, he associates Jesus's *power* with exorcisms (Luke 4:36) and healing (Luke 6:19). Jesus even gives the Twelve "power and authority over all demons and to cure diseases" (Luke 9:1).

Jesus's promise of power from on high, then, is more evocative than precise, more suggestive than specific. It seems to promise inspired speech, but inspired speech in connection with inspired power to heal and to exorcise demons.

▬ ▬ ▬

If the promise that his followers will be clothed with power from on high proves elusive, the preconditions of that promise do not. On this point, at least, Jesus is clear: they must wait in Jerusalem if there is any hope of receiving this power. The disciples do just that: return to Jerusalem and wait. As the curtain rises in the book of Acts, Jesus reappears to his disciples and reiterates this promise, ordering "them not to leave Jerusalem, but to wait there for the promise of the Father" (Acts 1:4). Still more waiting, still more work lies in front of them. But this time Jesus is finally willing to clarify, at least minimally, the vague hint of "what my Father promised" (Luke 24:49). "This," he says, "is what you have heard from me; for John baptized with water, but you will be baptized with the Holy Spirit not many days from now" (Acts 1:4–5). John the Baptist's prediction will finally be fulfilled, though now without judgment—without even a whisper of fire.

Then, when they ask him, "Lord, is this the time when you will restore the kingdom to Israel?" (Acts 1:6), perhaps hoping that the power promised to them will be expressed through a kingdom, Jesus redirects their concern to the Spirit. "It is not for you to know the times or periods that the Father has set by his own authority," he challenges them. "But you will receive power when the Holy Spirit has come upon you; and you will be my witnesses in Jerusalem, in all Judea and Samaria, and to the ends of the earth" (Acts 1:7–8).

As soon as he makes this promise, Jesus is taken up, and the disciples do exactly what Jesus told them to do—they return to Jerusalem and wait: "Then they returned to Jerusalem from the mount called Olivet, which is near Jerusalem, a sabbath day's journey away.

When they had entered the city, they went to the room upstairs where they were staying" (Acts 1:12–13). So serious are they about taking Jesus at his word, they do not even stay at the Mount of Olives but walk the mile and a half or so across the Kidron Valley to the old city of Jerusalem. It would be easier for them to bend the rules and sleep in the shadow of Jesus's ascension. They do not. They go back to Jerusalem and wait.

They wait, but not idly. Jesus's disciples are "constantly devoting themselves to prayer, together with certain women, including Mary the mother of Jesus, as well as his brothers" (Acts 1:14). Jesus's earliest followers stay put. They pray. They do not fill Jerusalem with frenetic activities, even good ones.

If the promise at the end of the Gospel of Luke is vague, the prerequisites are not. The disciples *wait*. They *pray* together. And they *study* the Scriptures together so that, when the Holy Spirit fills them, they fill the air with a litany of the praiseworthy acts of God.[8] Jesus did not command his followers to pray; he told them only to wait. But they have seen enough of Jesus—especially as he is portrayed in Luke's Gospel—to know that waiting means praying and praying means waiting. And Jesus did not order them to study, yet they have heard enough of Jesus's inspired teaching to know, from his first sermon in the synagogue at Nazareth, that Jesus was a student of Scripture. For an understanding of the Spirit, therefore, it is crucial not to rush past the promise at the tail end of Luke's Gospel to its fulfillment in the book of Acts, because to do so is to miss the essential insight that the process of waiting, the discipline of praying, composes the singular prelude to an experience of the Holy Spirit that effects powerful and effective witness to earth's ends.

Mouth to Mouth

The gift of the Spirit in the Fourth Gospel could just as well conclude each of the other Gospels. The usual elements are there. The disciples

8. We explored the significance of study in chap. 1, "Spirit and the Swell of Expectation," in the section "The Spirit and Simeon."

are huddled together. Jesus makes an appearance and greets them, acknowledging their fretfulness. The disciples recognize him. Jesus commissions them.

Each commissioning, of course, has its own unique features. In the longer ending of the Gospel of Mark, Jesus tells his disciples that five miraculous signs will accompany their worldwide proclamation of the gospel (Mark 16:14–18). In the Gospel of Matthew, Jesus sends the Eleven to make disciples of all nations, to baptize, and to teach everything that he has commanded them (Matt. 28:16–20). In the Gospel of Luke, Jesus urges the disciples to remain in Jerusalem to wait for "power from on high" before bearing witness "to all nations" (Luke 24:45–49). In the Fourth Gospel, Jesus commissions them in language typical of this particular Gospel: "As the Father has sent me, so I send you" (John 20:21).

The dominant trait of this scene in the Fourth Gospel could have been lifted from the pages of Matthew's Gospel. Jesus authorizes his disciples to forgive sins: "If you forgive the sins of any, they are forgiven them; if you retain the sins of any, they are retained" (John 20:23). This commission has a family resemblance to Jesus's words to Peter in Matthew's Gospel, which are spoken just after Peter has identified him as the Messiah: "I will give you the keys of the kingdom of heaven, and whatever you bind on earth will be bound in heaven, and whatever you loose on earth will be loosed in heaven" (Matt. 16:19). It mirrors as well Jesus's words to the church that appear exclusively in Matthew's Gospel: "Truly I tell you, whatever you bind on earth will be bound in heaven, and whatever you loose on earth will be loosed in heaven" (Matt. 18:18).

The introduction of the Holy Spirit into this traditional scene occurs in the typical language of the early church: "Receive [*labete*] the Holy Spirit" (John 20:22). The verb "receive" (*lambanein*) occurs several times in Acts (2:33, 38; 8:15, 17, 19; 10:47; 19:2) and Paul's Letters (Rom. 8:15; 1 Cor. 2:12; 2 Cor. 11:4; Gal. 3:2, 14) to describe the experience of the Spirit. The entire scene, therefore, is familiar, comfortable even—if a resurrection appearance can ever be comfortable.

A fresh element inveigles its way into this familiar scene. The traditional words, "Receive the Holy Spirit," are preceded by a distinctive act: "He breathed into them" (alt.). Jesus could spit on the eyes of the blind, lay his hands on the sick, have his feet caressed with hair and washed with tears, and even wash his disciples' feet, but nowhere else does this level of physical intimacy characterize Jesus's relationship with those for whom he cares so deeply.

The startling depth of that intimacy is reinforced by two sides of the same coin: breathing into and receiving. Jesus's breathing into and the disciples' receiving the Spirit are the same occurrence, occupying the same brief moment in time. Jesus's breathing into, in other words, is tied to their breathing in. In short, Jesus breathes *into* the disciples, not *on* them. Translations that adopt the preposition *on*—Jesus breathed *on* them—mask the intimacy, perhaps even the affection, that saturates this secluded scene.

This is a stunningly private scene to which the reader of the Gospel is privy. It occurs behind locked doors. It begins with a household greeting among friends. *And it involves what looks very much like an occasion of intimate contact*, by which the Spirit, the breath, the vitality of one is passed to another. This is the only means by which the disciples' *receiving* them the Spirit can coincide so closely with Jesus's *breathing into* them the Spirit.

Jesus's breathing of the Holy Spirit into his disciples is rich with Old Testament imagery. The verb "breathed into" (*enephysēsen*) is the verb that is used in the Greek version of Genesis 2:7: "And God formed man, dust from the earth, and breathed into [*enephysēsen*] his face a breath of life, and the man became a living being" (Gen. 2:7 NETS).[9] As God breathed into the face of the first man, Jesus breathes now into the faces of his disciples. Breathing into is not just a reconnection. It is a *re-creation*.

This is the verb also used in an Old Testament story detailing how Elijah revived the son of a destitute widow with whom he lived (1 Kings 17). The son grew gravely ill, "until there was no breath [*pneuma*] left in him" (3 Kings 17:17 NETS).[10] Elijah took him to his own room and set the boy on Elijah's own bed—intimate details of another closed room—and lay on the boy three times. In the Greek

---

9. For each of these three texts, I will refer to the Greek Old Testament as the suitable foreground to the use of a Greek verb in the Fourth Gospel.

10. In English, this verse appears in 1 Kings 17:17.

translation, Elijah breathed into the boy three times (17:21). Immediately, the boy sprang to life. In the Fourth Gospel, breathing into is not just a reconnection. It is a *revitalization*.

Ezekiel also envisaged the sort of breathing into that could bring the dead to life, although in his vision, the intimacy of Eden and Elijah's room is set aside to accommodate the formidable resurrection of a nation whose bleached bones lay lifeless in the desert of exile: "And he said to me, Prophesy to the breath [*pneuma*]; prophesy, son of man, and say to the breath [*pneumati*], This is what the Lord says: Come from the four winds [*pneumatōn*], and blow into these corpses, and they shall live. And I prophesied just as he commanded me. And the breath [*pneuma*] came into them, and they lived and stood upon their feet, a very great gathering" (Ezek. 37:9–10 NETS). For Ezekiel, the infusion of breath demanded a whirlwind movement of God's chariot-winds hustling from the four corners of the earth to resurrect a valley of very many, very dry bones. Against this background, what Jesus offers his friends is not just a reconnection. It is a *resurrection*.

The selection of this evocative verb, *breathe into*, which occurs in the New Testament just this once, suggests a creation, even a re-creation, of the disciples. Though formerly without breath, like a freshly formed *adam* in the dirt, like the widow's dead son on Elijah's bed, and like a nation reduced to a heap of bleached bones, the disciples into whom Jesus breathes his Holy Spirit become a new community charged with a new task: to forgive sins—extending the work of the Lamb of God, who takes away the sins of the world, to the whole world (John 1:29).

This is not only a theological act, though it is that. It is an *intimate* action. It would violate this story to move too quickly to an interpretation of this scene as the Fourth Gospel's version of Pentecost, for example, without first coming to grips with the essential element of closeness, the smack of intimacy, the sheer physicality of the Holy Spirit, and the pulsing breath of the resurrected Jesus that energizes his followers.

Conclusion

From the months before Jesus's birth, when his startled mother heard that she was pregnant, to his farewell words, we have garnered a sustained perspective on the Holy Spirit in the Gospels. So far, we have proceeded story by story, saying by saying. Now it is time to gather up the pieces into a coherent whole, or as coherent a whole as the Gospels allow, so that we may see how this book enhances—and challenges—our understanding of the Holy Spirit.

The Spirit, the Old Testament, and the New

We begin with a challenge to the errant belief that the New Testament is the testament of the Holy Spirit and the Old Testament is not.[1] We have seen time and again how the Gospel authors set Jesus within the current of the Old Testament rather than alongside or after it. The Gospels, understood in this light, belong to the stream of the Old Testament, even—or especially—with respect to the Holy Spirit.

From the start, the Gospel authors tether their understanding of the Holy Spirit to the Jewish Scriptures. The Gospel of Mark, probably the earliest of the Gospels, begins with a concoction of Malachi 3:1 and Isaiah 40:1 (Mark 1:11–12). The Gospel of Matthew takes

---

1. You will discover a trove of references to the Spirit in the Jewish Scriptures in my *A Boundless God: The Spirit according to the Old Testament* (Grand Rapids: Baker Academic, 2020).

in nearly the entire scope of Israelite history in its initial words: "An account of the genealogy of Jesus the Messiah, the son of David, the son of Abraham" (Matt. 1:1). The Gospel of Luke traces Jesus's genealogy all the way back to "Adam, son of God" (Luke 3:38). In our age, which values novelty and invention, in which the breakneck pace of life continues to accelerate, it may not be possible to grasp how intently the followers of Jesus pored over the *past* to ground their journey into the *future*.

When the drama begins in earnest, Matthew's birth story is hardly oblique: "Now the *genesis* of Jesus the Messiah took place in this way. When his mother Mary had been engaged to Joseph, but before they lived together, she was found to be with child *from holy spirit*" (Matt. 1:18 alt.). Possible allusions burst onto the scene with this introduction, from the spirit-wind that hovered over the abyss at the *genesis* of creation (Gen. 1:1–2) to the contrite, clean, and holy spirit for which Israel's psalmist once prayed (Ps. 51)—and which Mary now possesses.

The Jewish Scriptures saturate Luke's birth stories as well. The angel predicts that John the Baptist, filled with the Spirit, will labor in "the spirit and power of Elijah," who was one of Israel's earliest and most renowned prophets (Luke 1:15–17). The angel promises Mary, too, that "the Holy Spirit will come upon you, and the power of the Most High will overshadow you" (Luke 1:35)—the way God's pinions overshadow the vulnerable (Ps. 91:4), the way the cloud overshadowed the tent of God's presence in the wilderness, drenching it with so much divine glory that Moses could not even enter it (Exod. 40:35). Saturation with the Jewish Scriptures comes to a head in the story of Simeon, who is filled with the Spirit, is guided by the Spirit, and has received a revelation from the Spirit. Simeon encounters the baby Jesus and gushes with words that comprise a pastiche of phrases from the final chapters of the book of Isaiah, which imagined that Israel would finally be redeemed and released from Babylonian captivity (Luke 2:25–32). Simeon understands that the child in his arms is the harbinger of salvation, and he understands this salvation entirely in terms of the vision of Isaiah.

The Jewish Scriptures cascade through the remaining references to the Spirit in the Gospels. At his baptism, after Jesus hears words that capture the essence of Psalm 2:7 ("You are my Son") and Isaiah 42:1 ("In you I am well pleased"), the Holy Spirit descends like a dove—evoking Israelite images of the Spirit hovering at creation (Gen. 1:1–2)[2] or the dove sent out by Noah at flood's end (Gen. 8:8–12).

At his testing in Mark's Gospel, Jesus succeeds where Adam failed by living in harmony with the animals (Mark 1:12–13). In Matthew's Gospel, the Spirit leads Jesus *up* from the Jordan River, just as the pillars of cloud and fire led Israel *up* from Egypt (Matt. 4:1). In Luke's Gospel, the Spirit leads Jesus *in* the wilderness, as the pillars and angel once led Israel in the wilderness (Luke 4:1). The exodus of Israel and its sojourn in the wilderness are the indispensable foreground of the story of Jesus's test in the Gospels of Matthew and Luke. Yet there is a fundamental discrepancy between Israel's Torah and the Gospels. In the Jewish Scriptures, the *pillars*, an *angel*, and God's presence-face (*pānîm*) lead Israel, but in the Gospels, the *Spirit* leads Jesus. This apparent inconsistency evaporates in light of a lament buried deep in the final chapters of Isaiah (63:7–14), in which the Spirit takes over the prerogatives of the pillars, the angel, and the *pānîm*. This lament provides the perfect backdrop for the role of the Holy Spirit in the testing of Jesus in the wilderness.[3]

This prophetic lament provides the backdrop also for what may be the most disconcerting saying about the Spirit in the New Testament: blasphemy against the Holy Spirit will not be forgiven. The harshness of this saying does not dissolve, but it does become comprehensible, in the light of Isaiah 63:7–14. In the book of Exodus, God commands Israel not to rebel against God's guiding angel; in the later lament, Israel does precisely that, except that the author of the lament substitutes the Holy Spirit for the angel of the exodus: they rebel against not the angel of the exodus but God's Holy Spirit. In short, in the lament, Israel treats the Holy Spirit exactly as Israel was ordered *not* to treat the guiding angel. Consequently, the tragic poet notes, God turned and fought against them. Now, warns Jesus, echoing Isaiah 63, no one can escape if they too blaspheme the Holy Spirit.

2. In Deut. 32:11, a bird of prey *hovers* over its young; the verb is the same as in Gen. 1:1–2.

3. You will find a full study of Isa. 63:7–14 in my *The Holy Spirit before Christianity* (Waco: Baylor University Press, 2019).

Jesus's warning against blasphemy signals the indispensability of the Old Testament for understanding the Gospels. The Old Testament is not window dressing or beneficial but incidental background to Gospel sayings. Without the Jewish Scriptures, we would be left in the dark when it comes to such thorny sayings as Jesus's warning against blasphemy. With those Scriptures, we can see that Jesus himself situates the Holy Spirit in the context of Israel's story of the exodus from Egypt. In order to grasp Jesus's warning about blasphemy against the Holy Spirit, in other words, it is crucial to situate Jesus's saying about the Spirit in Israel's story. To allow his saying to float freely, jettisoned from the Scriptures that provide the bedrock upon which New Testament perceptions of the Holy Spirit are constructed, is to risk missing the thrust of Jesus's saying altogether.

Further dimensions of the Jewish Scriptures illuminate still other sayings about the Holy Spirit in the Synoptic Gospels. In his opening salvo in Luke's Gospel, launched from the synagogue in Nazareth, Jesus identifies himself with the anointed figure depicted in Isaiah 61:1–4, who will bring good news to the poor, release to the captives, recovery of sight to the blind, and liberation to the oppressed. Matthew, for his part, regards Jesus's healing as the fulfillment of Isaiah 42:1–4, which describes God's beloved as a light to the nations. The promise in Luke's Gospel that God will give the Holy Spirit rather than snakes and scorpions to those who pray (Luke 11:9–13) recalls Israel's sojourn in the wilderness, when God led the Israelites safely through a desert full of snakes and scorpions (Deut. 8:14–15).

━━   ━━   ━━

The role of the Old Testament in the Fourth Gospel's portrayal of the Holy Spirit is just as essential as in the Synoptic Gospels. When, on their last night together, Jesus familiarizes his friends with the paraclete, it is with an eye to the future, to his absence; it is better that he leave, he tells his unconvinced cohort, because the Spirit will guide them into the truth. But how? Here the process of truth grasping becomes tricky. They will find the truth not so much by looking ahead as by glancing back, not so much by seeking new truth as by discovering afresh the old truth, truth rooted in the life, death, and resurrection of Jesus. The Spirit will *remind* them of all that Jesus has said.

This backward expedition toward truth does not return only to the life of Jesus. It travels further back into the recesses of the Jewish Scriptures. In the Fourth Gospel, discovery of the truth about Jesus takes place in tandem with discovery of the truth of the Jewish Scriptures. During Jesus's lifetime, they could not understand what he meant when he said, "Destroy this temple, and in three days I will raise it up." Yet after he was raised from the dead, they "remembered that he had said this; and they believed the scripture and the word that Jesus had spoken" (John 2:19, 22). During Jesus's lifetime, they failed to understand his entry into Jerusalem on a donkey, "but when Jesus was glorified, then they remembered that these things had been written of him and had been done to him" (12:16). Twice the Jewish Scriptures become the lens by which the disciples grasp the meaning of Jesus's life after his resurrection. In the Fourth Gospel, this is the work of the paraclete—teacher, guide, reminder, steward of truth.

There is no single Old Testament foreground for the Spirit in the Fourth Gospel, no linchpin that unlocks its meaning. A kaleidoscope of texts lie under the surface of this ambiguous and mysterious Gospel. The psalmist, for example, prayed,

> Teach me to do your will,
> for you are my God.
> Let your good spirit lead me
> on a level path. (Ps. 143:10)

It is not difficult to detect that good Spirit skulking in the underbrush of New Testament portrayals of the Spirit, particularly in the Fourth Gospel, where the paraclete leads the disciples backward in their quest for truth. Revelations and visions, prediction and prognostication pale in comparison with the singular ability to understand Jesus in light of the Jewish Scriptures. The road ahead, the way of truth along which the paraclete travels, leads inevitably homeward, back to where the disciples of Jesus belong. It could hardly be otherwise in a Gospel beginning with first words that are at the same time the first words of the Jewish Scriptures: "in the beginning."

■ ■ ■

When we cast a protracted glance over the whole of the four Gospels, we can discern that the Jewish Scriptures are essential for interpreting the Holy Spirit in the New Testament. We can also fathom that no single strand in the Jewish Scriptures emerges as the solitary axis along which all conceptions of the Holy Spirit can be laid. Creation, exodus, wilderness wandering, the story of Elijah, and Psalm 51—each of these plays a role in shaping how the Spirit is portrayed in the Gospels. Yet among these there is one corpus in the Jewish Scriptures that appears to have been definitive for the portrayal of the Holy Spirit according to Jesus.

The later chapters of Isaiah contain raw elements that fuse in the Gospels. The many snippets of Isaiah 42 and 49 in Simeon's song, the allusion to Isaiah 42:1 at Jesus's baptism, the recitation of Isaiah 42:1–4 to underscore Jesus's ability to heal in Matthew's Gospel, the citation of Isaiah 61:1–4 in the synagogue at Nazareth—all of these signal how significant the later chapters of Isaiah were in helping the Gospel authors to convey the importance of the Holy Spirit in Jesus's life.[4] These texts together supply a credible foreground for Jesus's experience of the Spirit, according to the Gospels, since the inspired figure in these chapters of Isaiah is winsome—he is himself inspired—but also vulnerable to suffering and, eventually, a gruesome death. This foreground, then, is perfectly apt. Perhaps a more surprising—and no less essential—text to emerge from the later chapters of Isaiah is the lament in Isaiah 63:7–14, in which the Spirit takes over the role of agents of the exodus. It is no longer a pillar or angel or presence-face that leads Israel, as in the Torah, but God's own Holy Spirit. This lament offers an essential link between exodus in Torah and exodus in the Gospels by introducing the Spirit into the exodus tradition. Inconspicuous within the final chapters of Isaiah, this lament provides a singular foreground to the Holy Spirit's role in Jesus's exodus—his test in the wilderness—and his dire warning about blasphemy.[5]

4. Jesus's peaceful coexistence with the animals in Mark's account of Jesus's testing is reminiscent as well of Isa. 11:6–9.

5. The Gospel writers were not the first followers of Jesus to associate the Spirit with a new exodus. You will find detailed analyses of the association of Spirit with

The Spirit, the Gospels, and the Story of Jesus

Rather than preserving their understanding of the Holy Spirit in a creed or confession, instead of issuing a clear doctrinal statement, early followers of Jesus encoded their grasp of the Spirit in a distinctive narrative context—actually, in *four* narratives. They did not, at first, develop a doctrine ("The Holy Spirit is . . .") or distill that doctrine in a creed ("I believe in the Holy Spirit . . ."). They opted to situate the Spirit in the story of Jesus.

From this perspective, it is possible to appreciate how one Gospel ends (see chap. 10 above) with this promise and command: "All authority in heaven and on earth has been given to me. Go therefore and make disciples of all nations, baptizing them in the name of the Father and of the Son and of the Holy Spirit, and teaching them to obey everything that I have commanded you. And remember, I am with you always, to the end of the age" (Matt. 28:18–20). In these, the final lines of Matthew's Gospel, the relationship between Father, Son, and Spirit is not captured for posterity with the impeccable lucidity of trinitarian doctrine; the three join together to give ballast to the *practical* goal of a global mission grounded in the rich and robust teaching of Jesus.

Better yet, the relationship between Father, Son, and Spirit rises early in the Gospels (see chap. 3 above)—in Jesus's baptism, when the Spirit descends like a dove on him and he hears God's words: "You are my Son, the Beloved; with you I am well pleased" (Mark 1:10–11). There it is again in vivid story form: Father, Son, and Spirit

---

exodus in the letters of the apostle Paul in James M. Scott, *Adoption as Sons of God: An Exegetical Investigation in the Background of* ΥΙΟΘΕΣΙΑ *in the Pauline Corpus* (Tübingen: Mohr Siebeck, 1992); Rodrigo J. Morales, *The Spirit and the Restoration of Israel: New Exodus and New Creation Motifs in Galatians* (Tübingen: Mohr Siebeck, 2010); and Sylvia Keesmaat, *Paul and His Story: (Re)Interpreting the Exodus Tradition* (Sheffield: Sheffield Academic, 1999). The collection of reminiscences of the exodus in Gal. 4:1–7 prompts N. T. Wright to argue that Paul "is doing his best . . . to place the present predicament and puzzlement of the Galatian Christians on to the well-known map of the exodus narrative, in order to draw the moral: don't go back to slavery, but go on to your inheritance, led by that indwelling divine presence." See *Christian Origins and the Question of God*, vol. 4, *Paul and the Faithfulness of God* (Minneapolis: Fortress, 2013), 657. I offer a succinct discussion of the association of exodus and Spirit in New Testament literature, with a foreground in Isa. 63:7–14, in my *Holy Spirit before Christianity*, 112–22.

gathered together on the inauspicious shore of the Jordan River. This is not a tidy creed or a mature doctrine; this initial gathering of the lead characters in Jesus's story conveys in vibrant hues the fluid, even fledgling, relationship between Father, Son, and Spirit.

This realization about the inclusion of the Holy Spirit in the story—actually four stories—of Jesus has significant consequences. It is essential to gauge the depiction of the Holy Spirit in the contours of each Gospel, since the Holy Spirit is entrenched in four separate narratives of Jesus. Therefore, while we have looked at the Holy Spirit episode by episode, we should spend at least some time, at book's end, glancing back at distinctive features of the Holy Spirit in each of the four canonical Gospels.

Mark's Gospel, while providing the raw material for the Gospels of Matthew and Luke, has its own tenor. Beginning with John the Baptist's promise that Jesus would baptize in the Holy Spirit—a promise left unfulfilled in the Gospel of Mark—the Holy Spirit descends like a dove into Jesus. In a sense, Jesus is the object of John's promise: he is the only one who arguably could be said to be baptized in the Spirit. The tenor of this Spirit becomes clear when the Spirit expels Jesus into the desert—like a demon, like an errant eye plucked out, like money changers driven out of the temple precincts. The next reference to the Spirit in Mark's Gospel offers no more comfort to the Gospel's readers: blasphemy against the Holy Spirit is an eternal sin. Then, following a reference to David's inspired composition of Psalm 110:1, Jesus turns to the inevitability of martyrdom. He consoles the persecuted with the promise that the Holy Spirit will give them words of testimony but not words of release. This is good news for those followers of Jesus who regard testimony as a higher priority than survival.

Mark's Gospel, then, contains precious few references to the Spirit—and none that provides superficial comfort to those who hope to survive this life intact. Jesus himself is driven into the desert to be tested by Satan. Jesus warns against the eternal sin of blasphemy. Jesus promises a word of testimony rather than survival to martyrs.

Like the syntax of the Gospel, like the immediacy of its stories, the portrait of the Holy Spirit in the Gospel of Mark is raw—even menacing.[6]

∎ ∎ ∎

At first blush, references to the Holy Spirit found exclusively in Luke's Gospel—ones that do not occur in the other Gospels—suggest that Luke pays copious attention to the Holy Spirit. The overshadowing of Mary by the Holy Spirit and power of the Most High occurs only in Luke's Gospel (Luke 1:35), as does the claim that John the Baptist will be filled with the Spirit (1:15) and the spirit and power of Elijah (1:17). The praise and blessing that accompany the births of John the Baptist and Jesus (1:41, 47, 67), as well as Simeon's song at Jesus's dedication in the temple (2:25–35), are unique to the Gospel of Luke. Luke's Gospel alone also contains the return of Jesus to Galilee in the power of the Spirit after his baptism and testing (4:14); in this Gospel, too, Jesus claims in the synagogue at Nazareth to be the inspired figure of Isaiah 61:1–4 (Luke 4:18). Late in the Gospel, Jesus rejoices in the Spirit after the return of the seventy from a successful mission (10:21), and he shortly later promises the Holy Spirit rather than snakes and scorpions to those who pray (11:13).

All of these experiences and sayings contribute to the sense in Luke's Gospel that the Holy Spirit inspires praise and prayer, as well as prophetic speech and teaching, as in Mary's canticle, Simeon's song, and Jesus's teaching throughout Galilee. There is an ebullience in the Gospel of Luke when the Spirit fills or rests or reveals, typically resulting in inspired speech. Even Jesus, caught up in the Spirit, rejoices and prays (Luke 10:21–22).

This buzz of energy, especially in the first four chapters of Luke's Gospel, gives the impression that Luke's is the Gospel of the Holy Spirit. This is not quite true. Yes, there is a flurry of activity surrounding the births of John and Jesus and the baptism, testing, and earliest teaching of Jesus, but after Jesus's sermon at the synagogue in Nazareth, the Holy Spirit surfaces only three times in references

6. While chap. 10 of this book contains an analysis of the longer ending of Mark's Gospel, I do not include it here, because of its later date.

that are unique to the Gospel of Luke: in Jesus's rejoicing (Luke 10:21), in his promise of the Holy Spirit to those who pray (11:13; see Matt. 7:11), and in his veiled reference to the Spirit in a promise of power from on high (Luke 24:49) as the Gospel comes to a close.

Some sayings about the Holy Spirit found in other Gospels actually go missing from the Gospel of Luke. Luke detaches the quintessential expression of Jesus's power in the Gospels, the exorcism, from the Holy Spirit. When Jesus ties exorcism to the reign of God, he refers to the Spirit only in Matthew's Gospel (Matt. 12:28); in Luke's Gospel, Jesus claims to perform exorcisms, in a rich reminiscence of the exodus, by the finger of God (Luke 11:20). Neither can the saying about David's inspiration be found in Luke's Gospel (Mark 12:36; Matt. 22:43). Finally, Luke connects Jesus's warning about blasphemy with a promise of testimony for martyrs; what comprise two separate sayings in the Gospels of Mark and Matthew join to become a single saying about faithful witness to Jesus.

The initial burst of energy is hardly sustained, then, in the Gospel of Luke. In what may seem a measure of irony, the surge of inspiration that characterizes life *before* Jesus was born and at the *start* of Jesus's public life dissipates as his story continues. From 12:12 until 24:49, in fact, not a single reference to the Spirit surfaces in the Gospel of Luke. To put this scenario even more bluntly, Jesus says nothing and experiences nothing of the Holy Spirit, at least not explicitly, from his warning about testimony under pressure until *after* his death.

■ ▨ ▨

The commotion stirred by the Spirit's activity in Mary's pregnancy also occurs in Matthew's Gospel (Matt. 1:18–20). This Gospel contains two further references that occur nowhere else in the Gospels. Matthew alone sees Jesus's healing power as a fulfillment of Isaiah 42:1–4 (Matt. 12:18); like the servant, Jesus carries human diseases away. The authority of Jesus's exorcisms also arises from Jesus's experience of the Spirit (12:28). Matthew is keen to underscore the *authority* of Jesus—through healing and exorcism. Along this vein, the Gospel naturally concludes with the risen Jesus on a mountain, like Moses, telling his disciples that all authority on heaven and earth has been given to him. Therefore, they should preach the gospel—every jot and tittle of it—to all nations, baptizing them in the name of the Father, Son, and Holy Spirit (28:16–20). This final expression of authority caps off perfectly the emphasis in this Gospel on the authority of Jesus, who heals and performs exorcisms by the inspiration of the Holy Spirit.

———

The Fourth Gospel contains little in common with the other three Gospels. The appeal to birth from above (John 3:6, 8), the saying about giving the Spirit without measure (3:34), the association of the Spirit with truth (4:23–24), the contrast of the Spirit and the flesh (6:63), the conjoined statements that the Spirit will gush from within (7:37–38) and that the Spirit was not yet given (7:39)—all of these are unique to the Fourth Gospel. These sayings also share the character of the Fourth Gospel. Like so much in this Gospel, they represent dualities: birth from above versus birth from below, truth versus falsehood, and Spirit versus flesh. These are two worlds. These are sharp contrasts. There is no room in the Fourth Gospel for compromise, no cause for concession.

And like so much in this Gospel, the experience is lavish: the wrenching drama of new birth, the springing up of the Spirit, the giving of the Spirit without measure, and the gushing of the Spirit from a cavity deep within. There can be no question in the Fourth Gospel of whether someone has experienced the Spirit, since it gushes and pours and springs up. If this is a document of the second or third generation of Jesus's followers, it has not lost the sense that sensation is part and parcel of the Holy Spirit—not sensation for the sake of spectacle (this is the Spirit of *truth*, after all) but a palpable presence undeniable in its reality, inevitable in its impact.

Then there are the sayings about the paraclete spoken on Jesus's last night with his closest followers (John 14:16–17, 26; 16:7–11, 13–15). These promises, too, suit the Fourth Gospel. What Jesus pledges that the paraclete will do looks a good deal like what God and Jesus do in the Gospel: abiding, instructing, judging, guiding into truth, and glorifying. These sayings also share the character of this Gospel more generally, with their emphasis on truth and their contrast between believers and the world.

It is not difficult to glimpse a disjuncture between the first part of the Gospel and the last. In chapters 1–12, the Spirit gushes and flows and springs. In chapters 13–16, the Spirit convicts and teaches and guides. Has the cerebral replaced the visceral? Has the intellectual superseded the experiential? It would seem that way if we fail to realize that Jesus early on stresses the necessary connection between Spirit and truth in his daytime tête-à-tête with the Samaritan woman. When he refers on his last night to the Spirit of truth, it is hardly a surprise that his disciples have paid attention.

What happens to the gush and flow and springing and giving of the Spirit without measure in the story of Jesus's final hours? Has it disappeared? It would seem so. Jesus is concerned with teaching, reminding, and convicting. He shows no interest whatsoever in what his disciples will feel. He cares about only what his disciples will *know*. And what they will know is his story refracted through the lens of his death and resurrection. The Spirit *is* about truth, and the truth is generated by the Spirit.

Truth, it appears, has won out over experience—so it would seem until Jesus rises from the dead. Entering the upper room and encountering his huddled friends, he does something remarkable—so startling, in fact, that translators shy away from the sheer physicality of the scene. The final appearance of the Spirit cements the intimacy that is inevitable for those who have touched and heard this occasionally cantankerous and invariably exceptional figure. In this private scene, we are privy to a moment of unusual tenderness: Jesus breathes the Holy Spirit *into*—not just upon—his daunted disciples (John 20:22).

■   ■   ■

Each of these Gospels, then, has its own unique qualities and associations. The Gospel of Mark is *unsettling* in its portrait of a Holy Spirit that, freshly descended like a dove, drives Jesus into the desert and gives words of testimony but not survival to Jesus's followers.

The Gospel of Luke contains the lion's share of inspired *speech*—praise, prayer, and prophetic teaching—though most of it is in the earliest chapters. The Gospel of Matthew associates the Holy Spirit with Jesus's *authority*; his healing and exorcisms offer raw testimony to this authority, to which he lays claim in his final commissioning of the disciples. The Fourth Gospel sets the Spirit within the context of its *dualities*: its penchant for truth and its vitality from above. Yet there is something visceral, too, in the Fourth Gospel, a Gospel that incarnates truth and drives readers back to the Word made flesh in the inhabited world below.

The Spirit, Jesus, and an Intractable Quest

When they wrote each of these Gospels, the ancient authors did not uncover Jesus; they *interpreted* Jesus. This reality means that there is a difference between the historical Jesus—the Jesus of history—and Jesus as he is interpreted in each of the Gospels. For example, the Spirit acts differently in each of the Synoptic Gospels when Jesus is tested in the wilderness. In Mark's Gospel, the Spirit drives or expels Jesus *into* the desert. In Matthew's Gospel, the Spirit leads Jesus *up* into the desert. In Luke's Gospel, the Spirit leads Jesus *in* the desert. Each of these offers a unique interpretation of Jesus's experience of the Spirit (see chap. 4 above). The subtle differences between these interpretations render it difficult, if not impossible, to discover Jesus's experience of the Spirit at that moment. We have only the Gospel writers' *interpretations* of that experience.

In the early twentieth century, some scholars attempted to uncover Jesus's experience of the Holy Spirit behind the Gospels. Oskar Holtzman asked if Jesus was an ecstatic—and answered his own question with a measure of ambivalence.[7] Hans Leisegang traced conceptions of the Holy Spirit in the Synoptic Gospels to Greek mysticism.[8] Daniel Frövig explored the relationship between Jesus's consciousness

7. Oskar Holtzman, *War Jesus Ekstatiker?: Eine Untersuchung zum Leben Jesu* (Tübingen: J. C. B. Mohr, 1908).

8. Hans Leisegang, *Pneuma Hagion: Der Ursprung des Geistbegriffs der synoptischen Evangelien aus der griechischen Mystik* (Leipzig: Hinrichs, 1922).

of being sent and the Spirit.[9] Friedrich Büchsel argued that Jesus was singularly a pneumatic—a *Pneumatiker*. Büchsel grounded this characterization in Jesus's prophetic authority, his ascetic bent (Jesus's fast in the desert and his repudiation of family), and his visionary experiences.[10]

Half a century later, James D. G. Dunn revisited the question of Jesus's experience of the Holy Spirit. Any quest for Jesus's experience of the Spirit—rather than the Gospels' interpretation of that experience—must begin with this exemplary study. In *Jesus and the Spirit*, Dunn drills to the bedrock of "the religious experiences of Jesus and of first-generation Christianity."[11] Because Dunn reasons that "the more public teaching of Jesus about God is easier to track down and has frequently been treated in modern studies of Jesus' life and ministry," he puts his effort into the more difficult quest for "Jesus' more private experience of God."[12] When the dust has settled, Dunn has discovered the heart and soul of Jesus's consciousness of the Spirit in his initial experience at the Jordan River, in his ability to address God intimately in prayer as Abba, and in the power of exorcism, which provides evidence that Jesus has fulfilled the prophetic vocation envisaged in Isaiah 61:1–4.

Despite bringing enormous erudition to the task of uncovering Jesus's consciousness of the Spirit, Dunn is compelled to concede that his conclusions are only provisional: "All we can say is that he lived out of a consciousness of sonship and power, of commissioning and authority, which seems to have transcended the ordinary prophetic experience of inspiration. By how much it transcended ordinary human experience we cannot say—qualitatively or quantitatively,

9. Daniel Frövig, *Das Sendungsbewußtsein Jesu und der Geist: Ein Beitrag zur Frage nach dem Berufsbewußtsein Jesu* (Gütersloh: Bertelsmann, 1924). In *Theologische Literaturzeitung* 22 (1926): 544, Rudolf Bultmann pans the book as "eines der typischen apologetischen Bücher, die möglichst viel vom traditionellen Jesusbild aus dem Feuer der Kritik retten wollen" (one of the typical apologetic books, which as much as possible want to rescue the traditional picture of Jesus from the fire of criticism).

10. Friedrich Büchsel, *Der Geist Gottes im Neuen Testament* (Gütersloh: Bertelsmann, 1926).

11. James D. G. Dunn, *Jesus and the Spirit: A Study of the Religious and Charismatic Experience of Jesus and the First Christians as Reflected in the New Testament* (Grand Rapids: Eerdmans, 1977), 6.

12. Dunn, *Jesus and the Spirit*, 11.

metaphysically or existentially, we cannot say. These questions can only be answered in the light of the first Easter—and even then the answers will only be a little less tentative."[13] The best that scholarship has to offer is captured, in the end, in a concession twice repeated, that "we cannot say" how Jesus's experience of the Spirit mirrors the experience of ordinary humans.

In a more popular take on this question, Gerald F. Hawthorne, in *The Presence and the Power*, tackles the same question about Jesus's experience of the Holy Spirit.[14] Hawthorne tries "to answer the question of why it was that the Holy Spirit played such an important role in the experience of Jesus."[15] To answer this question, Hawthorne works his way carefully through the role of the Spirit in the conception and birth of Jesus, the boyhood and youth of Jesus, the baptism and temptation of Jesus, the ministry of Jesus, the death and resurrection of Jesus, the kenosis or self-emptying of Jesus, and the lives of those who follow Jesus.

In what is no doubt unacceptable to many of his evangelical readers, who trace Jesus's power to his divinity, Hawthorne contends that Jesus had given up powers associated with divinity—this is the essence of kenosis—and lived instead like other human beings. "Jesus possessed the power himself," concludes Hawthorne, but "by a preincarnate deliberate decision the eternal Son of God chose that all his intrinsic powers, all his attributes, would remain latent within him during the days of his flesh and that he would become truly human and limit himself to the abilities and powers common to all other human beings. Therefore he depended upon the Holy Spirit for wisdom and knowledge and for power to perform the signs and wonders that marked the days of his years."[16] This deliberate preincarnate decision meant that Jesus "*needed* the Spirit's power to lift him out of his human restrictions, to carry him beyond his human limitations, and to enable him to do the seeming impossible."[17]

13. Dunn, *Jesus and the Spirit*, 91.
14. Gerald F. Hawthorne, *The Presence and the Power: The Significance of the Holy Spirit in the Life and Ministry of Jesus* (Dallas: Word, 1991).
15. Hawthorne, *Presence and the Power*, 1.
16. Hawthorne, *Presence and the Power*, 218.
17. Hawthorne, *Presence and the Power*, 219.

Jesus was, admits Hawthorne, different from other human beings because he received the Spirit "without measure," because he offered none of the natural resistance exercised by those scarred by sin, and because the Spirit "was always central and perfect in Jesus, while this is never so in all others of us." Having conceded this sort of uniqueness to Jesus, Hawthorne goes on to claim that "apart from these differences, which certainly are considerable, Jesus was nevertheless a human being commissioned to do the will of God in this world, and filled with and empowered by the Holy Spirit to bring it all to a successful completion."[18]

These are significant studies of Jesus's experience of the Holy Spirit, the one scholarly, the other popular. Yet the qualms Dunn is compelled to confess ("by how much it transcended ordinary human experience we cannot say"), along with the theological assumptions Hawthorne is compelled to import (for example, "a preincarnate deliberate decision") into his reading of the Gospels, allow us to see how fraught and formidable the task can be of exploring behind the Gospels in a quest to discover Jesus's historical consciousness of the Holy Spirit.

The Spirit, the Cross, and an Unconventional God

Early in the life of the church, just decades after Jesus's death, the apostle Paul offers some of his earliest written reflections on the Holy Spirit. In a letter to the Corinthians, Paul recollects, "When I came to you, brothers and sisters, I did not come proclaiming the mystery of God to you in lofty words or wisdom. For I decided to know nothing among you except Jesus Christ, and him crucified. And I came to you in weakness and in fear and in much trembling. My speech and my proclamation were not with plausible words of wisdom, but with a demonstration of the Spirit and of power, so that your faith might rest not on human wisdom but on the power of God" (1 Cor. 2:1–5). The pairing of Spirit and power in this text suggests signs and wonders, as in Romans 15:19, where Paul describes the obedience of

18. Hawthorne, *Presence and the Power*, 219.

the nations that have been won "by the power of signs and wonders, by the power of the Spirit of God." Yet something else is at play in 1 Corinthians; the Spirit inspires the *content* of Paul's preaching: "For I decided to know nothing among you except Jesus Christ, and him crucified" (1 Cor. 2:2). Paul is perfectly clear about the source of this message: he preaches what "God has revealed to us through the Spirit" (2:10). And the substance of his preaching? The cross. The cross is what the rulers of this age cannot grasp. The cross is what the Spirit, which "comprehends what is truly God's," transforms into a powerful message (2:11).

The writers of the Gospels, with the apostle, grasped the power of Jesus Christ and him crucified. Whether they believed this message was revealed to them through the Spirit they do not say. But that they grasped the power of Jesus Christ, *and him crucified*, is undeniable. Even the Fourth Gospel, which stands apart from the others with its depiction of the paraclete, sets this mysterious figure from the start in the shadow of the conflict that led to Jesus's crucifixion: "And I will ask the Father, and he will give you another paraclete, to be with you forever. This is the Spirit of truth, whom the world cannot receive, because it neither sees it nor knows it. You know it, because it remains with you, and it will be in you" (John 14:16–17 alt.). This is the Spirit of truth, not the spirit of deceit known from the Dead Sea Scrolls. This is the Spirit of truth, whom the world cannot receive. Though subtly, the struggle between truth and deceit, believers and unbelievers, light and dark, seeps into a promise that portends hostility.

▬   ▬   ▬

The forbidding character of the Holy Spirit, seen in the light of Jesus's conflict-laden life and death, is especially evident in several sayings and stories in the Gospels of Matthew, Mark, and Luke:

- John the Baptist's prediction that Jesus will baptize with the Holy Spirit—and fire;
- the descent of the Holy Spirit like a dove after Jesus's baptism in the Jordan River;

- the warning against blasphemy; and
- the promise of the Spirit in the context of severe persecution.

There is an edge to each of these, a foreboding, a grimness.

At the start, these are gentle rumblings, distant thunder. In the Gospel of Mark, John the Baptist promises that Jesus will baptize in the Holy Spirit. In the Gospels of Matthew and Luke, whose authors may have had another version of these sayings, Jesus will baptize with Holy Spirit *and fire*—with *fiery judgment*. John is not the only one to demand penitence, redirection, change, or to set the ax at the root of the tree. Jesus, too, will burn the dross, refine the impurities. Jesus will baptize with Holy Spirit *and fire*.

These rumblings seem to soften in the next scene, as the Spirit descends on Jesus like a dove. The dove evokes images of the Spirit hovering over the abyss (Gen. 1:1–2). It is redolent of the dove returning with an olive branch in its beak, a sign that the tragic flood is finally over (8:8–12). The dove signifies hope, promise, anticipation. Only the voice that Jesus hears hints at the road ahead: Jesus will be king, yes, but also the servant who, in the final chapters of the prophetic book of Isaiah, will speak quietly—leaving bruised reeds intact and dimly burning wicks alight—and suffer just as silently (Isa. 42:3; 53:7).

Which is why the next scene is so jarring. In the Gospel of Mark, the Spirit casts Jesus out—like a demon—into the desert. The Spirit is no longer companionable, intimate, congenial. The gentle descent of the Spirit turns on a dime when the Spirit hurls Jesus violently away, seemingly against his will, from the bucolic shores of the Jordan River to the utterly inhospitable confines of the desert, from the bliss of a vision to the bane of hunger and heat and cold and snakes and scorpions—and Satan.

The lesson of Mark's Gospel, though it is succinctly told, could hardly be clearer. This first work of the Holy Spirit in Jesus's adult life is vicious, cold, and heartless. It had to be so, because Jesus could not test his dual vocation as king and servant in the serenity of a beatific vision. Only in the severity of the desert, in the heart of hostility and inhospitality, could his vocation be tested, so the Holy Spirit cast him out, like a demon, to the desert for forty days.

This is a grim scenario. We might have expected Jesus, freshly inspired by the Spirit, to speak an inspired word on the riverbank, pray an inspired prayer, utter an inspired blessing, preach an inspired sermon, perform a first work of inspired healing. These would be signs of the Spirit with which we could easily reckon. But he does not. Instead he goes, seemingly against his will, where the Spirit leads—into the desert.

Matthew and Luke, with another version of the story at hand, soften the blow by having the Spirit lead him *up* to the wilderness (Matthew) or *in* the wilderness (Luke). This is exodus language: just as the angel and pillars led Israel in a wilderness for forty years, now the Spirit leads Jesus so that he can succeed where they failed. But the desert is still full of snakes and scorpions. It is still Satan's lair. It is still the locale where Jesus is forced to test his mettle—no less than three times—in the Gospels of Matthew and Luke.

Gone is the gentleness of a dove, the sweet descent, the divine words whispered through the broken clouds. Gone is the revitalization of river water. Gone is the camaraderie of John the Baptist. Gone is what we might come to expect from a reading of Paul's Letters: "The fruit of the Spirit is love, joy, peace, patience, kindness, generosity, faithfulness, gentleness, and self-control" (Gal. 5:22–23). In the desert, the list looks different: the fruit of the Spirit is isolation, trial, conflict, and endurance. Kindness, generosity, and gentleness play no role in Jesus's survival in the desert. Only faithfulness and self-control remain as fruits of the Spirit in the face of Satan.

— — —

Grimmer still is the next reference to the Spirit—Jesus's warning about blasphemy against the Holy Spirit, which occurs in all three Synoptic Gospels *and* the Gospel of Thomas. This was clearly a difficult saying for even the authors of the Gospels. In the Gospels of Matthew and Mark, Jesus warns his *opponents* not to attribute to Satan what Jesus does by the Holy Spirit; in the Gospel of Luke, Jesus warns his *followers* not to blaspheme the Spirit that has the words they are to say under the compress of trials. To make this shift, Luke transports this saying to another context altogether and sets it alongside the promise of the Spirit for martyrs—effectively transposing the people at which it is aimed from Jesus's opponents to Jesus's followers.

There is no way to avoid the grimness, to avert the darkness, to circumvent the foreboding of this warning. Blasphemy is called an eternal sin in the Gospel of Mark and a sin that extends to the age to come in Matthew's Gospel; this warning against blasphemy makes the Holy Spirit dangerous and daunting, like the angel that led Israel through the wilderness.

███ ███ ███

Nor is it possible to avoid the grimness in the next saying in all three Synoptic Gospels, in which Jesus promises—though *promise* is hardly the right word—that the Holy Spirit will speak through Jesus's followers when they are on the verge of martyrdom. The Spirit will come to them in an era of unprecedented hostility, when brothers will have brothers put to death, children will make martyrs of their parents, and parents will betray their children. This is hardly reassuring. Jesus offers no hope for liberation, no pledge of release from prison, no promise of rescue from martyrdom.

To put the matter bluntly, Jesus does not promise that his persecuted followers will preach spellbinding sermons when the Spirit inspires them. He does not promise that his mistreated band will find legal loopholes that lead to their vindication when the Spirit inspires them. He does not promise that his battered brothers and sisters in faith will miraculously be released when the Spirit inspires them. No, the truth of this promise is grimmer still: those who endure to the end will be saved (Mark 13:13).

To that end, and to that end alone, the Holy Spirit inspires the faithful. That is why, in the Gospel of Mark, Jesus says, "As for yourselves, beware; for they will hand you over to councils; and you will be beaten in synagogues; and you will stand before governors and kings because of me, as a testimony to them. *And the good news must first be proclaimed to all nations*" (Mark 13:9–10, italics added). Inspiration is for testimony—not release. Inspiration serves the good news—not good feelings. Inspiration comes to the faithful—not the successful.

From the perspective of social standing or personal health or adequate wealth, this is a grim business. From the perspective of Jesus, who lived through a growing conflict, betrayal, trials, floggings, and crucifixion, there may be a different definition of *grim*. *Grim* is failed testimony. *Grim* is the lost opportunity to experience and exhibit the inspiration of the Spirit in an age of betrayal. *Grim* is the fizzling out of the good news.

There is a realism in this promise—a realism that suffuses so much about the Spirit in the Gospels. Jesus knew that his fate would be his followers' destiny too. He once asked them, "Are you able to drink the cup that I drink, or be baptized with the baptism that I am baptized with?" They replied, "We are able." So Jesus, ever wary and always wise, responded cannily: "The cup that I drink you will drink; and with the baptism with which I am baptized, you will be baptized" (Mark 10:38–39). He might well have asked them, "Are you willing to be inspired by the Spirit that inspires me, to be baptized with the Spirit that has baptized me?" What Spirit is that? The Spirit that the apostle Paul seems to have grasped intuitively, or at least through his own brutal experiences, as the source of a message of Christ crucified (1 Cor. 2:1–5). The Spirit, that is, that took Jesus to the desert, the Spirit we should never dare to blaspheme, the Spirit that arrives at just the right time, and not a moment before, to aid the persecuted—not with solace and certainly not with release but with endurance, faithfulness, and the unconventional but ultimately good news the nations so desperately need.

Appendix

Relevant References to *Pneuma* in the Canonical Gospels

	Matthew	Mark	Luke	John
Birth and upbringing				
Mary pregnant	1:18		1:35	
Mary pregnant	1:20			
John the Baptist to be filled			1:15	
John in the spirit and power of Elijah			1:17	
Elizabeth filled			1:41	
Mary's spirit rejoices			1:47	
Zechariah filled			1:67	
John strong in spirit			1:80	
Simeon filled			2:25	
Simeon receives revelation			2:26	
Simeon guided			2:27	
Baptism				
John's prediction	3:11	1:8	3:16	(1:26–27)
Descent at baptism	3:16	1:10	3:22	1:32–33

	Matthew	Mark	Luke	John
Wilderness testing				
Wilderness testing	4:1	1:12	4:1 (2x)	
Return to Galilee filled			4:14	
Sayings and miracles				
Isaiah 61:1–4 at Nazareth			4:18	
Jesus rejoices			10:21	
Gift of Holy Spirit			11:13	
Isaiah 42:1 (healing)	12:18			
Exorcism	12:28			
Blasphemy against	12:31–32	3:29–30	12:10	
David's psalm	22:43	12:36		
Persecution	10:20	13:11	12:12	
Born from above / spirit blows where it will				3:5–6, 8
Spirit given without measure				3:34
Spirit and truth				4:23–24
Spirit, not flesh, gives life				6:63
Spirit not yet given				7:37–39
Paraclete saying #1 (Spirit of truth)				14:17
Paraclete saying #2 (paraclete, Holy Spirit)				14:26
Paraclete saying #3 (paraclete, Spirit of truth)				15:26
Paraclete saying #4 (Spirit of truth)				16:13
Troubled, etc., spirit				
Jesus perceives in his spirit		2:8		
Poor in spirit	5:3			
Deceased girl's spirit returns			8:55	
Jesus sighs in his spirit		8:12		
Disturbed in spirit at Lazarus				11:33
Disturbed in spirit				13:21
Spirit is willing	26:41	14:38		
Death				
Gave up his spirit	27:50		23:46	19:30
Jesus the ghostly spirit			24:37, 39	

	Matthew	Mark	Luke	John
Resurrection				
Five signs (no spirit)		(16:9–20)		
Father, Son, Holy Spirit	28:19			
Promise of the Father			(24:49)	
Breathing into				20:22

Scripture and Ancient Sources Index

Subject Index